THE DEATH OF INNOCENCE

On the morning of March 19, 2000, Thomas Soria Sr. woke up early to add to his journal. "I want to plan how I'm going to rape a milky-white blond-haired, blue-eyed kind in the forest. I need to rape and possibly kill a woman. I enjoy raping and hurting and killing women and little girls. It's what they deserve in life and what they're good for. I will tell her limp body it will do everything that I want it to do."

After he was finished he said to his nineteen-year-old son, T.J., "Go get me a girl."

A few hours later, T.J. came running back into the apartment and announced, "I have a girl for you."

"Well, go bring her up," Soria Sr. replied.

<u>BOOK YOUR PLACE ON OUR WEBSITE</u>
<u>AND MAKE THE</u>
<u>READING CONNECTION!</u>

We've created a customized website just for our very special readers, where you can get the inside scoop on everything that's going on with Zebra, Pinnacle and Kensington books.

When you come online, you'll have the exciting opportunity to:

- View covers of upcoming books

- Read sample chapters

- Learn about our future publishing schedule
  (listed by publication month *and author*)

- Find out when your favorite authors will be visiting a city near you

- Search for and order backlist books from our online catalog

- Check out author bios and background information

- Send e-mail to your favorite authors

- Meet the Kensington staff online

- Join us in weekly chats with authors, readers and other guests

- Get writing guidelines

- AND MUCH MORE!

**Visit our website at
http://www.kensingtonbooks.com**

LIKE FATHER, LIKE SON

ROBERT SCOTT

PINNACLE BOOKS
Kensington Publishing Corp.
http://www.kensingtonbooks.com

First Printing: December 2002
10 9 8 7 6 5

Printed in the United States of America

ACKNOWLEDGMENTS

For helping me gather material for this book, I would like to thank Investigator Beder Clifton, Investigator Rory Planeta, Detective Tom Lee and Sheriff's Technician Erin Inman. Also, thanks to Christy Chalmers, Belinda Grant, David Stafford, John Stafford and Shelley Stafford for all their help. Special thanks to Deputy District Attorney Thomas Perkins of Douglas County for his support and help on this project. Lastly, I would be remiss if I didn't thank my wonderful literary agent Damaris Nicole Rowland and my terrific editors at Pinnacle, Karen Haas and Michaela Hamilton.

ACKNOWLEDGMENTS

ONE

"Uncle Tom"

Lake Tahoe, Nevada, Fall 1999

The nineteen-year-old man could look straight down his street to one of the most beautiful sights on earth: pristine Lake Tahoe in Nevada, surrounded by snow-capped mountains, and with waters so deep it appeared to be almost purple. Mark Twain and John Muir had sung its praises and the local Washoe Indians held it sacred. There were 101 things for a teenager to do in the area. In summer he could fish or hike, and in winter he could go skiing right behind his apartment at Heavenly Valley, one of the preeminent ski resorts in the nation. And if he got tired of the outdoor life, there were dozens of clubs along the lakeshore that beckoned with pulsating beats and rocking nightlife.

The young man had curly brown hair, hazel eyes and was of medium build. When he smiled, his eyes tended to light up. He had a friendly, open nature and was talkative. On the flip side, he also spent time reflecting about his life and could be quite withdrawn. When he got into this frame of mind, the reflections usually concerned his father. Life should have been paradise up at

Tahoe, but the needs of his father tended to over-whelm everything else.

The young man's thirty-eight-year-old father lived with him in the Lake Park Apartments on Kahle Drive, and his dad was always wanting something. The young man was all too aware that these desires generally took on the aspect of wanting sex with young girls. He heaved a sigh whenever these urges surfaced because he knew that sooner or later they would involve him. The young man would rather not get involved, but what could he do? To his mind, his father was the only person in the world who truly loved him. It had always been this way. Hadn't his dad even told him that his own mother never cared for him? She would call him "you little bastard" or "you son of a bitch." There was almost never a kind word for the boy coming from his mother.

To better serve his dad's "special" needs, the young man took on the job as a counselor at the Tahoe Boys and Girls Club. He was kind and friendly to the kids and they really liked him. Especially the young girls. He would play with them in the club house and on special occasions he would even take some of them to meet his dad. But he never introduced the man as "father." In-stead, he referred to him as his uncle. In fact, without any irony, he called his dad "Uncle Tom." He let it be known to the girls that Uncle Tom had lots of nice toys and games for them in the apartment. Uncle Tom liked kids and would play with them and keep them company. To girls between the ages of eight and twelve, the young man and his uncle were lots of fun. It was just strange that sometimes Uncle Tom liked to touch them. But then he was a friendly man.

One of the young girls at the Tahoe Boys and Girls Club was eight-year-old Sandi Taylor. She knew the young man well and liked him a lot. He was somebody you could trust. The young man introduced her to Uncle Tom and before long she was comfortable around him too. She lived in the same large apartment complex with her mother and she often saw the young man in the parking lot. Sometimes she saw Uncle Tom as well. He always said hello and was very friendly.

One day, in the autumn of 1999, Taylor was walking her dog when Uncle Tom, who lived in apartment 22, said that his sister had a dish for the puppy and invited her into his apartment. The man had dark curly hair, brown eyes and a nice smile. He smiled a lot when she was around. Even better than that, he had lots of fun toys, games, dolls and stuffed animals in his computer room. It was just like being in a toy store.

When Taylor walked into the computer room that day there was a "funny" picture on the computer screen. It was of a woman and she wasn't wearing any clothes. Uncle Tom said that they should be like the woman in the picture. It was fun sometimes not to wear any clothes. He took Taylor by the hand and led her into the bedroom and stripped off her clothing. He laid her down on some blankets on the floor and began to lick "her private spots"—the places where she "peed" and "pooped." He seemed to like doing this a lot. Something funny happened to him. It happened between his legs. He looked different there when he did this. She felt funny about this, but she didn't tell him to stop. He was so happy when he did these things. The only time she didn't really like it was when he dug his fingers into the place where she peed. It hurt.

After he was done, he allowed Taylor to get dressed and told her he had cancer and would die soon, so she shouldn't tell anyone about what had just happened. If she did, he would die a lot sooner. She liked Uncle Tom and didn't want him to die.

Uncle Tom checked the hallway before Taylor left the apartment, and when he saw it was all clear, he let her leave.

A week later, Sandi Taylor was back at apartment 22. Uncle Tom gave her a dish for her puppy, just as he said he would do. There were a few people in the living room, including the nice boy from the Boys and Girls Club. She liked the boy and Uncle Tom because they were always friendly to her.

Taylor kept going back to apartment 22 because Uncle Tom had so many nice toys and games. He once gave her a twenty-dollar bill just to take off her clothes so that he could touch her. He liked to touch the private spots. He said he gave her the twenty-dollar bill because she was a "good Christian girl." Then he reminded her she wasn't supposed to tell anyone about this. It would make his cancer very bad and he would die even sooner.

The nineteen-year-old knew very well what was going on in the bedroom between his father and Sandi Taylor. He didn't particularly like it, but there had always been secrets between him and his father. In fact, his father told him everything that went on between himself and young girls. It had been going on for years. If the young man was "good," he was even allowed to watch. All of this made him feel a little guilty about working at the Tahoe Boys and Girls Club. But if his dad said it was all right—well, his father had always known best.

By October 1999, Dad had his eyes on the young man's fifteen-year-old friend named Donna Orlando. This made the nineteen-year-old feel even worse than the incidents with Sandi Taylor. The young man liked Donna so much that he wished Donna would be his girlfriend. He knew that Donna liked him and was romantically inclined toward him. But when Dad wanted something, he usually got what he wanted. And he definitely wanted Donna Orlando. Even his stepmom, Lupe, who lived with the young man and Dad, didn't object. She was old-fashioned in one respect. She believed that the man was king of his own castle. His stepmom was kind of strange, but at least she was better than his mother. Lupe didn't hate him the way his own mother did. Lupe was often kind to him.

But the whole "Donna Orlando thing" bothered the young man. He knew how frail she was, both physically and emotionally. She seemed more like a little child than fifteen years old. She was fairly naive and had young girl's fantasies about him. But then Dad's wants and needs came first. It had always been that way.

One day, in October 1999, Dad simply said, "Get Donna for me."

"How?" the young man asked, trying to put him off.

Dad grinned and said, "Tell her I have a brain tumor. Tell her that having sex with me is the only way to relieve my stress and keep me from dying."

The young man sighed but did what his father said. He was a good "bullshitter" and the fifteen-year-old girl was so naive. He convinced Donna Orlando that it would be an act of kindness to have sex with Uncle Tom. (The young man had never told her that Uncle Tom was really his father.) Reluctantly she complied. She didn't particularly like Uncle Tom, but she did like the young man so much she would do anything he asked her to do, even this. Maybe if she went along, the young man would make her his girlfriend someday.

Orlando followed the young man to apartment 22,

where he stopped in the living room as Uncle Tom escorted her into the bedroom. Uncle Tom undressed himself and attempted to remove her clothes, but she pushed him away and said that she could take off her own clothes. She looked at the clock. It was 4:00 P.M. Orlando removed her shoes, socks, pants and underpants, leaving her shirt and bra on. She lay down on the bed and Uncle Tom followed. He began fingering her and licked her left outer thigh. He became very excited. After almost a half hour of this, he put his head down between her legs and began sucking and licking her vaginal area.

Orlando was watching the clock above the bed the whole time. It was now 6:10 P.M. and she became worried that Lupe would return home and catch them. Uncle Tom told her not to worry. Lupe wouldn't come into the bedroom if she saw the door was closed. Besides, she wouldn't mind if she saw them anyway. She knew what he liked.

After Uncle Tom was through with her, he allowed Orlando to get dressed. Then, just before she left, he reminded her once again not to tell anyone or he would get so upset that it would make his brain tumors explode. Orlando was naive enough to believe him.

Strangely enough, Donna Orlando came back a few more times to be molested by Uncle Tom, even though she hated it. Perhaps she hoped that the young man would take pity on her and make her his girlfriend. Or maybe she just wanted to be close to him. Whatever the reason, Orlando allowed Uncle Tom to grope her and run his hands all over her body.

The young man was no happier about the situation than Orlando was. He liked Donna a lot. But what could he do? Father's wishes came first. And besides, he was aroused by the "animal noises" coming from the bedroom. Sometimes he would sit on his own bed, unzip his pants and masturbate. It reminded him of the times when it was *he* whom father wanted.

Dad would take him into the master bedroom from the time he was six years old and climb into bed with him. Dad would tell him that his mother never wanted him and that only he truly loved his boy. Then Dad would gently undo his pajamas and run his hands all over his body. It was a pleasure beyond description. He would make the boy run his hands over his body as well. Then Dad would have him roll over and enter him from behind. Dad liked that a lot. It hurt, but he eventually got used to it.

They were close like that, father and son. Some people noticed they were almost inseparable—Thomas Soria Sr. and Thomas Soria Jr., better known by his nickname, T.J.

But as T.J. climaxed on the couch as he listened to his dad having sex with Orlando, he didn't know one thing that was coursing through his father's mind at the moment. Thomas Soria Sr. enjoyed having sex with the naive fifteen-year-old all right, but he wanted girls who were even younger. He wanted a young, petite, blond girl to torture and cut as he had sex. He wanted to chop parts off her body as he molested her. He wanted to slit her throat as he came. The journal he'd been amassing on his computer attested to his wildest fantasies and it was about time to put them into practice.

One thing Thomas Soria Sr. knew for certain. When the time came to act, he could count on his son, T.J.

TWO

A Horrible
Way to Die

Thomas Soria Sr. was born on January 27, 1961, and might have had a normal childhood if his parents hadn't divorced. That in itself wasn't so catastrophic, nor was the fact that his mother, Jayne, better known as Janey, married a man named Duane Mozingo. But the fact that Duane had a son, Ronny, would spell disaster for them all. Ronny's violent nature was like a hurricane sweeping through all of their lives.

Ronald "Ronny" Mozingo was born on February 24, 1957. He had two siblings, brother Roger and sister Linda. In one regard, Ronny's outbursts mirrored the age-old question "Which came first, the chicken or the egg?" Did the alleged beatings by his parents turn him violent, or were the beatings in response to his violent nature? Perhaps it was a little of both. Whatever the reason, by the age of nine he was already on the path to uncontrolled discipline problems. He disrupted his classmates at school. He got into unprovoked arguments and fights. He even bothered and molested young girls. Before Ronny was ten years old, he had molested a young girl and assaulted her with a rock. This latest outburst of violence got him shipped off to juvenile hall.

A psychologist for the D. W. Harkness School in Sacramento later said about Mozingo's outbursts in 1967, "It was so tragic, you could almost read what was going to happen to him. He is someone who slipped through cracks in the system."

But it wasn't for lack of trying on the part of the parents or counselors. Nothing they did seemed to work. In 1968 one doctor said Ronny had "strong sado-masochistic tendencies." In fact, three months later, he molested another young female. From the age of eleven to fifteen, Ronny Mozingo was sent to various boys' homes in Southern California. But even there, Ronny continued his string of petty thefts and fighting.

After this, he was returned home to his father's house. But this was to have dire consequences for his eight-year-old stepbrother, Thomas Soria. On at least two occasions, Ronny suggested homosexual activity with Thomas. Tom later claimed that Ronny actually followed through on these suggestions. This latest outrage got Ronny thrown right back into another boys' home.

He was placed in Guadalupe Home for Boys in Yucaipa, California, in 1971. And he claimed later, "I experienced child abuse and beatings. I never saw a psychiatrist the whole time there. I ran away, was caught and experienced more beatings."

He was shuffled from one home to another. In 1973 he was placed in St. John's Home for Boys in Palm Springs, where he claimed to be the victim of more beatings and abuse. Finally ending up at Napa State Hospital for the Mentally Ill, he said later, "I was placed in a ward with thirty-six beds among long-term, mostly schizophrenic and autistic patients. After my initial psychiatric examination, no other therapy was ever done. I was too young to understand why I was there and terrified to be placed in a ward with these extremely disturbed individuals."

He was sent to the California Youth Authority for a while and got married after his release. But even this didn't straighten him out. He and his wife were arrested for grand theft in trying to rip off his landlord. Just before he was to begin serving time for this incident, Ronny got into even more trouble. Outside a Sears store, he assaulted a security guard by pulling a gun on him. The guard thought it was a .357 Magnum. But when Ronny was arrested for this disturbance, it proved to be only a .22 pellet gun. He received a misdemeanor for the crime.

Before long he was back on the streets of Sacramento, having learned nothing behind bars to stem his violent nature. In 1975, at the age of eighteen, while hanging out at a shopping mall, he noticed a young girl walking alone. Mozingo followed her, put a knife to her throat and dragged her into a vacant field. Then he ripped off her clothes, forced her to orally copulate him, sodomized and raped her. Afterward, he said he was going to kill her, but the fourteen-year-old girl lied that she liked him and if he let her go, she wanted to see him again. Ronny believed her and let her go. But the only person she wanted to see was a policeman. The girl hooked up with an officer and it wasn't long before Ronny Mozingo was under arrest once again.

He'd really gone overboard this time, and was shipped off to the State Hospital for Mentally Disordered Sexual Offenders at Atascadero, California. He was evaluated for one year there, until they determined that they couldn't do anything for him and he was summarily sent to a regular prison at Soledad to serve out his term.

Mozingo didn't seem to cause as much trouble in prison as elsewhere, and on August 20, 1979, he was released. However, two weeks before his release, he had seen a movie on television in Soledad State Prison that was to have dire ramifications for him and everyone in his orbit. He watched a movie called *The Brotherhood*, starring Kirk Douglas and Alex Cord. It was a movie about the Mafia, a precursor to *The Godfather*. One scene in particular grabbed Mozingo's attention.

Kirk Douglas took a man who had ratted on his gangster father to an empty garage. He tied the man's hands behind his back, placed him on his stomach and wrapped rope around his neck. The rope was then strung from the man's neck to his legs, which were arched above his back. As the victim's legs slowly dropped, he strangled himself to death.

Ronny Mozingo wasn't sickened by this scene. In fact, it excited him and he stored away every detail in his memory.

In the long run, the real tragedy wasn't what happened to Ronny Mozingo. The real tragedy was what happened to everyone else around him. Like a single domino tipping over and striking all the others in a line, his outbursts of violence wouldn't stop until years later when a totally innocent young girl was raped and murdered and left in a blood-soaked garbage bag. She may not have died by Ronny Mozingo's hands, but she certainly died from his legacy.

Ronny's entry into Soledad State Prison had been a reprieve for Thomas Soria. His family got back to a semblance of order and his grades improved. By now, they lived in a small older home in a modest neighborhood on Wah Avenue in Sacramento's south side.

As Thomas's grades picked up, so did his outlook on life. He was resilient enough to put his stepbrother Ronny's molestations behind him and move on. In 1979 Thomas Soria was accepted to the University of California, Sacramento. He looked forward to the college life and all that it implied.

Tom also had a very close relationship with his mom at this time. They went bowling together and to restaurants. She got up in the morning just to fix him breakfast before he went to school. He practically worshiped her. He would speak later about what a good relationship they had, how she loved him and wanted what was best for him in life.

But before Tom barely got started at college, there was a specter on the horizon in the form of his stepbrother who had just been paroled. Ronny's mind seethed with enemies, real and imagined, that he wanted to dispose of; in his mind, one of the worst was his forty-one-year-old stepmother, Janey. In a twisted way, he hated her and desired her. The beatings she had given him as a child angered and aroused him. He not only wanted to kill her, he wanted to have sex with her. By September 1979 he decided to do both.

The events of Tuesday, September 25, 1979, became seared into Thomas Soria's mind for the rest of his life. He woke up around 7:00 A.M. as usual and went down the hall to the bathroom. His mom was already up and he noted she was wearing a long green lounging dress. He knew that later on she planned to go for her workout at a nearby spa, which she did every Tuesday. After he finished brushing his teeth, Janey came into the bathroom and curled his hair with a curling iron. This was just one more aspect of how close they were.

Tom grabbed a quick bite to eat before heading out the door and peeked into her bedroom just before he left. He saw that Janey had gone back to bed and he told her good-bye. Then he left through the front door, climbed into his blue Toyota sedan and drove the few miles to Sacramento State University. At 8:00 A.M. he attended his first class in Mrs. Cannon's health education class. His last class that day was accounting and ended just before noon. But as he was attending classes on the quiet campus, all hell was breaking loose at his home on Wah Avenue, not far away.

On September 25, 1979, Ronny Mozingo was living with his sister, Linda, and her husband, Kent Smith, a reserve Sheriff's deputy, on Atlas Avenue in Sacramento. He got up that morning and related later that he said to himself, "This is the day I will kill." He had been thinking about it for four years in state prison.

He showered, dressed and hopped on a borrowed ten-speed bike for a ride over to the Department of Motor Vehicles to obtain an identification card. He then pedaled over to Janey Mozingo's neighborhood on Wah Avenue. Between 9:30 and 10:00 A.M., one of Janey Mozingo's neighbors, Manuel Ramirez, looked up from mowing his lawn and noticed a young man ride up the street on a bicycle, turn around and park the bike in the Mozingos' driveway. He saw that the young man had longish hair and was wearing a brown coat.

What happened next can only be pieced together by statements later made by Ronny Mozingo and physical evidence. Ronny said that he knocked on the door and Janey answered it. His father, Duane, and his stepbrother, Thomas, were gone. Janey let him in and immediately ignored him. She went back to fixing her hair and applying makeup in the bathroom. Her dismissal of him angered Ronny.

He related, "I came up behind her and put my hand

over her mouth and said, 'I don't like what you did to my family.'

"She answered, 'Do whatever you want.'

"I took this to be sexual."

Whether she actually said this to try and save her life, only Ronny Mozingo knows for sure. Whatever her intent, he did drag her into Thomas Soria's bedroom, pulled off all her clothing and raped her on the floor. Or as he put it, "I boned her."

But if Janey thought he would leave her alone after he had raped her, she was sadly mistaken. He remembered how graphic and exciting the execution scene had been in *The Brotherhood.* He told her to stay on the floor and don't move. He then obtained some wiring from Thomas Soria's Atari game and stereo speakers. He also jerked the cord out of Thomas's electric clock. It stopped at exactly 11:06 A.M. Ronny Mozingo bound her wrists behind her back with the Atari wire and stereo wire and ran the cords down to her ankles. Then he tied more wire from Janey's neck to her ankles and placed her on the bedroom floor. She was placed in such a position that if she dropped her legs, the wire would choke off her air supply.

Janey struggled with all her might to keep her legs erect. But minute by minute, her muscles grew more tired. Even as she flinched and tried to raise her legs back, gravity and tiredness were taking their toll. She couldn't have had many illusions about the final outcome. Her agony and grief must have been profound. She turned her head and body away from Ronny so that he wouldn't see her die. Ronny Mozingo, however, was totally untouched by her struggles or muffled cries. He sat back and watched the show.

Janey's face turned red, then purple as the wires cut off her air. Slowly but surely, her legs dropped. By the time ten minutes had elapsed, she went into her final death spasms. Ronny watched with rapt attention as she jerked one last time and lay still.

Ronny went to the bathroom and got a towel. He didn't cover her body with it, just her face. Then he simply walked out the front door and rode away on his bicycle.

Just before noon that day, Thomas Soria returned home from California State University, Sacramento. He knew something was amiss when Janey didn't come to the door to greet him as she always did. He parked in the driveway next to her silver sedan and looked in the window to see if she was there, but he did not see her. He then walked through the front door of the house and called her name, but got no response in return.

Wandering into the kitchen, he noticed a Pepsi bottle on the drain board and a can opener nearby. But the Pepsi bottle was unopened and getting warm. He looked for Janey in the dining room and her bedroom, to no avail. But as he walked down the hallway toward his own bedroom, he spotted something unusual on the floor. It took an instant for the image to sink in. He was viewing the nude body of his mother lying on the floor with a towel draped over her face and wires on her body.

In an absolute state of shock, Thomas didn't call the police but rather ran to the back door and yelled upstairs to a unit rented by Ernest Berry. "Did you hear any screams or anything unusual?" he bellowed.

"No," Berry answered.

Thomas then phoned his stepfather, who operated a service station only a few blocks away. Thomas screamed into the phone, "You'd better get the fuck home! Something's wrong with Mom!"

Much later, Thomas Soria admitted, "I called my

stepfather instead of emergency personnel because I was scared. I wasn't thinking right."

Some claims could be made that he would never "think right" from that moment forward. It was as if the image of his defiled and murdered mother had been burned into his brain. He would always speak of having nightmares from that time on. His whole world had been ripped apart by stepbrother Ronny Mozingo.

After phoning his dad, Thomas went into the living room and just stood there for a couple of minutes in shock. Ernest Berry came downstairs and peeked into the window, calling out to Tom. Thomas didn't answer him; he didn't move at all until his stepfather arrived home.

In almost a daze, Thomas Soria would remember later, "I stepped out the door a little bit and told him (Duane Mozingo) to come in. I told him there was something wrong with Mom. [Then] I pointed to the hallway and said, 'In there.' He started to go into the master bedroom, but I said, 'No' and pointed toward my room. He went to my bedroom and I went with him. He pulled the towel off. I remember him cutting the cord that was going to the video game. He listened for a heartbeat. Still in shock, I picked up my clock. And then set it back down. [Duane] went into the closet and got out a blanket. My mom would use it in the living room. He put it over her."

Thomas and Duane went back to the living room. While Duane Mozingo called the police, Tom was at least aware enough to notice that none of the door locks had been tampered with. Whoever had entered the residence to kill his mother must have been let in by her.

The police arrived in less than ten minutes and questioned both Tom and Duane. Sheriff's Deputy Robert Williams wrote in his report, "Sacramento Police radio advised this office of the discovery of a homicide victim. Upon arrival at the scene, Lt. Taylor of the Homicide Division advised investigators that he had summoned CSI for photographs and a videotape crew. He also requested a pathologist and a criminalist to respond to the scene. Officers were advised that the subject had last been seen by her husband, Duane Mozingo, at approximately 0930 hours. The subject's son came home from school at approximately 1200 hours and discovered the subject. He phoned Mr. Mozingo who came home from work immediately. Mr. Mozingo then phoned the police."

Detectives Tom Lee and de Borba were the next to arrive at the crime scene. Detective Lee's report began:

> Approximately 12:00 hours 9-25-79 this department was notified of the discovery of a victim's body in her own residence. Uniformed officers responded and confirmed that victim was dead and foul play evident.
>
> Approximately 1239 hours [I] and de Borba arrived on the scene and examined the remains of the body. The body, identified as one Janey Mozingo, female, forty-one years old, was observed to be completely nude, lying on her back, and several electrical cords were used to bind her. Cords were observed wrapped tightly around the neck, leading down the back to her wrists and wrapped around several times around the wrists, binding her hands behind her back. The cords continued downwards to her ankles which were also wrapped several times. This method of restraint places or increases pressure around the neck when resistance is attempted.
>
> An examination of the victim also disclosed two

recent bruises on the upper part of her right arm.
The only other visible evidence of trauma would
be the flow of blood from the nasal and oral
openings. A check of the residence disclosed no
items to have been tampered with outside of this
room nor were there any items missing, though
guns, jewelry and a large amount of cash was discovered in the residence.

R/Os (recording officers) discovered no signs
of forced entry and according to person who discovered victim (Son—Soria, Thomas), the front
door was locked and the rear door leading to the
garage was closed but unlocked.

R/Os determined that one cord was forcibly
ripped apart from a nightstand clock, another
was attached to a T.V. Atari set and another cord
was possibly taken from the room is used for
stereo equipment.

Detective de Borba noted in his report:

The victim's face was completely made up
[with] make-up and false eyelashes. The victim's
body was face up, her head to the south. The victim's hands were behind her back and her feet
were bound and drawn up under her buttocks.
The victim's body had not set up in rigor. Her ex-
tremities were flexible and rigor did not appear
to be setting in at this time. The victim appeared
to be wearing a gold necklace and one ring.
Noted on the victim's abdomen, approximately
one or two inches below the navel, was a single
black possible pubic hair approximately two and
one half inches long. This hair was taken to be
processed by Kvick, County Criminalist. The hair

found on the victim's abdomen did not appear to be consistent with her pubic hairs and for this reason was taken. Kvick also took a similar hair from one of two pillows that were laying on the floor in the room, but the origin of these hairs is also uncertain.

Detective Lee Murphy, who was also now on the scene, interviewed Thomas Soria. A neighborhood canvass of the area was made by several detectives and uniformed officers. Detective Murphy contacted a neighbor named Manuel Ramirez. As de Borba's report went on to state:

Ramirez said that while he was working on his front yard at approximately 0930 hours, he saw a subject riding a ten-speed bike past his residence heading in the direction of the victim's residence. The subject passed victim's residence, turned around, and rode up on victim's driveway. This subject parked his bike behind victim's vehicle and walked toward the front door. Ramirez described the subject as follows: twenty-two to twenty-five, 5'8", medium build, collar length blond or light brown hair and appeared to have blemishes on face. Subject was thought to be wearing a light brown sports coat, white dress shirt and gray slacks.

Ramirez did not concentrate his observations on the subject and thus did not see this subject actually enter the victim's residence. However, approximately forty-five minutes later, Ramirez did glance in the direction of victim's residence and noticed that same bike was still in the driveway.

Between 1000 to 1015 hours the bike was still there.

During an examination of the crime scene, R/Os noticed that the clock from which the cord was pulled apart, displayed a time of 1106 hours.

While the detectives talked to Ramirez, Detective Jean Burchett interviewed Ernest Berry, the victim's neighbor, who lived upstairs in the same complex. Berry related that he was at work during the morning hours and returned home at approximately 11:30 A.M. but did not observe anyone around Janey Mozingo's residence.

Meanwhile, Detectives Lee and de Borba contacted another neighbor named Kathy Campos, who told them she'd seen a young man of average build with shoulder-length blond hair riding away on a bicycle sometime after 11:00 A.M.

Another investigator who arrived on the scene was pathologist Pierce Rooney. He wrote:

I arrived on the scene at approximately 1:40 P.M. The nude body of a brown-skinned female was present on the floor of a room in the southwest corner of the residence. She was situated on her back with her arms behind her buttocks, and her legs flexed at the knees. The left foot was situated under the buttocks. The right foot was situated under the left leg. The legs were spread. Bloody fluid was present in the nose and mouth and had exuded down over the right side of the face and some of the left. Multiple electrical cords indented the subject's neck in ligature fashion. Similar cords were present about the wrists and ankles. There was some blood on a towel situated near the subject's head. Situated just below her umbilicus was a brown hair approximately three inches long. At 2:00 P.M., Criminalist Gus Kvick removed the hair from the abdomen. Also at approximately 2:00 P.M. the subject's rectal temperature was 97.8 degrees. The thermostat in another room read 80 degrees at approximately 2:00 P.M.

The subject showed no rigor at the time I arrived. She was still warm to the touch and lividity was very minimal over the dorsal aspects of the body. It blanched readily.

I advised the investigators that the subject was possibly dead for about three hours, plus or minus.

If pathologist Rooney's estimation of death was correct, Thomas Soria had missed walking in on the torture and murder of his mother by only about an hour.

After the investigators were through with Thomas Soria, he could no longer stand to be in the house. He went across the street and stayed all afternoon at Mrs. Clem's house. Then when night fell, he went to stay with some relatives in Vacaville. He refused to return home again for two weeks. And even then, he would only go into his old bedroom to take things out. He would not sleep in there.

The investigation went on, despite Thomas Soria's absence. At 2:24 P.M. Detective de Borba said:

The victim's body was moved to examine any possible physical evidence under her body. No physical evidence was found to be under her body, although there was a white fluid under her buttocks area and was possibly expelled from the victim's body unvoluntarily prior to or following death. Regarding this clear fluid, the rug that was on the floor is a throw rug type and that entire rug was picked up by Lee and myself, and booked into evidence.

At approximately 1455 hours the victim's body was removed from the crime scene by Coroner Deputies Williams and Bowers.

The next day, Detective Lee again contacted Duane Mozingo and asked about his sons. Mozingo told him that he thought both of his sons were still serving time in prison. But Detective Lee checked the records and noticed that Ronny, 131 pounds with blond hair, had been released on August 20, 1979.

What was even more interesting to Detective Lee was the report concerning Ronny Mozingo's rape of the fourteen-year-old girl near the shopping mall. It stated, "He (Mozingo) grabbed the victim from behind. Victim was led to a vacant field on foot where he forced victim down and forcibly removed her clothes. Acts of oral copulation, sodomy and rape occurred. Suspect Mozingo also looked into victim's purse, but did not take anything."

The next day, pathologist Pierce Rooney performed an autopsy on the body of Janey Mozingo. He wrote in his report:

The subject is 5'5" and weighs 126 pounds. It is the body of a well-developed and nourished brown-skinned female. Rigidity is complete at this time. The scalp is covered with abundant curly dark brown hair. There are bruise marks on the right buttocks.

The epiglottis and laryngeal mucous show numerous petechiae above the level of the ligature. The posterior tongue is markedly hemorrhagic and this apparently accounts for blood in the mouth and nose. The tongue is clenched firmly between the teeth. The vagina shows no lacerations or abrasions or contusions. But the vagina contains one half cc of whitish thick milky liquid.

A few days later, a very interesting conversation took place at Linda Smith's home on the evening of September 28, 1979. While Ronny Mozingo and his sister were watching television, he suddenly said to her, "I've got to tell you something."

Just by his tone, she knew it must be something bad. "I don't want to hear it," she replied.

But Ronny was insistent. "I've got to tell you anyway. I've got to get this off my chest." And then he blurted out that he'd been at Janey Mozingo's residence on the morning of September 25. He'd ridden his bike there, knocked on the door and she'd let him in. But once she began to ignore him, it set him off. He'd grabbed her, disrobed her and raped her. Then he described how he'd killed her. He even went so far as to demonstrate his actions by lying on the floor on his stomach, arching his back and pretending like his legs were tied to his throat. He told his sister he'd watched until he was sure Janey was dead.

Linda was incredulous and only half believed him. But she did ask, "Why Janey? Why not Duane?"

Ronny answered, "She was there."

"Do you feel sorry now?" she asked.

He gave a one-word reply, "No."

Things became jumbled at this point. Linda Smith

recounted later that she'd seen a newspaper report about the murder and began to believe Ronny's story. She believed it enough to tell her reserve Sheriff's officer husband, Kent, and he contacted a friend of his in the Sacramento Police Department.

But Ronny contended something quite different happened. He said later that the authorities contacted him independently of anything Smith might have said. Whatever the case, Detective Lee did contact Ronny Mozingo's parole officer, Bob Palo, on October 5, 1979, at 2:05 P.M. Officer Palo informed Detective Lee that Ronny Mozingo was residing with his sister and her deputy husband out on Atlas Avenue.

At 4:00 P.M. Detective Lee contacted psychologist Sorensen by phone and learned that Ronny Mozingo saw him for bimonthly therapy sessions. He also related that Detective Lee would be able to have access to a summary of Ronny Mozingo's crimes.

Detective Lee went to Sorenson's office in downtown Sacramento and reviewed Ronny Mozingo's crimes, noting the similarities between them and the murder of Janey Mozingo.

At 11:05 A.M. on October 6, Kent Smith returned Detective Lee's phone call and said that he did suspect Ronny Mozingo for the murder. He told Lee that Ronny had access to a ten-speed bike and that Ronny didn't own a brown jacket, but he could have taken one of his. He agreed to talk with Ronny and try to convince him to go down to the station for elimination prints and questioning.

Kent Smith noticed that for days his wife, Linda, had been in a funk. When he finally questioned her about it, the whole story of what Ronny had told her came tumbling out. Through an intermediary, Kent told Captain Thomas Stark of the Sacramento Police Department about everything he'd just heard. He also related that Linda was not willing to help police in the arrest of her brother.

Nonetheless, Ronny Mozingo did phone Detective Lee at 10:00 A.M. on October 7, 1979. He was very reluctant to talk and told Lee that he might say something that would incriminate him and therefore wanted a lawyer present. Detective Lee replied that wasn't necessary because Mozingo wasn't under arrest and the police were questioning all family members. But Ronny countered that he had a past record and that one police officer had said he had a violent temper, which would tend to incriminate him. Against Detective Lee's advice, Ronny said that he wanted to discuss the matter some more with his sister before coming in for questioning.

At 12:50 P.M., on October 7, Linda Smith did show up at the Hall of Justice, but Ronny did not accompany her. Even without him, she divulged everything she had been told covering their conversation of September 28. She described the murder of Janey Mozingo as "an execution-style" killing.

At 1:40 P.M., on October 7, Detectives Lee, Burchett, and Mamuyac went to Ronny Mozingo's address on Atlas Avenue, but by then he'd already flown the coop, destination unknown.

A probable-cause arrest warrant was drawn up by Detective Lee stating, "Suspect Mozingo, Ronny, has been linked to the use of a ten-speed bike during the morning of the murder, Mozingo's general description matches the subject seen by witnesses Ramirez and Campos; similarities to the method of the crime which Mozingo was convicted of in November 1975, Mozingo's access to clothing similar to that described by witness Ramirez, incriminating statement made to suspect's sister, Linda Smith, and husband Kent Smith verifying the crime scene's other evidence."

By this time, Ronny Mozingo was long gone. According to statements he made later, he either stole a car or hitchhiked to southern California, first to Long Beach and then San Diego. But for whatever reason, Sacramento pulled him back like a homing beacon. Ronny Mozingo returned to Sacramento, where he hid out at a fellow parolee's apartment.

But if he thought he was safe there, he was sadly mistaken. The law enforcement authorities soon got wind of his whereabouts and a heavily armed crime suppression unit surrounded the apartment and used a bullhorn to order him outside. As Ronny Mozingo later told his sister, if there hadn't been a two-year-old child in the apartment at the time, he would have resisted, which certainly would have meant gunplay. Instead, he surrendered peacefully to officers.

As Ronny Mozingo's trial got under way, he was represented by court-appointed attorney Peter Fatros. Mozingo did not get along with his attorney at all and thought he was not receiving adequate representation. Mozingo filed a brief to be his own attorney, but was denied. Then he tried to change his plea from not guilty to guilty by reason of insanity. But he was dissuaded from taking this course.

During the trial's jury phase, Deputy District Attorney Kenneth Peterson asked Thomas Soria several questions in his attempt to show that Janey Mozingo had not been murdered in a burglary gone bad and that she must have known her attacker.

Q.—As a result of this incident, after coming back to your house, did you ever find anything missing of any property . . . any money, any weapons, any valuables, any stereo equipment, anything missing at all from the house?

A.—No.

Q.—Showing you seventeen-A, do you recognize this piece of clothing?

A.—Yes.

Q.—What do you recognize this to be?

A.—That's a leotard.

Q.—Is this the type of clothing that your mother would wear underneath her shorts when she would go to the spa?

A.—Yes.

And then Deputy DA Peterson asked Thomas a question that elicited a very curious response.

Q.—Do you know Ronny Mozingo?

A.—I remember him.

This was the most that Thomas Soria would say about the stepbrother who used to torment and sexually abuse him. The same stepbrother who had just murdered his mother. It was as if he were trying to expunge all memories of Ronny Mozingo from his mind.

Meanwhile, Ronny Mozingo's attorney, Peter Fatros, was trying to lay blame for the murder of Janey Mozingo much closer to home. His target was the Mozingos' upstairs neighbor, Ernest Berry. He drilled in on this theme with a series of questions to Thomas Soria.

Q.—Did you tell any officer or anybody that day that you had seen Mr. Berry peeking through the windows?

A.—I can't remember.

Q.—How long have you known Mr. Berry?

A.—Approximately ten or eleven years.

Q.—Now from that moment you saw Mr. Berry until you yelled up to him from downstair of the stairwell, did you see Mr. Berry again?

A.—Yes, I did.

Q.—And where was he when you saw him at that time?

A.—He was looking through the dining-room window.

Q.—So did he stare through this window very long, or was it just sort of a momentary glance?

A.—Momentary glance.

Q.—Was he standing still when he was looking in, or was he just walking by to get to his doorway?

A.—He was standing still.

Q.—Is there anything unusual in that area that he would have a reason for standing there to peek in?

A.—He normally did that.

Q.—He would normally just be peeking around the house?

A.—Yes, he's just a nosy person.

Attorney Fatros went on to key in on the fact that Berry's car was not running at the time and he had to ride around on a bicycle. Perhaps it was Berry whom Manuel Ramirez had seen riding away from the Mozingo residence after the murder.

But the most damaging testimony against Ronny Mozingo came from his own sister, Linda Smith, who detailed their conversation on the evening of September 28, 1979, where he confessed to her. It didn't take the jury long to find Ronny Mozingo guilty of the murder of his stepmother, Janey Mozingo.

At sentencing in April 1980, Mozingo had a chance

to speak on his own behalf. He told the judge, "I feel strongly myself that I didn't get no fair trial in this courtroom for the simple fact, you tell twelve citizens that this guy has already been an ex-convict and that he was supposed to have stolen a car to leave Sacramento and that's supposed to show that he's a hardened criminal. I feel I have never in my life been put through so [much] agony and depression as in this courtroom.

"I got a DA who went all the way. Acted immature when I was on the stand making facial expressions. It was really unnecessary. I have a judge who shouldn't even be a judge to allow such things in the courtroom. And I've got an attorney who didn't know nothing about a murder case."

Judge Lloyd Phillips Jr. had seen things quite differently and said so at sentencing: "The murder was of the first degree and that the murder was especially heinous, atrocious and cruel, manifesting exceptional depravity in that the murder was a conscienceless and pitiless crime which was unnecessarily torturous to the victim. . . . It is the order of this court that you shall suffer the death penalty, said penalty to be afflicted within the walls of the state prison at San Quentin, California."

There was only one thing keeping Thomas Soria from going completely off the deep end after his mother's murder—his girlfriend, Francine. He had been interested in her since they met at a junior-high study room. She related later, "When in this class (the study room), we started hanging out together. I was reserved. It seemed like Tom had a lot of friends. He was nice to me. We became good friends."

When Fran's family moved to another part of the Sacramento area, Tom was undeterred. He went to the local post office and found out where Fran's family had moved. Then he tracked her to Roseville High School. Fran said, "I thought it was romantic at the time. He said I was the most fascinating person in his world and that he just couldn't live without me. It made me feel great."

Fran had been born in 1961 at Sacramento's County Hospital. And just like Thomas Soria's parents, her own had divorced and she was now living with her mom and stepfather. She said of her stepdad, "He was very strict. We weren't close and had our share of arguments. He once told me, 'You'll probably grow up to be a lawyer. You're too headstrong to be anything else.'"

But Fran was also frequently sick as a child. She had allergies and asthma and had to stay indoors a significant amount of time during her youth. She said it made her be a "stay-inside" kind of person who read a lot and did puzzles.

Even though her stepdad forbade her to date during high school, she sneaked out anyway to meet Thomas Soria. She did this two or three times a week since her stepfather worked nights and didn't have an easy time tracking her movements. Fran said, "I remember [how] once Tom and I parked up on a hill. It was a lot of orchards and things like that. We were checked by the cops. It was embarrassing."

Even though Fran thought of her teenage years with Thomas Soria as "the good times," she also had a dark secret in her past concerning her stepfather, the way he did concerning his stepbrother Ronny. She related years later, "My stepdad exercised too much control. He was a security guard. I had a bad dream once when I was a child that my stepdad handcuffed me and locked me in a closet. I cried and kicked the door. I couldn't remember later if it was a dream or real. From that time on, I was claustrophobic. I would run in to a walk-in closet and run out when I got my clothes. I had a fear of all confined spaces."

When Fran was eighteen years old, her stepfather found out that she was meeting Tom on the sly; there was a huge argument. In response, she grabbed all her clothes and moved across the street to a neighbor's house. A few days later, she moved in with Thomas Soria.

Of this time, she said later, "I loved it. He was going to college, and even though it was difficult for him and me because his mother had just been murdered, we somehow coped. It was his opinion that Ronny did it because she'd taken his mother away from him."

Fran went with Thomas to the detective's office during the investigation. But she said she mainly sat in the hallway while he went inside. She also said, "He (Tom) never really talked to me much about the case. I know that he was devastated by it. He didn't want to go into that room where she was murdered. That room was always closed. He would run in there to take out some clothes, and then run back out."

But at least Thomas Soria seemed to be performing normally on some levels. Fran remembered later about her first sexual experience with him, "It was very gentle. Very romantic. He took his time."

Tom and Fran were married in 1979, and even though he didn't stay in touch with any of his Soria relatives, he did contact a few of his Mozingo relatives, especially Aunt Josie and Aunt Carmen. In fact, there were lots of Mozingos in the Sacramento area. Unfortunately for Thomas Soria, his uncle Douglas Mozingo was even more violent and dangerous than Ronny Mozingo. And it would further add to Thomas Soria's bleak outlook on life and feeling that he was cursed. His connection with certain Mozingos would poison him until he became as bad as the worst of them.

THREE
Bloodbath

Thomas Soria's step-uncle Douglas Mozingo, not unlike Ronny Mozingo, had been an angry young man. He swore that while growing up in the small Central Valley town of Galt that his father beat him with a rubber hose for the slightest infraction. Born in Sacramento County, on April 22, 1953, Douglas Mozingo was the youngest of eleven children of Earl and Esther Mozingo, who were then fifty-one and forty-one years old. Court documents revealed that Douglas Mozingo considered his father to be old-fashioned and an ardent disciplinarian. He said later, "He (my father) was a very strict and rigid individual. He was away at work most of the day. He was very set in his ways."

The father's regime of discipline included the children not leaving the yard except to go to school. "The kids left anyway," Douglas said, "knowing that they'd face further restrictions and beatings with a belt or rubber hose." The most rebellious of the lot was Douglas himself.

Douglas Mozingo later told a counselor that his mother was very weak in regard to his father. He said, "Mom seemed hard on us kids in our younger years.

But she was a very sweet and loving person, considering the life she had to live."

Douglas Mozingo attended Archoe Elementary School in Galt and eventually Galt High School, where he had severe discipline problems. School records show that he had an explosive temper and attacked other students without provocation. Mozingo even admitted that he was obtaining liquor and drinking to excess, even though he was underage, which only fueled his already substantial inner rage. His high-school counselor wrote, "[Douglas] is a bully and potentially dangerous. He is paranoid and very rebellious." The counselor recommended that the parents seek counseling for their son. But the elder Mozingo was too old-fashioned for that. He decided to take care of the "problem" in his own manner, which meant more severe punishment. By the time Douglas was in the eleventh grade, he quit school before earning his diploma.

Douglas joined the army as soon as he turned eighteen. But he was just as much a discipline problem in the military as he was in civilian life. He constantly went AWOL and was lax in following orders. After tenth months of this, the U.S. Army grew tired of his insubordination and booted him out with an "undesirable discharge."

With little training and less schooling, Douglas hired on as a ranch hand back in the Galt area. He took on a common-law wife and her two daughters, and it was the first genuinely stable relationship he had ever known. He later said of her, "She was the only person I could express my feelings to. And she expressed her feelings to me." But despite the good relationship with this woman, Douglas soon fell back into drinking too heavily. He said, "I was up to about three six-packs of beer a day. Then I went to scotch. About four fifths a day."

In November and December 1974 his antisocial behavior finally spilled over into crime. In a series of armed robberies at the Victoria Station Restaurant on Tribute Road in Sacramento, Mozingo waylaid patrons as they left the establishment. While demanding a wallet, he told one man, "I'll blow your fucking head off."

Another couple said of their attack, "He said he would shoot us if we didn't cooperate." Because of the pattern of the robberies, the Sacramento Police Department decided to stake out the location. They didn't have long to wait long for Mozingo's next play. On December 23, 1974, Mozingo robbed a prominent Sacramento physician and his wife at gunpoint. He took $118 from the man and started to make his getaway by car. But he didn't get far. A police vehicle pulled him over before he'd gone two blocks and he was caught red-handed.

Unlucky in his pattern of robberies, Mozingo was at least lucky on the judicial front. The deputy district attorney trying the case let him plead to only two robberies instead of five. Soon after that, California's "Use a gun, go to prison" policy went into effect. This would have added more years to his sentence. Instead, Mozingo received only two years at the Deuel Vocational Institute in Tracy, one of California's more lenient penal institutions.

A Department of Corrections official said of Mozingo's time there, "He was a near-model prisoner. He followed the rules and gained a reputation as being very responsible. A good worker. A man who can maintain employment in the community." During his stay at Deuel, Mozingo learned the art of cabinetmaking. In fact, he got to be quite good at his craft.

On March 27, 1977, Douglas Mozingo joined a work furlough program at the Valley Community Corrections Center in Sacramento, which was even less restrictive. Before long, he was completely free of the penal system and working in a furniture store. He moved into a pleasant tree-shaded house in Sacramento's south area with Tanya Reyes and her two daughters. He even set up a workshop in the garage and turned out some very good cabinets for extra money. Their landlord thought Mozingo was a good tenant and remarked on how he always paid the rent on time and kept the place neat.

After a calm period in his life on Sacramento's south side, Douglas Mozingo, Reyes and her daughters moved up to Idaho for what he thought would be greener pastures. But this didn't work out, and before another year was through, Mozingo and the others were back in Sacramento, this time in the north area on Sunnyslope Drive. They moved into a typical suburban house, and everything looked normal from the outside.

But once again, Douglas Mozingo went back to his bad habits of drinking to excess. When he got into those drinking binges, he lost all sense of restraint. One of his neighbors later told a *Sacramento Bee* reporter, "He's (Mozingo) always drunk. He said vulgar things to the girls in the neighborhood. All he did was sit outside with his dog and his beer and get blitzed."

During July 1982 there was a block party in his neighborhood, and according to one neighbor, Mozingo hassled many of the women at the party. One said, "He bothered my sister. Proposed things way out of line."

Even Mozingo's relatives were frightened of him when he drank. One of them later told a *Sacramento Union* reporter, "I always felt a little fear of the guy. If you know him, you know what he's [capable] of doing."

Asked by the reporter if his family was afraid of him, the relative said, "Oh, sure."

One person not afraid of Douglas was his cousin Ronny Mozingo, killer of Thomas Soria's mother. For some reason, these two hit it off, and Douglas even went to visit Ronny in prison. Perhaps their violent natures attracted each other. They certainly didn't attract Thomas Soria. He was still reeling from the murder of his mother and wished Ronny "in hell." But one thing Thomas Soria couldn't have known at the time was that his uncle Douglas Mozingo was about to become much more famous than his murderous stepbrother. Douglas Mozingo lived only about a mile from the Mother Lode Bar, and on the afternoon of Friday, October 1, 1982, he climbed into his car and headed toward that drinking establishment.

On October 1, 1982, the Mother Lode Bar was throwing an "end of summer" party. The bar itself was not much to look at from the outside. Tucked into an area of small businesses and warehouses, it had a Western motif and a wagon wheel above the door. It was a friendly, congenial place. Owner Ron Muller said of the tavern, "It's kind of a comfortable place where people take their wives and mothers. Everyone's on a first-name basis. Because of the party, there was a larger crowd than usual."

Among the patrons that afternoon was Randy Sherwood, twenty-eight years old, who had grown up in the wilds of Alaska with his parents. He was a skilled mason, but when he moved to California, he decided there might be more money to be made as a hairdresser. While at a hairdresser school, he met his future wife, Sharon, and they both went to work at a department store beauty shop after graduation. They did this for a few years until Randy decided to open a tavern called

Journey's End, not far from the Mother Lode Bar. He bartended at his establishment and occasionally did masonry work on the side to earn extra cash.

On October 1, 1982, Randy did some brick work in Vacaville, California, while his dad, James Douglas Sherwood, tended bar at the Journey's End. They agreed to meet at the Mother Lode Bar just to drop in and have a few drinks and see how the party was going. Randy called his wife, Sharon, and told her he would only be there for a little while.

Another patron that afternoon was Pamela McCoy, twenty-seven, who lived in nearby Placer County. She was an artist who made leather goods and jewelry items. She also worked part-time at a convenience store to earn extra money. She stopped by the Mother Lode Bar after work and talked a friend of hers, twenty-six-year old Rhonda Faye Lyons, into joining her.

Rhonda, initially a native of South Dakota, had moved to Sacramento ten years earlier. Like Randy Sherwood, she was a hairdresser. She had long blond hair and was noted for her smile and love of jokes. She played in a softball league and also was a gifted pianist. Rhonda was not a regular at the Mother Lode Bar and only showed up that afternoon because Pam McCoy had invited her.

One more patron wandered into the Mother Lode Bar at about 3:00 P.M. on October 1. He was Douglas Mozingo. He arrived with someone he called his "brother," but others there thought it was a term of comradeship rather than any familial relationship. These two ordered quite a few drinks and even bought a round for the other patrons. The owner, Ron Muller, had seen Mozingo before but didn't know his name. The two men stayed until about 4:30 P.M. and then left quietly.

Muller looked up from the bar at about 5:00 P.M. and noticed that the two men were back, sitting on a bar stool. Mozingo ordered more drinks, and as he continued drinking, he became more and more belligerent. One patron asked Mozingo what he did for a living and Mozingo answered, "We're mercenaries. We haven't had a good fight lately. We'll have to do something about that."

This comment was greeted by a rejoinder to the effect of "Oh, bullshit." Mozingo took umbrage at the remark and an altercation ensued. Muller wanted no fighting in his bar and asked Mozingo and his "brother" to leave.

Muller followed Mozingo out of the parking lot and asked him what the fight was about. Mozingo forgot all about the mercenary remark. He said, "Because some-one jumped my wife and pulled her to the floor by her hair."

Muller was confused by this remark. Mozingo hadn't been sitting with a woman and nothing like that had happened. He wondered if Mozingo was all there in the head or if he was high on some drug. Then Mozingo slurred a regret, and Muller said, "He was almost apologetic when he left."

The Mother Lode Bar returned to normal after the altercation and everyone looked forward to the country-and-western band that was ready to start playing. There was a festive atmosphere in the establishment and the clientele seemed to be enjoying the "end of summer" party. Then at 9:26 P.M. a single man opened the front door and just stood there for a moment. It was Douglas Mozingo, and he had something long, dark and cylindrical in his hand.

Without warning, Douglas Mozingo lifted a .30-cal-iber semiautomatic rifle and began spraying the entire bar with bullets. There was instant pandemonium. Twelve people were struck as others dived for cover. The large mirror behind the bar shattered and pelted everyone with shards of glass. One man crawled into the bathroom down a long corridor while a woman hid behind cases of beer. A waitress said a bullet zipped by her and smashed a pitcher of beer on her tray before she hit the deck. Band members tumbled off the stage as if a hurricane had hit them. There was screaming and the loud reports of the rifle echoing in the confined space as Mozingo fired away like a manic robot.

Then as suddenly as it began, the firing ceased. It was deathly quiet except for the moans of gunshot victims and cries of fear from the more fortunate. In less than a minute, Douglas Mozingo had killed two people, wounded one so seriously that she would soon die, and wounded nine others. He surveyed the damage for only a moment and then walked back out the door without uttering a word. He left behind a scene of incredible carnage.

Randall "Randy" Scott Sherwood, the owner of the Journey's End, was dead, shot through the throat, arm and chest. Pamela McCoy, the artist, was dead, shot through the back and chest. And Rhonda Faye Lyons would soon die, shot through the chest.

Nine others had wounds of various intensity. Kenneth Neal McGuire, twenty-eight, was shot through the shoulder and stomach. Michael Joseph Pesut, thirty-two, had been hit in the head, arm and hand. Raymond Prather, fifty-one, had been struck in the right knee. James Douglas Sherwood, Randall's father, had been shot in the lower back. Ronnie Reed, forty, had been grazed on his left side by a bullet. Jake Renfro had been shot in the buttocks. Ricky Linn Wolfe was hit in the chest. Randolph Wooley had been shot in the chest. Michael Ynostroza, twenty-eight, had been hit in the leg.

Within minutes, police were on the scene and opened the doors to a veritable slaughterhouse. Officer Tim Dunham told a *Sacramento Bee* reporter, "There were bodies everywhere. No one was standing. All were lying on the floor. It looked like they dropped where they stood. They didn't have time to react."

Bar owner Ron Muller was even more graphic: "There was blood and bodies everywhere."

The entire neighborhood became a sea of police cars, ambulances and flashing lights. A cordon of officers was set up just to control the crowd of onlookers who soon gathered. There was also a gunman to catch—with a lot of alleyways and nearby buildings to hide in. Fortunately for the police, they had a good description of the man, but his route of escape was still a mystery. Some of the shocked witnesses said the man climbed into a vehicle with someone else at the wheel. Others thought he had driven off by himself. Another person thought he had merely taken off on foot. At this point, nothing could be discounted.

Jimmy Reynolds, who lived a half block away, told the police he had been watching television when he heard a *"pop, pop, pop"* noise coming from the Mother Lode Bar. He stepped outside and saw a man holding a gun walk out. Then Reynolds said the man had taken a shot at a passing car before leaving in a vehicle.

The officers searched the area around the Mother Lode Bar and came up empty-handed. But they did run into some people who knew the shooter and gave them a name, Douglas Mozingo. Now all they had to do was find him. But this was easier said than done. Mozingo wasn't at home, and they couldn't find him hiding in the neighborhood despite an intense search.

The entire area was by now awash with cruising cop cars, ambulances with sirens screaming and television news crews with their bright lights.

And then a very strange incident happened in the early-morning hours of October 2 that would lead the police directly to their quarry.

Fireman/medical technician Duane Doglieto with the Pacific Fire Station was on duty after midnight on October 2 when a call came in about an overdose victim on Green Tree Drive in Sacramento. When Doglieto and another technician arrived, they found a middle-aged man slumped on the floor of a suburban house. He was unconscious with very weak vital signs. As Doglieto related to a *Sacramento Bee* reporter, "I didn't know the victim's name. Two guys who said they were the victim's brothers told us he wanted to kill himself. Said he took a bunch of pills and drank a lot of alcohol. They didn't know what type of pills he had swallowed. The two brothers kept saying he was 'crazy.'"

Doglieto deposited the victim at the University Medical Center about 12:30 A.M. and then went back to the station. Around 7:30 A.M. he picked up a local newspaper and nearly dropped it on the floor. He read about the slaughter at the Mother Lode Bar, and the physical description of the gunman matched his "suicide" victim to a T: Hispanic, about 5'8", 150 pounds, with a reddish beard. Doglieto phoned the police; when they arrived at the University Medical Center, they discovered that the semi-comatose man was indeed their gunman, Douglas Mozingo. In fact, Mozingo had managed to end up in the same hospital as some of his gunshot victims. Michael Pesut was there undergoing brain surgery. Ronnie Reed was there for treatment of his wound. And Rhonda Lyons was there, soon to succumb to the bullet wound in her chest.

At University Medical Center and in hospitals across town, gunshot victims and their families spent an anguished night. Viola Sherwood had the distinction of having two members of her family cut down by Douglas Mozingo. Her husband was wounded and her son was dead. She had found out about their plight through a friend who had been watching television and phoned her. The friend had heard the name Sherwood mentioned by the reporter.

Within the corridors of the University Medical Center was Juanita Pesut, mother of Michael Pesut, who was undergoing intercranial surgery at the Neurosurgical Intensive Care Unit. When she learned that the shooter, Douglas Mozingo, was in the same hospital, she told a *Sacramento Bee* reporter, "He should have done it (committed suicide) last night before he went to the bar. What the hell. They won't do anything to him. Maybe a couple of years [in prison]. That's what's so disgusting."

Mother Lode Bar owner, Ron Muller, took up this same cry of anger at the judicial system in California. After all, this was an era when the lenient decisions of Rose Bird's court still had great ramifications in the state. He told a *Sacramento Bee* reporter, "In this country, it seems easier to get away with murder than drunk driving. We can't let creeps like this run the country. This is the kind of thing you expect to happen anywhere but your home or your home away from home. Something has to be done with our justice system before it's too late."

In fact, something was already in the works that August day in Sacramento. Douglas Mozingo could have hardly picked a worse time to go on his rampage. The state legislature was dealing with tougher death penalty laws, and Mozingo's bloodbath only added ammunition to Governor Deukmejian's stance on the "Briggs Initiative." This would make it easier for juries to vote for a death penalty conviction.

The ramifications of Douglas Mozingo's massacre even spread out into unexpected quarters and may have claimed one more victim in a roundabout way. The day after Pamela McCoy was pronounced dead, a coworker of hers, Daniel Barton, twenty-eight, shot himself to death. It was hard to say if the death of Pamela McCoy sparked his suicide, but it certainly played a part in it.

While Douglas Mozingo lay on a bed in intensive care, he was charged with three counts of murder and nine counts of attempted murder. Police spokesman Sergeant Bob Burns said, "He has positively been identified as the shooter. We're sure we have the right person."

Mozingo was being held at the hospital's detention ward, where he was still in serious but stable condition. By Monday, October 4, Mozingo was coherent enough to give police detectives a lengthy statement, including the fact that he had tried to kill himself after the rampage.

On October 6, 1982, a dazed-looking Douglas Mozingo was arraigned on three counts of murder and nine counts of attempted murder. He appeared to be recovering slowly from the overdose of pills and huge intake of alcohol. As he leaned heavily on the railing at the prisoner's dock, Judge Allen Fields of the municipal court read the twelve-count list of charges. Mozingo's public defender, Michael Bigelow, entered no plea at that time, but the prosecutor let it be known that they would be seeking the death penalty against him.

Meanwhile, various memorial services for his murder victims were being held across town. Melann McCoy,

Pamela McCoy's sister, said, "It's just an overall tragedy. It's a tragedy for us and for him (Mozingo) and his family. I feel sorry for everybody involved. My sister didn't even know that man."

At Rhonda Faye Lyons's memorial service, her friend Carol Hrimnak was not so forgiving of Mozingo. She said, "I don't care how drunk you are or what problems you have. You don't go around killing people. It's sickening."

One person who was not asked about all of this was Douglas Mozingo's step-nephew, Thomas Soria. The news was everywhere in the Sacramento area; it was in newspapers, on radio shows and on television. He couldn't have escaped it if he tried. By now, the name Mozingo was absolutely toxic to him. He had endured the rape and murder of his mother by a Mozingo, and now this. Asked about it much later by his wife, Francine, she would say, "The death of his mother affected him deeply. He never got over it. As each year passed, it didn't get any better. It was just as fresh as the year before."

As hard as he tried, Thomas Soria could not cast off the shadows that Ronny Mozingo and Douglas Mozingo cast over his world. But he and his fellow Sacramento residents had not heard the last of these two. Both would cause headlines to be splashed across the front pages of newspapers in years to come, even as Thomas Soria struggled to maintain his own sanity.

FOUR

Breakout

One thing became crystal clear as far as Douglas Mozingo and the criminal justice system were concerned—he would battle them every step of the way. Mozingo became a master at using every constitutional tool to delay his day of reckoning. His very first preliminary hearing in Sacramento County set the tone for everything to follow. He was bound over to the superior court after a hearing at the municipal court. But this was soon set aside when it was learned that the municipal court judge allowed Mozingo to be represented by an attorney with a conflict of interest.

It was back to square one before the prosecutors were barely out of the gates. In fact, the case was soon to be bounced back and forth between various judges. The first judge had to release the case because of retirement, and the next two kept shifting the case back and forth between themselves because of calendar problems. Even the deputy district attorneys got into the act. Before long, district attorney number three was working on the Monzingo case, and like all the others, he had to be brought up to speed. It was a trial that was going nowhere fast.

By 1984 everything finally looked ready to go, but
then Douglas Mozingo pulled the rug out from beneath everyone. He decided to fire his defense
attorneys and represent himself. More time was wasted
as Mozingo was given the appropriate documents and
a primer in legal terms. Then Mozingo decided just as
suddenly to "rehire" his attorneys. More time was
wasted in the process. Some of the cynics around the
courthouse said that Mozingo would die of old age before this case ever came to trial.

In July 1985 the whole mess took a bizarre twist as
cousin Ronny Mozingo and his lawyer got into the act.
Ronny Mozingo had been languishing in San Quentin
Prison and waging an appeal battle of his own as the
whole Douglas Mozingo matter was making its way
through the Sacramento County court system. Ronny
Mozingo's lawyer, who was dealing with the appeal in
Sacramento, saw a big opening in his own case because
of the notoriety of Douglas Mozingo. Ronny's lawyer
argued before the Third District court of appeals that
his client was not likely to get a fair hearing in Sacramento County because of the "spillover effect" from
the Douglas Mozingo case. The Third District court of
appeals agreed and stopped all proceedings in both
cases while the matter was sent up to the California
supreme court.

Vince Adeszko, the latest prosecutor in the Ronny
Mozingo case, was beside himself. He told a *Sacramento
Bee* reporter, "I litigated pretrial motions for three
months, and one day before we were ready to start se-
lecting a jury, the supreme court issued a stay."

Both Mozingos had been separated by a distance of
eighty miles for the last two years, but things were
about to change. Ronny Mozingo had been in San
Quentin Prison, on the shores of San Francisco Bay,

and Douglas Mozingo had been in Sacramento County Jail. But as Ronny Mozingo's appeal came up, he was transferred to Sacramento County, not far away from his notorious cousin.

Their close proximity was to be short-lived, however. Douglas Mozingo couldn't control himself in jail any better than he could on the outside. He'd already been in several fights in the Sacramento County Jail. When he got into a major scuffle that summer and bit off another inmate's ear, Douglas Mozingo was summarily shipped off to the Amador County Jail, up in the Gold Country.

Things only got worse there. Douglas got into one fight after another with inmates. Sergeant Emmett Rettagliata of the Amador County Sheriff's Department said, "There was an awful lot of tension in the cell block and we sent him back to Sacramento."

Nobody wanted violent, half-crazed Douglas Mozingo. It wasn't long before the Sacramento County Jail shipped him off to neighboring Placer County and its new multi-million-dollar jail facility. It was hoped that Mozingo's violent nature would be dampened there.

Meanwhile, just across town, Ronny Mozingo was embroiled in his own brand of mayhem. At the Sacramento County Jail, he struck Deputy Stephen Budrow in the throat with a closed fist. When a second deputy, Michael Dunbar, joined the fracas, Mozingo fought so violently that he made a deep gash in Dunbar's forehead, requiring ten stitches. A third deputy had to be called in just to restrain Mozingo.

New charges contending the felony assault of a police officer were filed against Ronny Mozingo.

If the Mozingos weren't battling it out in the county jails, they were battling it out in court with lawyers as their proxies. By now, both of them had their cases

under appeal at the Sacramento superior court, only
two doors apart. It was unparalleled in Sacramento
County history to have two close family members fac-
ing the death penalty on unrelated crimes. Both men's
lawyers were asking for the same outcome in proceedings, that each man be given a change of venue
because of the intense publicity in the area. Of all this,
Fran Soria said, "Tom knew all about this publicity and
such. But he tried to ignore it the best he could. It
made him think about his mother."

Ronny Mozingo's lawyer, William J. Owen, argued,
"My client may become a victim of guilt by association.
The name Mozingo itself is so well known and so asso-
ciated with wrongdoing in Sacramento that there is a
likelihood Ronny Mozingo cannot get a fair trial. He's
a Mozingo. That alone is a factor in favor of a change
of venue."

Meanwhile, Douglas Mozingo's lawyer, James Thomas,
conducted a survey and found that eight out of ten
prospective jurors in his case recognized the case and
four out of five had prejudged it. The results, he said,
were unmistakable. The case must be moved out of
Sacramento County.

By now, the legal wrangling had gone to such ex-
tremes that Raymond L. Brosterhaus II, the attorney
general of the state of California, weighed in on the
issue. He said, "Sacramento County with 574,000
prospective jurors is large enough to handle both
Mozingos. Any spillover effect can be cured during the
jury selection process. Even if you accept the defense
figures that forty-nine percent of the jurors have prejudged the case, that leaves us with a quarter-million
prospective jurors."

A three-justice panel took up the issue of the change
of venue for Douglas Mozingo. While the three men

debated, Douglas Mozingo was making plans of his own, and they had nothing to do with lawyers, judges or legal briefs.

Douglas Mozingo was in the brand-new Placer County Jail in October 1985. It had cost over five million dollars and was a state-of-the-art facility just north of the city of Auburn. At the time of its completion, it was hailed as one of the most secure jails in the state. It had a centralized remote-control system that included cameras, electronically controlled doors, movement detectors and other devices. But inmates are always looking for ways to break out of jail, and Douglas Mozingo, in the fall of 1985, was in the company of some desperate and innovative prisoners.

Mozingo's time in the Placer County Jail placed him in some very interesting and dangerous company. He rubbed shoulders with Frank Morrell, who was a parole violator from Oregon. He also came into contact with George Jackson Newton, who had been accused of killing a Concord man and dumping his body along the American River. Perhaps the most dangerous of the bunch, besides Mozingo, was David Dominguez, who was awaiting trial for having killed two people in Roseville in September 1984. These four men plotted in secrecy, trying to ascertain the best means for a breakout.

Luckily for them, there was a prisoner who had proved that a jail break was possible. On June 30, 1985, convicted rapist Gary Lee Freeman had scaled the wall of the exercise yard, run across the roof of the jail and leaped downward over a chain-link fence. He then shimmied through a tight space in a bundle of razor wire and lit out over the fields. He was recaptured a week later, but he proved the "state-of-the-art" jail was not invulnerable.

On the evening of October 27, 1985, Douglas Mozingo, David Dominguez, Frank Morrell and George Newton were ready to do Freeman one better.

The four men should have been in the recreation room or the television room with the other inmates that evening. Instead, they all quietly made their way toward a fire door that led to the exercise yard. The door was usually electronically shut and locked, but for some reason there was a glitch that evening in the new computer system. The door was not only unlocked but the motion sensor was deactivated as well. No one in the central command center knew a thing as the quartet of inmates quietly opened and closed the door on their way to escape.

Their plan was as bold as it was simple. They carried bundles of bedsheets and blankets with them. Once they reached the twenty-foot-high fence, which was topped with razor wire, they threw the blankets over the wire and used the sheets as ropes to climb over the top without getting cut. They dropped down on the other side, unseen, and made their way across a darkened field southwest of the jail.

Somewhere in the dark, George Jackson split off from the others. Douglas Mozingo, David Dominguez and Frank Morrell headed in another direction. They knew they couldn't go far dressed in their bright orange prison jumpsuits. However, there were no houses in the immediate vicinity and they had to cross three miles of forested foothills in the dark before they came upon a house on Vernon Road.

The trio of convicts entered the house and tied up the family and discovered that the house was a treasure trove of just what they needed. They donned civilian clothing and found some firearms. Best of all, there was a silver Camaro in the driveway and they soon had the keys. It was an escaped prisoner's dream come true.

The three men fired up the Camaro, Douglas Mozingo at the wheel, and headed down the road toward Interstate 80. But the long trek across the countryside had cost them valuable time. At 9:20 P.M. a head count at the Placer County Jail showed that four prisoners were missing. Almost immediately an all points bulletin (APB) was put out about the escape. In the local area, a dozen Sheriff's officers with dogs scoured the rugged foothills while a California Highway Patrol helicopter hovered overhead.

It was now a race against time for the trio in the Camaro as more and more police agencies sent out men in the search. The one advantage the escaped convicts had was that dozens of roads spread out everywhere in the hilly countryside. Even better was that they had shed their prison garb. One thing they hadn't counted on, though, was another member of the family returning home to find the other members tied up. He soon gave a phone call to the police, and the authorities knew to be on the lookout for a silver Camaro.

Douglas Mozingo and the other escaped convicts headed down Interstate 80 toward Sacramento when he discovered that the gas gauge was low. Mozingo turned onto an off-ramp into the small town of Rocklin, confident that their anonymity was still intact. But the word was out now, and Officer Mark Scott of the Rocklin Police Department happened to be cruising by in the area when he spotted the little silver Camaro at a gas pump. He knew that the convicts were armed and dangerous, so he did the wise thing: called for backup. Only in a grade-B Western did a lawman take on three escaped, armed convicts by himself.

As Douglas Mozingo and the others left, Officer Scott followed them toward Sacramento on I-80 as other police cars rushed to the area. At Riverside Boulevard in Roseville, Officer Scott's reinforcements arrived. A sudden blaze of lights and wail of sirens pierced the night as police officers ordered the Camaro to pull over. Instead, Mozingo hit the gas.

Mozingo roared onto the city streets of Roseville, the little silver Camaro fishtailing like a frisky colt with a half dozen police cars in hot pursuit, with more on the way. Mozingo figured he was a dead man anyway and had nothing to lose. The Camaro zigzagged through passenger cars and pickups as if they were standing still. Innocent bystanders looked on in amazement as the silver streak spun around corners with a police car pursuit roaring along behind in a game of dangerous crack-the-whip. Mozingo careened the car all over Roseville, up side streets and down major boulevards. Everything was lit up with flashing red and blue lights and the screech of tires echoed off the surrounding buildings. It was a chase that would have made movie hero Bullitt proud.

Douglas Mozingo was driving a pattern so erratic that no one could guess where he would go next. Even he didn't know for sure until he spun the wheel, nearly sideswiping vehicles, and heading off in some new direction. Despite his best efforts, Mozingo could not shake his pursuers. At the corner of Antelope and Riverside Boulevards in Roseville, Mozingo took the corner too fast and the Camaro skidded off the road into a barbed-wire fence.

Even though the trio of convicts was totally surrounded, they still refused to come out of the car. It was an incredible scene of flashing lights and officers crouching behind squad cars, guns at the ready.

Mozingo, Dominguez and Morrell had their own weapons in the car; it seemed as if all hell would break loose at any moment.

But eventually reason prevailed. It wouldn't have been much of a shoot-out anyway as far as the convicts were concerned. Mozingo was caught up in his seat belt and Morrell was hurt. The trio had about as much chance as Bonnie and Clyde against the lawmen. All three decided they could die now or die later. They chose later.

Douglas Mozingo and David Dominguez were escorted back to the Placer County Jail, and Frank Morrell was shipped off to Auburn's Faith Hospital for treatment. Meanwhile, escaped convict George Jackson Newton was having an adventure of his own. After splitting off from the other three, he had made his way to Baxter Road, near Auburn, where he stole a vehicle. Newton's race for freedom lasted until 3:30 A.M. on Saturday morning when he was spotted on I-80 and pulled over near the town of Newcastle. His capture was much less dramatic than that of the other three.

Everyone at the county jail was red-faced after this escape attempt from the new multimillion-dollar jail facility. It was supposed to be state of the art with its electronic doors and computer-aided equipment. In fact, the door left open at the jail had not been detected at all by the computer system. It was so bad that Lieutenant Larry Newman, jail supervisor, told a reporter, "Authorities are considering replacing it with a manual-type system."

Sheriff Don Nunes exclaimed to a *Roseville Tribune* reporter, "We cannot totally rely on the electronic circuitry system and are having to do several things manually and intend to put at least one additional night shift supervisor over there. The system failed and is the same circuitry that has frustrated jail staff from time to time over the last month."

Then he lashed out at the men who had designed and built the expensive jail: "I am strongly considering a lawsuit against either designers, contractors or subcontractors to correct these deficiencies. We've had the whole computer system down for as long as forty-eight hours and the jail's two hundred eighty-six doors all had to be opened manually with keys, which created some havoc."

Stung by all the criticisms, county architect Ted Cook, who'd helped design the facility, shot back: "The sheriff forgets he was involved in the entire planning process. It was a cooperative effort on the part of a lot of people to go through the design and development of this jail project. It is not as if it was designed and dropped on the Sheriff's department and we said, 'Here, you operate it.'"

Once again, Douglas Mozingo had a knack for stirring up controversy, but it was nothing compared to the hornet's nest he was about to unleash.

Douglas Mozingo was far from willing to cooperate with the authorities after his capture. If he couldn't escape by conventional means, he would do it by much more drastic methods. Only one day after his return to the Placer County Jail, Douglas Mozingo was found dead—hanging by a strip of bedsheet knotted into a rope and tied around his neck. And just like everything else he did, it would set off a wave of controversy about what had really happened.

After his return to the Auburn Jail, Mozingo had been placed in a double-locked, single-man cell. Then on the morning of October 28, other inmates down the hall informed a guard that Mozingo had not touched his morning plate of food. When the guard went to see what was wrong, he discovered Mozingo hanging by his neck.

Somehow Douglas Mozingo had managed to tie his hands behind his back before stepping off his bunk into eternity. At least that was the official version. Inspector Johnny Smith said that Mozingo's hands were very loosely bound. Smith said he had used slipknots, tying one hand and inserting the other through a loop. Smith went on to say that Mozingo could have saved himself at any time by simply stepping back onto the bunk. Mozingo had apparently stuffed a gag in his own mouth so that he couldn't change his mind and call out for help.

But Chief Deputy Larry Stamm, who had twenty-seven years with the Sacramento Sheriff's Department, said that he'd never heard of anyone tying their hands behind their backs in jail before committing suicide. He didn't say it was impossible; he simply said he'd never heard of it.

The implications of foul play hung in the air pretty thick after that.

Even more vociferous in his contention of guard-induced murder was one of Douglas Mozingo's relatives. The relative asked a *Sacramento Bee* reporter, "How can you tie your own hands behind your back? Maybe it's possible. But I feel deep down inside that the police did it."

Over in a jail cell across town, Douglas's cousin Ronny Mozingo agreed. He said about the standoff in the Camaro and Douglas's suicide: "Now, if he had a gun and wanted to die, why wouldn't he (Douglas) have held court there on the street instead of going back to a single cell and kill himself?"

Inspector Smith tried to quash that theory by stating that Douglas Mozingo probably couldn't get to the rifle from the front seat when he was wound up in his seat belt. He added, "Just about every officer in Placer and Sacramento Counties must have been there."

Doubts still simmered, though, in many people's minds about what actually happened in Douglas Mozingo's isolation cell.

Whatever the reason for Douglas Mozingo's death, there was one group of people who held a celebration when they learned of his demise. They were the survivors and friends and family of victims who had suffered through Douglas Mozingo's rampage at the Mother Lode Bar. As a *Sacramento Bee* reporter noted, "The mood at the Mother Lode bar Sunday night was a bittersweet drink of restrained joy and sorrow stirred by laughter and tears and the knowledge that a three-year nightmare of tangled legal maneuvers was over."

It was a private wake at the bar among Mozingo's survivors and their friends; naturally, their memories drifted back to the terrible evening of October 1, 1982. The woman bartender who had been there that night told the reporter, "This is the first day of the rest of my life."

David Wooley, the father of victim Randolph Wooley, said, "I'm just glad the situation is over so that the living victims don't have to be dragged back into court and live through the hassle and the runaround."

Wooley's comments were greeted by muted applause and raised glasses and beer bottles.

Then he added, "The supreme court stinks."

Survivor Tom Smith agreed heartily and blamed the whole judicial system for the years of frustration and delayed justice. He said, "A lot of people are living well out there because they don't settle things like this."

Doris Crowe chimed in, "I think if the judges had been here to see those bodies taken out, they would have changed their opinion."

"What would have happened," David Wooley asked, "if a judge's son or daughter had been here that night? Would justice have happened sooner?"

Owner Ron Muller said, "I hope some of the rumors are true that the jailers hanged him. We may never know. Either way, he got what he deserved."

Mixed in between the grief and anger was a sense of relief that the Douglas Mozingo slaughter could be put behind them. Either by suicide or other means, he was finally out of their lives.

But the patrons of the Mother Lode Bar would have been astonished that night if they could have been privy to Ronny Mozingo's thoughts as he lay back on his Sacramento County Jail bunk that evening. As his lawyer noted, "He is a Mozingo." Ronny was cooking up plans to do his cousin one better. Within a matter of days, he'd have everyone all over town talking.

FIVE

Over the Top

Ronny Mozingo was anything but contrite in the years since his conviction for the brutal rape and murder of his stepmother, Janey Mozingo. His appeals process had been like a roller-coaster ride. Initially sentenced to death, he'd been residing at San Quentin Prison since 1980. Behind those walls, he had stabbed two other prisoners in fights. Mozingo was just as much a disciplinary problem as he had always been.

He was also becoming a proficient jailhouse lawyer, claiming that his defense attorney Peter Fatros had not done an adequate job at his trial. Mozingo said, "After speaking with some other convicts (during his trial in 1980), I decided to change my plea to insanity, but [my attorney] said it was too late and that the judge said it would be improper for me to change my plea at that time."

Mozingo's appeal was that he had not received a fair trial. Judge J. Spurgeon Avakian of the Alameda County superior court looked into the matter and, amazingly, agreed with Mozingo that he had not received adequate counsel. Judge Avakian wrote, "The trial counsel failed to act in the manner expected of a reasonably competent attorney acting as a diligent advocate thereby depriving [Mozingo] of a potentially meritorious defense."

The California supreme court agreed with Judge Avakian's assessment and scheduled a new trial for Ronny Mozingo. With any luck, he would get off death row in San Quentin. And by 1984 his chances improved even more. It was in November of that year that the California supreme court ruled that hypnosis-induced testimony was illegal. This brought the testimony of Mozingo's sister, Linda Smith, directly into question. She had undergone hypnosis as had Janey Mozingo's neighbor Manuel Ramirez. Mozingo's attorneys quickly brought forth a motion to overturn Ronny's conviction, contending that key testimony was tainted by hypnosis. They argued that since "the testimony of any witness who has been hypnotized to restore or improve memory is inadmissible as to all matters that are the subject of the hypnotic sessions." Manuel Ramirez's recollections of seeing Ronny Mozingo on a bicycle near the scene of the crime on September 25, 1979, was particularly aided by the help of hypnosis.

Now it was up to Judge Joseph A. De Cristoforo of the Sacramento superior court as to whether Ronny Mozingo's conviction should be overturned on this technicality. De Cristoforo did not take the matter lightly. He conducted a seventeen-day hearing that addressed the whole issue of the California supreme court's ruling. At the end of this time, De Cristoforo concluded that the specific issue before him in the Mozingo case was the one issue that the California supreme court did not rule on: "Whether there should be an exception allowing a witness to testify to facts he remembered before he was hypnotized." De Cristoforo ruled that Ramirez, who was hypnotized, could testify to the facts he related to police before his hypnotic sessions.

De Cristoforo acknowledged that his ruling on Ramirez was a close call, but he had no reservations about the testimony of Mozingo's sister, Linda Smith. Her hypnosis sessions had been performed long after the trial and were for therapeutic reasons rather than for testimony.

Charles Bloodgood and Fern Laetham, Ronny Mozingo's lawyers, were disappointed with the ruling, but they indicated they still held out hope for yet another trial in the murder of Janey Mozingo.

Just like his dead cousin Douglas Mozingo, Ronny Mozingo was back in the Sacramento County area because of this new round of legal maneuvering. And like his infamous cousin, he planned to take the matter of freedom into his own hands. If the judicial system couldn't free him, he would do it himself. Just like Douglas, Ronny had some pretty rough company in jail; soon they were plotting together about how to escape.

While in the Sacramento County Jail on Seventh Street, Ronny Mozingo got to know Rocky Boatwright and Jimmy Ray Williamson. Boatwright was in on a federal charge for manufacturing methamphetamines. Williamson was more in the Ronny Mozingo mold. He had a whole string of convictions against him. During several months, he had managed to perpetrate thirteen separate criminal incidents. When arrested, he garnered eleven counts of burglary, nine counts of robbery, eight counts of false imprisonment, seven counts of kidnapping, five counts of assault with a deadly weapon and one count each of sodomy, rape, receiving stolen property and intent to commit a sex crime. Only twenty-two years old, Williamson had been a busy young man.

Williamson was busy once again in early December 1985. Along with Ronny Mozingo and Rocky Boatwright, Jimmy Ray Williamson was ripping apart the bottom of his jailhouse mattress and weaving the shreds into rope. The material was very strong—strong enough, in fact, to hold the weight of a man when woven together. This factor was key, since the trio planned to escape via the rooftop of the jail, six stories above the street. In one regard, they had a leg up on Douglas Mozingo's escape plans. They wouldn't have to find a car, one was coming directly to them. Ronny Mozingo had talked his wife, Mary, into joining the escape plot. She would drive her car into the area and be waiting when they made their daring escape.

The plan was as bold as it was imaginative. The trio convinced and threatened other inmates into leaving the rooftop recreation room while they wove the bits of mattress into rope. They worked night after night until they each had twenty-foot sections of rope. Another individual came into their orbit named Roger Joel Mackrill, although it's not clear how much he became a part of their plans to escape. Mackrill was in jail for violating his probation by carrying a gun. One thing was for certain, though, Mackrill knew Ronny Mozingo's reasons for wanting to escape. Ronny told Mackrill, "I want to get the witnesses in my death penalty case." Mackrill understood "get" to mean "kill."

At 8:00 P.M., on December 4, 1985, everything was set to go. Mary Mozingo was stationed outside the jail in her station wagon. Jimmy Ray Williamson and Rocky Boatwright had lengths of rope tied around their waists, while Ronny Mozingo had fashioned a brace from a Ping-Pong table into an eight-inch shank, pointed at one end to serve as a knife. As the men were escorted to the elevators on the fifth floor for their ride to the sixth-floor recreation room, there seemed to be no suspicion on the part of the guards. But just on mere chance, and according to regulations, one of the guards performed a pat down on the inmates. He was just as surprised as they were when he felt foreign material underneath their jail clothing.

The ropes and weapon were discovered, and the commanding officer on duty ordered an immediate search of the streets below, just in case the men had an accomplice on the outside. One of the deputies sighted Mary Mozingo sitting in her 1976 station wagon only a few steps away from the jail. He recognized her because she had been visiting her husband in jail on a regular basis. The deputy spotted a gun inside the car. Other deputies soon arrived and they ordered twenty-five-year-old Mary Mozingo out of the car at gunpoint, at which time she surrendered.

Inside the vehicle was an eye-opening amount of incriminating evidence. There was a loaded .22-caliber rifle, four boxes of ammunition, and a .25-caliber automatic pistol with fifty rounds of ammunition. There was also changes of clothing for four men, men's toiletries, a small amount of methamphetamines, cocaine and six hundred dollars in cash. Mary Mozingo had definitely come to play.

Mary Mozingo was arrested on the spot for aiding and abetting an escape and being in possession of a concealed and deadly weapon. Her excuse for being there at that time of night sounded pretty lame to the officers. She said she was only in the area to deposit some money at the jail in her husband's name.

When it came time for Ronny Mozingo to face the new charges of planning an escape and carrying a concealed weapon, there was one man to whom he wished he had never spoken, Roger Joel Mackrill. With a videotape camera rolling, Mackrill told the prosecutor that Mozingo's main target was "a man who lived next door to his (Mozingo's) dad." The "man" most likely was Manuel Ramirez.

Mackrill was being videotaped just in case he couldn't make it in person to the actual trial. Mackrill was no longer an inmate but feared retribution by Mozingo so much that he had failed to appear in court on two previous occasions to testify against Ronny. Taking no chances now, the prosecutor Vince Adeszko recorded Mackrill's statements on videotape in front of Judge Richard Backus before a jury was even impaneled. Adeszko didn't want to have Mackrill somehow disappear before his testimony became a part of the court record.

Mackrill testified reluctantly in front of the camera that his life had been threatened by Ronny Mozingo if he ever told about the plans that were made before the escape attempt. He then went on to identify two "ropes" made of the mattress strips and torn bedsheets. He went on to tell how the prisoners had fashioned the ropes in the recreation room. Mackrill related how Mozingo was going to use the shank to overpower any guard who happened to be on the roof and how the inmates were going to "pop" a link in the chain-link fence that surrounded the roof area. After that, it would be a daring scramble down the side to the street where Mary Mozingo would be waiting in a car packed with civilian clothing. He did not go into details about whether he was part of the escape attempt or just an innocent bystander.

After all these new revelations, Ronny Mozingo still wasn't through impacting the Sacramento County court system. In fact, as the time approached for his third trial in 1987, his daring rooftop escape plan seemed to have infected others in the jail. On the night of January 27, 1987, Darrel Donat and Stephen Sanders climbed down a wire dangling from the side of the new jail on H Street to the fifth floor of the old jail. Unfortunately for them, they tripped an alarm and it wasn't long before officers streamed onto the fifth floor and captured them.

Ronny Mozingo seemed to have a knack for getting other people into trouble. So far, they had included his wife, Mary, Rocky Boatwright and Jimmy Ray Williamson. All of them had suffered by following his lead. But it was supremely ironic that the man prosecuting him would also be in hot water by May 1987. Deputy District Attorney Vince Adeszko had just stepped over the line with Judge Richard Backus and was soon to feel his wrath.

Back on April 9, Judge Backus had issued a court order expressly forbidding out-of-court comments on the evidence. But on May 19 Deputy DA Adeszko had spoken to a *Sacramento Union* reporter and said, "Roger Mackrill is a hero. Everything he said about what Mozingo told him came true. Mackrill's testimony shows that Mr. Mozingo was attempting to suppress a witness in his murder case. You don't try to kill a witness if you're innocent."

Charles Bloodgood, Mozingo's attorney, cried foul, saying that Adeszko's comments were "inflammatory." He went on to say that his client could no longer get a fair trial in Sacramento County because of all the publicity.

On May 29, 1987, it was Deputy District Attorney Vince Adeszko's turn to be "in the hot seat" as Judge Backus convened a disciplinary session. The judge stated that Adeszko had specifically gone against his instructions to suppress all statements of innocence or guilt as to any party in the case. Adeszko sat quietly and chastened at the prosecutor's table as Judge Backus read him his constitutional rights. Charged with violating the gag order, Adeszko waived his rights and asked for an immediate resolution of the contempt citation. In his own behalf, he did say that his comments to the *Sacramento Union* reporter were based on evidence presented in open court.

Judge Backus zeroed in on Adeszko's most "inflammatory" statement to the reporter: "You don't try to kill a witness if you're innocent." Backus said that one statement violated three separate paragraphs of the gag order, including the provision barring out-of-court comments on the guilt or innocence of the defendant.

In the end, he gave the deputy district attorney only a verbal reprimand for his actions. Judge Backus said that he was convinced that Adeszko's statements concerning the violation rang true as more inadvertent than willful. He declined to administer harsher sanctions against Vince Adeszko.

Ronny Mozingo must have been laughing up his sleeve at the prosecutor's discomfort. He would have been even more pleased to find out that slowly but surely the deputy DA's case was falling apart through the summer of 1987. When Mozingo's defense attorneys learned what kind of hypnosis the prosecutor's star witness, Linda Smith, had undergone, a whole new can of worms was opened in the case that never seemed to end. Mozingo's sister, Linda Smith, had not only been hypnotized but she had been involved in séances as well to call back the spirit of her stepmother, Janey Mozingo. With the knowledge of this fact, her entire credibility was called into question.

Between Douglas Mozingo and Ronny Mozingo, the taxpayers of Sacramento County had already spent millions of dollars for court costs. The Mozingos had gone down just about every judicial avenue possible and enraged countless people. But on August 7, 1987, it all came to an abrupt and surprise ending.

Ronny Mozingo decided to use a little-known decision recently handed down by the United States Supreme Court in a North Carolina case. In that decision, a person had pleaded guilty with protestations of innocence. In other words, Mozingo could profess his innocence while still being found guilty. By this means, he could leave the door open for further appeals down the line. It also meant that the death penalty against him would cease to be a valid sentence. It would save Mozingo his life and it would save the taxpayers of Sacramento County further millions of dollars. In the end, it seemed to be a good compromise for everyone involved.

Deputy District Attorney Vince Adeszko didn't make any comment to reporters about the decision. He was keeping his mouth shut now, having already been burned once. But Mozingo's defense attorneys, Charles Bloodgood and Fern Laetham, commented, "We're real pleased. It saved Ronny Mozingo's life."

On October 2, 1987, the whole Ronny Mozingo case in the murder of Janey Mozingo, finally came to an end. Judge Richard Backus sentenced Mozingo to a twenty-five-year term for the murder of Janey Mozingo and a further eleven years for the 1985 escape attempt. If Mozingo behaved himself in prison, he would be eligible for parole in twelve years.

One person who was not pleased by this sentence was Ronny Mozingo's own father, Duane. He told a *Sacramento Bee* reporter, "I think Ronny should have received the death penalty for his actions."

Another person not pleased about this sentence was

Ronny Mozingo's stepbrother, Thomas Soria. There was no doubt that the shock of his witnessing back in 1979 the defiled and murdered body of his mother on the floor had altered his life forever. The rampages of his uncle and stepbrother only furthered his sense of alienation in a city where the name Mozingo had begun to stand for murder and mayhem.

But what form Thomas Soria's mental torment would take went beyond the realm of imagination. It led him down dark and twisted corridors that only a gifted psychologist could unravel. Instead of rejecting everything Ronny Mozingo stood for and had done, Thomas Soria would emulate him. He would take his stepbrother's sick and depraved nature and ratchet it up a notch to such unspeakable deeds that they would defy description. In a horrible and twisted fate, Thomas Soria would become the mirror image of the stepbrother he so despised.

SIX

"Daddy's Boy"

The first years of the marriage between Thomas Soria and Fran had been fine. Francine was still in love with him and willing to put up with some of his demands. Tom's mother had always spoiled him and so he expected the same treatment from her. She did admit later, "I would say that he was a manipulative person. Tom wasn't so much dominating as selfish. Everything was for him. And this is when I had two jobs. I worked the graveyard shift and would get three or five hours' sleep in the afternoon. I was still cleaning house and cooking meals."

These kinds of things might have been part of any normal marriage, but Thomas Soria's internal mechanisms could never be normal after what had happened to his mother. The strains soon came out in different ways; the chief one was in his sexual life. Fran said later, "We weren't having the right kind of sex, according to him. Like sodomy. I didn't want to do it. I tried it a few times to please him. But it hurt and I didn't like it."

She also related, "He wanted me to urinate on him. I told him, 'No! No way! That's not my thing.' But then

he would insist and say, 'You'd do it if you love me.'
Sometimes I would do it just to get him off my back."

There were also problems about having children.
Tom desperately wanted a little girl. Perhaps he wanted
to turn her into a replacement of the mother he had
lost. Instead, they had a son, Thomas Soria Jr., nick-
named T.J., in Carson City at the Carson-Tahoe
Hospital on August 9, 1980. They lived for a short time
in Round Hill, Nevada, and then moved to the Sacramento area.

Tom still wanted a girl, but Fran now had complica-
tions conceiving. She said, "After two D and C's I told
him, 'No more.' He was disappointed, but he didn't
press me on it." She noted, though, that their sex life became less frequent after that. She said, "After that, the
sex went downhill. We didn't do it that often anymore."

There were also troubling signs elsewhere in the
marriage. They moved to Lake Tahoe and there was an
incident with their next-door neighbor. The neighbors,
who had a son and daughter, complained to the police
that they had spied Thomas Soria standing naked outside their home. They called the police, and when an
officer arrived at the Soria home, he confronted Tom
about it. Thomas told the officer that the whole thing
had been "a cooked-up thing" because of some antag-
onism between himself and the neighbors. But it must
have been more than just that. Twenty years later, the
daughter still had nightmares about Thomas Soria
standing outside her window exposing himself.

Fran believed Tom's version of the story because she
was still in love with him. Unable to find concrete
proof, the officer let Tom off with a warning, but the
incident seemed to sour the Sorias on Lake Tahoe.
They began to move around a lot. The trek took them
from one residence to another; first to Cartan Drive in

Sacramento, next to Carmichael, then Foothill Farms and finally the community of Antelope, California. Tom didn't pester her anymore for the sex he wanted, but it didn't mean he hadn't been gratifying himself elsewhere.

At some point, Thomas Soria went to visit a cousin's family on a ranch in the Central Valley of California. Their daughter remembered vividly one incident when she was not yet a teenager. She walked behind the barn and found Thomas masturbating. Instead of being embarrassed about it, he seemed to be glad that she was watching. It freaked her out.

There were other incidents as well with other members of his extended family. But the dates and circumstances have become clouded with time and an exact accounting can't be reconstructed. All of this seemed to accelerate after Fran decided that they couldn't have a daughter. In point of fact, Thomas Soria had a thing for young girls by the early 1980s. He began playing a coin game with Andrea, whom Francine sometimes baby-sat. Andrea was six years old at the time. The rules of the game are now obscure, but the object of the game was to have Andrea pull down her panties. She recalled "playing" this game with Thomas Soria on several occasions. She also remembered that he liked to touch her.

And then there was T.J. Soria. It can be said in retrospect that Thomas Robert Soria Jr. never had much of a chance in life. By the time he was old enough to understand, he had heard from a very early age a litany of complaints from his mother, Francine. She was holding down two jobs and earning most of the money for the household, as well as doing the cleaning and the cooking. She began to resent T.J. about as much as she did Thomas Soria Sr. It was as if she had to baby-sit two kids instead of one. Within T.J.'s hearing, she often told Thomas Soria Sr., "He's your son" and other derogatory remarks.

Things really went downhill fast when Fran took on a third job for NutriSystems. By then, she had moved out of the master bedroom and was sleeping on the couch. She said later, "Tom and I would pass each other in the hall and that was about it. The house wasn't as clean as it should have been. I don't know. We just started drifting. It wasn't any one thing."

She was also drifting away from T.J. He had always been a "Daddy's boy," and Fran felt a wall going up between herself and her son. She said, "It was about the time I got the job at NutriSystem. It was subtle at first. Then I noticed T.J. would go to his dad when he wanted something, instead of me. They didn't seem to be more affectionate than was normal. They just seemed like they were the best buds. I felt like a third wheel."

In truth, though, T.J. and his father had been a lot more than just "best buds." She suspected Tom was having some kind of an affair, and he had even told her, "If you won't make me happy, I'll find out someone who will." Fran never dreamed that the someone was their own son, T.J.

The sexual contact between T.J. and Thomas Soria started in 1985 when T.J. was five years old. Thomas Soria had a fixation about young girls; in some twisted way, he attempted to turn his son into one. His moral compass had been knocked off kilter by the murder of his mother and it short-circuited his last chance at a normal sex life. He still had nightmares constantly of what he had seen. His grasp of reality was further eroded by Douglas Mozingo's infamous mass murder. It was as if he had become tainted by the depredations of his stepbrother and stepuncle. In fact, by now, Thomas Soria Sr. had passed the boundaries of all normalcy and would take T.J. down with him. If Francine wouldn't fulfill his sexual needs, then T.J. would.

Sometime in 1985, Thomas Soria Sr. asked T.J. to come into the master bedroom while Fran was away at work. He had T.J. remove his clothes and began to fondle him. T.J. may have been frightened at first, but then the sensation felt good. And besides, his father had constantly been telling him that he was the only one who loved him. He told the young boy that his own mother called him a bastard and a little son of a bitch. Whether this was true or not, T.J. began to believe it. It was psychological warfare on a young mind that could hardly differentiate fact from fiction. Thomas Soria told T.J. that Fran had often said she never even wanted him. Here was the only parent who "loved" him.

As Soria senior fondled his son, he told the boy to do the same to him. As the boy's hands roamed his body, Thomas Soria Sr. became excited. He taught T.J. where to place his hands. He taught T.J. where to place his mouth. Nothing was off limits.

Years later, T.J. would admit that his father sodomized him. He recalled that his dad required him to lick his armpits, stomach, testicles, penis and anus. Soria senior would then do the same to T.J. He would roll him over and insert his "thing" in his behind.

T.J. said, "He was my dad. He was the only one who loved me. I didn't know it was wrong. He (Thomas Soria Sr.) explained how Mom didn't care at all. (That they both had sex). Why should she?"

Soria senior rarely forced himself on the boy roughly. It was much more subtle and sinister than that. In an almost polite voice, he would tell T.J. what they were going to do and then they would do it. It was much more exciting than sex with Francine had ever been. He was in charge here. He had control. It was something that had been missing from his life.

T.J. was asked about the experience years later by law enforcement authorities. They asked, "Didn't it hurt?"

He simply answered, "No."

"Didn't you tell him to stop?"

"No, I didn't."

"Why didn't you?"

"He was my dad."

One thing Thomas Soria Sr. constantly drove home to young T.J. was that he must never tell anyone outside the immediate family about this. Nothing to other students or teachers or especially school counselors. He told T.J. that if he ever did, then they would take him away from his father and he would have no one who loved him. The prospect of that was too crushing to bear.

All of T.J.'s young life revolved around his father. Several times a week, the molestation would occur, but he though it was all part of a normal family life. His father told him lots of families were like this—they just didn't talk about it. Asked later if his mother, Francine, knew about the sex with his father, T.J. answered, "Yeah, she must have known, because we would always go back in the room and lock the door."

In fact, Fran may not have known. She was working three jobs at the time and already on the outs with both T.J. and Thomas senior. And she told authorities later, "I had no idea this was happening."

To gain even more control over the boy, Thomas Soria Sr. constantly reinforced the negative image about Francine. He told him, "Your mother doesn't love you. But I'll always be there for you."

In this case, "being there" meant rape.

There was really only one woman in the Soria family that young T.J. cared for and missed; ironically, it was someone he had never met. The person was his dead grandmother, Janey Soria Mozingo. Tom senior told him about Janey and how she would have loved him. He told him about all the virtues she had. T.J. would cry himself to sleep at night over the grandmother he never had known. The fact that some woman in the family would have loved him was almost too painful to bear. His murdered grandmother took on a status that his own mother never had—that of a caring guardian. He was sure his own mother hated him. His own father abused him. Only the ghost Janey Soria Mozingo was there to love and protect him.

The molestation of T.J. continued for years. It was the one constant in the boy's life. By now, he was so dependent on his father for affection that it had taken on the aspect of mind control. And at one point, the molestation moved from the disgusting to the truly bizarre. While T.J. was taking a bowel movement one day, his father came into the bathroom and scooped out the feces before T.J. flushed the toilet. Tom senior then took a bite out of the feces and swallowed it. He said it was proof that they always would be connected. He asked T.J. to do the same for him; in this one instance, T.J. did it at least one time to please his dad, but he didn't like it. He later said, "It was nasty." Deep inside, he instinctively knew this was wrong.

By 1995 T.J. had reached puberty, and the lust by Soria senior for his son began to wane. It was replaced by a further yearning for young girls. By now, T.J. was almost robotic in answering his dad's needs. It was way beyond a normal child-and-parent relationship. But the one thing Thomas Soria Sr. had not extinguished in T.J. was the hope for a normal life. T.J. did all right in school, and like any other teenage boy, he noticed girls. He even held out the almost forlorn hope that he might one day have a girlfriend. And in 1995 that possibility came to fruition.

When T.J. was fifteen years old, he met a fourteen-year-old girl named Carla at the Circus Circus Casino while on a trip to Reno with his family. There is a large arcade area there for teenagers, and while Francine and Tom senior went to gamble, T.J. went to play in the arcade. As he related later, "I was nervous. But [Carla] came right up to one of the racing games and I said hi and started talking to her." Almost to his amazement, she seemed to like him. They kept on talking and T.J. told her he had a room upstairs at the Circus Circus.

He went on to say, "I asked if she wanted to come up with me. And she said okay. We sat on the bed and I just kind of scooted closer and put my arm around her. She was responsive." They eventually had sex, and he said that he didn't do anything she didn't want to do.

Afterward they went outside and walked by the Truckee River. They strolled through the older part of town and sat on a bench in a park beneath the cottonwoods. T.J. and Carla held hands and kissed. Something so ordinary for other boys was almost like a miracle to T.J. The fact that she was a girl his age and liked him blew his mind.

He said, "We went down by the river and just enjoyed each other's company."

Many years later, he was asked by law enforcement agents about Carla: "Did you think she could be your girlfriend?"

T.J. answered, "Yes."

"Did she feel like you were her boyfriend?"

"Yeah."

"Did you think maybe someday she could be your wife?"

"Yes."

Suddenly sex took on a whole new meaning. It could actually be the connection between himself and a girl he loved. And more than that, it was a window toward normalcy.

When they went up to Reno again, his dad even had the decency to leave the room, knowing what was going to happen between Carla and his son. T.J. said later, "She and I French-kissed and things like that. She would reach down into my pants and feel me. And I would do her. I had vaginal sex with her. I didn't do anything to her butt, though I thought about it. I didn't think she would feel comfortable with it."

But the shadow of his father was always looming on the horizon. Thomas Soria Sr. knew what was going on between T.J. and Carla, and he knew it had to be short-circuited if he was ever to retain control over "his boy."

T.J. said later, "Eventually my dad was doing a lot of things for us. Taking us places. Buying us decent meals and stuff. Buying her groceries. They were kind of a poor family. I knew what he was up to. We just went up and met her at her house. He told me, 'If things don't work out between you and her, then I would like to try and have a relationship with her.'"

T.J. also said, "This upset me." But he didn't tell his dad to back off.

In fact, T.J. said, "It ended up I brought up the idea to her about this. She kind of liked the idea. I think part of it was because of the financial gain. Things that were being given to her. We were going up to Reno every weekend. Sometimes we would leave Sacramento at one or two in the morning and head up to visit her.

I said to her, 'He's interested in you. He would like a relationship as well.' She was a little bit surprised. But it
didn't seem like she was that surprised. It was just kind
of worked into. He started spending more time with us.
And he would kiss her as well. They would French-kiss
in front of me. In a way, it was kind of invigorating.
Then eventually we three had sex together. It was in the
truck (Chevy Blazer). She went down on me while she
was having sex with him. Once we were both finished,
she got out and went home.

"He had given her money before, but not at that
time. But she was always asking for money because they
needed food and stuff. I think she might have done it
for money. The three of us only did something one
time. [Later] he would penetrate her vagina. I tried
mentally blocking it out over time. Just trying to forget
about it. In the end, I kind of ended up being hurt by
it. She said she didn't want to see me anymore. She said
I wasn't normal."

But Carla didn't say the same thing about Thomas
Soria Sr., who was giving her money and buying her
groceries, after all. In fact, he and Carla were having
sex exclusively now. T.J. felt edged out and said, "They
had a relationship over a period of time. It bothered
me. I mostly just kept it inside. It [went on] with him
until the end of summer and she went back to school."

T.J. did eventually tell his dad how much this had hurt
him. His dad's response was "There will be others."

By the time Thomas Soria Sr. was taking over T.J.'s
girlfriend, Fran had just about had it in the Soria
household. She apparently didn't know about Carla,
but she suspected some kind of disloyalty on Tom's
part. She said of her marriage, "I was sleeping when he

came home. I would never see him. I would actually see him happier when I didn't see him. When we did see each other, we would just kind of growl."

It didn't help that she was sick a lot from allergies and asthma and he would get upset at her maladies. She claimed he never hit her, but there were other, more subtle abuses. Especially his constant strategy to turn T.J. against her. She said, "T.J. hardly ever spoke to me anymore." Over time she began to block T.J. out just as much as he did her. It was way beyond a teenager's rebellion against his mother and her response to the negative attitude. She had become almost a ghost floating through the Soria home, barely acknowledged by Thomas Soria Sr. and junior. The only interactions with Tom senior were the arguments, they occasionally had. She said, "When we got into verbal arguments it wasn't about hurting me. It was about hurting himself. He'd say stuff like 'I'll kill myself if nobody will do what I like. Why live if I can't have what I want?' Like with sodomy."

All of this was becoming too much for Fran Soria by the mid-1990s. She said, "It finally hit me; this isn't working. I should be happier than this in my life. Why should I stay in something that's obviously not working? Neither T.J. nor Tom would talk to me much. Finally [Tom and I] had a discussion about it. I told him, 'You know and I know this is not working. One of us has to leave and I can't afford to take care of the house. Then I will leave because T.J. has decided he will stay with you.'"

According to T.J., he and his father moved to the house of a friend of Thomas senior's before Fran split. They paid rent there for a while until Fran had moved all her things out of the house. T.J. said there was never a chance he would go back with his mom and related, "At that time, I was old enough so that the court saw that I wanted to stay with my dad and they granted that."

After Fran was gone, T.J. and his dad moved back to their house.

Fran Soria separated from Thomas Soria Sr. in 1995 and the divorce was final in February 1997. Her leaving removed all restraints from what Thomas Soria Sr. could do under his own roof. He no longer had to keep things secret from her. He could have T.J. anytime he wanted now. But by this time, his sexual lusts had changed. Part of the reason was that T.J. had reached puberty and Tom Soria Sr. wanted younger children, especially girls. And T.J. had changed in other ways as well. He had yearnings of his own that had nothing to do with his father.

With Fran out of the picture, T.J. related, "I had a lot of friends over and stuff. Guy friends mostly. Watching rock videos. Listening to music. My dad worked days. I tried to introduce [my dad] to some high-school girls. And he was trying to get some of the guys to introduce him to some girls. He told me that he was interested in getting a relationship with a young girl. In high school or whatever. I mostly asked the guys if they knew anybody. For them to kind of ask around. But I didn't have any takers. I was occasionally having sex with him. He'd ask me every so often to do something for him. Like orally. 'Cause he was depressed or whatever. The anal sex had pretty much stopped."

Around this time, Thomas Soria Sr. met a woman named Guadalupe, who generally went by the name Lupe. For someone so enamored with young girls, it was surprising that he went for a woman his own age. According to T.J., "Some coworkers at the California Lottery (where Tom senior worked after Fran's departure) wanted to set him up with somebody. One

particular gentleman thought it was going to be a joke-
type thing. Trying to play a joke on my dad. I guess
'cause she's considered overweight and stuff. He knew
Lupe's sister and that's how he set it up. [Dad and
Lupe] went out to a mall or something like that and a
restaurant. Eventually they got together. They ended
up going together on a couple of dates and taking a
trip down to San Francisco."

Thomas Soria Sr. and Lupe got married about a year
after their first date. T.J. said, "I was kind of happy. She
seemed like a real good person and everything."

But life under the Soria's roof was never going to be
anything like the Cleaver residence on *Leave It to Beaver.*
This was definitely no ordinary suburban household.
According to T.J., "After I got to bed one night, my dad
came and asked me if I wanted to join them. Have sex
with him and Lupe. And I went ahead and agreed. She
was a little big. Big breasts . . . but I was attracted to her.
I found her a little bit sexy. I just kind of got into bed
with them and started feeling her breasts and stuff. It
just kind of went from there. I sucked on her breasts
and I went down on her and made her have orgasms.
And I eventually fucked her. My dad was holding her
hand. Later, he asked me if I enjoyed myself. I said I
would be interested in doing it again."

Asked later on if his dad was offering Lupe as a gift,
T.J. answered, "I guess it was for incidents like the girl
in Reno. To show he would do the same for me."

It was during this time that Thomas Soria Sr. bought
a small neighborhood video store. He made T.J. work
in the store, even though T.J. wasn't that keen on the
idea. But something unexpected occurred while T.J.
worked there. A lesser soul than his might have been
totally crushed by losing the girl in Reno to his father,
but T.J. must have had more resiliency than many knew

he possessed. It was true that both Thomas Soria Sr. and T.J. were by now both damaged individuals, acting out a bizarre scenario of their own devising. But against all expectations, T.J. found another girlfriend. And this one lived in the neighborhood.

Her name was Natasha and she was bright, articulate and funny. T.J. related, "I met her through the video store we owned. Her mom was a video renter. Her mom sent Tasha to meet me 'cause she wanted someone like me who had a positive influence. Who wasn't into crime or such. Tasha was kind of a gang-banger. A rough woman. But she was actually a bit mellow. It was a bit difficult 'cause she still wanted to hang around with her old friends."

But Tasha, T.J.'s nickname for her, also had a soft spot beneath the rough exterior and was someone with a lot of feelings. T.J. and Tasha ended up walking through the park one evening and he said to her, "I care for you."

Her reply was "I know I shouldn't, but I care for you, too."

It wasn't long before she and T.J. were very much in love. In fact, they wrote love letters to each other despite the lack of distance between them. It was something they had to put down in words. Especially Tasha. She was a perceptive girl and could see the unnaturally close contact between T.J. and his father. In one letter, she wrote that she wished they could have their own secrets without T.J. telling his father about them. She wrote, "You don't have to pass everything on to your Dad. I'm close to my Dad, and love my Dad, too, but I don't tell him absolutely everything."

As time went by, she wrote, "I think your Dad is starting not to like me."

The reason was obvious. The more T.J. became en-

amored of Tasha, the less control his father would have
over him. Besides, by now T.J. and Tasha were having
sex, and that was a definite threat to Thomas Soria Sr.

Tasha was a strong person in her own way and loved
T.J., but she had problems of her own. And the chief
of these was drugs. Tasha was hooked on crank
(methamphetamines). She needed it so much that
she wouldn't just snort it, she injected it for a quicker
and more powerful result. Unfortunately for both of
them, T.J. started to do drugs too. She hated that
he would start. She even wrote in one letter, "Baby,
it really hurts me every time I push a needle into your
arm. Don't get involved in drugs like me. I don't want
to be on it. I'm sorry baby."

But the drugs were stronger than Tasha's will to re-
sist or even her love for T.J. She needed them like she
needed air. In her desperation to get more, even when
there was no money, she manipulated T.J. into getting
some the only way she knew how. She said, "Go give
that drug dealer down on Eighteenth Street a blow job
and get some crank. Give a blow job to that guy 'cause
that's how you'll pay for it."

T.J. desperately needed Tasha in his life so much that
he acceded to her request. He did this even knowing
that the drug dealer in question was HIV positive. It
didn't matter. He would risk his own life with this dis-
ease rather than lose Tasha.

Thomas Soria Sr. initially didn't show much interest
in Tasha. He liked thin, submissive little girls, and she
certainly wasn't either of those things. But according to
T.J., "He finally did one night. Me and Tasha had kind
of gotten into some bad drugs. Crank and stuff. I
wasn't able to perform [with her]. And I asked her if
she would be interested in him because she really
wanted to do something. She was a little bit nervous

about it. But I went and called him out into the hallway and asked him and he said, 'Just a minute.'

"And eventually he came in and fondled her tits and stuff. And he eventually penetrated her vagina. I was lying on the bed next to her. I was holding her hand. Then I fondled her breasts as well. I ended up leaving after a little bit. Afterward she seemed to regret it."

A short time after this incident, an unexpected thing happened. On December 12 T.J. found out that Tasha was pregnant. He was sure he was the father, and not his dad. He said it made him feel happy.

The senior Soria also said he was happy for T.J. and Tasha. But according to something Tasha overheard in a conversation, she swore that he had other reasons for wanting them to have a baby. She related that Thomas Soria Sr. intended to use the baby as a "sex toy." When T.J. learned about this, he said, "Well, I guess I shouldn't put anything past him."

In the long run, whether Thomas Soria Sr. really intended to use T.J.'s baby as a sex toy became a moot point. Tasha lost the baby.

SEVEN

"What Do You Want Me to Do to You?"

Even with the threesomes of Lupe and T.J., and Tasha and T.J., this type of sex was not enough for Thomas Soria Sr. By 1998 he had impulses that he couldn't restrain. He worked at GTECH, the security arm of the California State Lottery, in Sacramento. And it was there that he came into contact with women he desired but could not have. He decided that if he could not have them in the flesh, he would do it through his fantasies via the telephone.

Julie Drayton was a supervisor at GTECH, and on January 20, 1998, she picked up her telephone receiver to hear a man's voice say, "I want to see your breasts." He seemed to be pleasuring himself while he said it. At 4:30 P.M. the phone rang again and the same man announced, "Julie, I want to rape you."

Three days later, Julie Drayton answered the phone at 2:30 P.M. to hear, "You smell good when you walk by." Then he abruptly hung up.

The next day, at 5:10 P.M., he said, "Hi, Julie," then nothing more.

On February 3, at 2:34 P.M., the man's voice pronounced, "I like to hear you pissing and cussing in your office." Then at 2:44 P.M. he said, "I bet you're playing with yourself while you're listening to me."

She demanded to know who he was.

He replied, "It's a secret. I can't tell you who I am. I work with you at GTECH, obviously. We work together. Hold on. I'll have to call you back."

At 3:14 P.M. he was back on the line answering her question of who he was by saying, "Don't be concerned with figuring out who I am. I'm going to bash your fucking head in. I'm watching you. What do you want me to do to you?"

At 4:45 P.M. he said, "I want to smell your cunt. Your boyfriend doesn't have to know. I want you real bad. I'm going to follow you home to see where you live. I have to go back to work now."

At 5:09 P.M. he was on the line again. "We can do this the easy way and you cooperate, or we can do it the hard way and I rape you over [*garbled*]. Either way, I get what I want."

She cussed him out and he responded, "I like it when you talk dirty. See you outside."

At this point, Tom senior either became nervous about his calls to Julie Drayton or just decided to switch his target. Instead, he began to call a woman named Sara Stein at the California Lottery headquarters. He did it from a phone within the building.

At 4:20 P.M. Stein picked up her phone to hear, "Hello, Sara. You smell good. I want to smell you down there."

At 4:31 he called back and said, "I just need to be raped inside my [*garbled*]. I'll see you later."

Then at 4:35 P.M. he announced, "Sara, you're beautiful. I want to put my face up your butt."

There were other phone calls to her as well, with de-grading messages she couldn't remember with great clarity. But Sara Stein was scared enough by the phone calls to contact the police. In turn, they set up a phone trap with the Pacific Bell Anonymous Call Bureau. They didn't have to wait long. The harassing caller phoned Sara Stein once more and it was determined that the call was coming from a phone booth on North Tenth Street inside the lobby of the California State Lottery headquarters.

It took a while for the path to lead to Thomas Soria Sr., and in the meantime, he was calling two other women at work and sexually harassing them as well. The investigation narrowed the possible field of callers to someone working either at GTECH or the Califor-nia State Lottery who knew Julie Drayton and Sara Stein. Neither one of these women ever gave out their first names on the phone or on their voice mail.

Eventually Detective Mudderig got around to talking to a middle-aged Hispanic man who worked for GTECH by the name of Thomas Soria Sr. Under ques-tioning, he admitted that he had made sexually explicit phone calls, but he said he thought he was talking to his wife at the time and had dialed the wrong number. He said this was a routine of theirs. That she liked the "rape scenario."

"You know, warm her up before I get home." He then repeated phrases that Julie Drayton and Sara Stein had heard: "I want to see your breasts. I want to smell your cunt. I'm going to follow you. See you out-side." These phrases were exact matches to some of the other calls.

Detective Mudderig didn't buy the "phone call to the wife" routine. When a voice match of Soria to the phone traps was analyzed, it was determined that he was the harassing caller. On June 4, 1998, Peace Officer Nelson was dispatched to arrest Thomas Soria Sr. on the charge of making annoying phone calls with a threat of injury.

Initially Tom Soria Sr. was going to get off fairly easily with just some probation for the phone calls, but then it was discovered that he had also harassed the two other women besides Stein and Drayton. And Sara Stein was scared enough to write a letter to the judge who would pronounce sentence.

She wrote about his case and upcoming sentencing. She said she had received obscene phone calls starting at approximately 4:20 P.M. She said, "After I received the calls I was very upset, scared and confused."

She immediately notified her supervisor, who contacted security and had a security officer walk her to her car. Little did Sara know at the time that the obscene phone caller worked in security. In her letter she wrote, "I did not know if (the caller) was someone I spoke to at work, someone I may have just casually met, or some I knew in my neighborhood. And because of this it scared the hell out of me, because I did not know if he would try to attack me, rape me or even worse, kill me."

Stein said that she was scared for weeks to be alone, and she was suspicious of everyone. She was afraid that someone would jump out from behind a corner and hurt her. She wrote, "What makes the whole situation even worse is the fear that I was looking for security to help me, and it turned out the calls were coming from someone in security."

She asked the judge to take all of this into consideration when it came time to sentence Thomas Soria Sr. She pleaded in her letter, "Please do not take what Mr. Soria did lightly, because he did change my life and needs to know this. Do not let Mr. Soria put anyone else through this as the next time he may not be caught and someone may end up hurt, raped or killed."

Sara Stein could not have known at the time just how prophetic these last words were.

The letter to the judge did, in fact, have the desired effect as far as she was concerned. The judge, instead of just giving Thomas Soria Sr. probation, ordered him to spend seventy-five days in jail and pay $3,800 in restitution to the victims. Also, because of the decision, Thomas Soria Sr. was terminated from his job at GTECH.

According to T.J., Thomas Soria Sr. and Lupe moved out of Sacramento at this time to escape the stigma of being an obscene phone caller. They moved up to the Lake Park Apartments in Stateline, Nevada, where Lupe got a job doing secretarial work at the Horizon Casino and Thomas received unemployment benefits. Tom Soria Sr. was supposed to start serving his time in jail soon, but Paul Commisky, his lawyer, was writing a letter to the judge as well. In the letter, he stated:

> Thomas Soria Sr. is receiving $920 a month in unemployment benefits. And Lupe receives about a $1,000 a month from her job. . . . Their rent comes to $671 a month, $247 for truck payments, $154 a month for truck insurance, $300 for food, $100 a month for utilities and $210 a month for storage of items in Sacramento. . . . They as a family are just barely making it at this time. If Mr. Soria has to serve this time in jail, he will lose the unemployment benefits and it would put his wife out on the street. He is currently making efforts to find employment and is planning to enroll soon in the counseling programs that the probation department has prescribed for him.

He has left the state of California out of sensitivity and concern for the victims in this matter and also to avoid any further problems and to get a new start on life.

The letter did the trick as far as jail time was concerned. Thomas Soria Sr. was ordered to serve out his time instead by joining the El Dorado Sheriff's Work Program, near Lake Tahoe. This consisted of working one day a week on a road crew, mainly picking up trash. He was to report by 8:00 A.M. and work until 4:00 P.M., with a one-hour lunch break. He was to wear suitable clothing and shoes for outside work. He wasn't to wear sandals or offensively designed clothing. He was to provide his own work gloves and lunch, since none would be provided. Insubordination or failure to follow orders would lead to his immediate removal to the El Dorado County Jail.

Meanwhile, down in Sacramento, T.J. was finally away from his father's dominance. He said, "When I was with Tasha, I did kind of rebel. I got upset with [dad] and I felt like he was making me run the video store. That's when we had a real big argument in the store. That's when I left and went out on my own with Tasha."

But it was a dangerous life hanging around with Tasha and her friends. Living on the streets was not easy and certainly not lucrative. T.J. had no high-school diploma and very little in the way of marketable skills. Sometime in the spring of 1999, he began passing bad checks. This came back to haunt him when some checks he passed in the downtown area led to his arrest. For the first time in his life, he found himself up against the law.

Just like his father, he decided to plead nolo contendere. Because he had no prior arrests, the judge

decided to be lenient. Instead of jail time, the judge set
down a series of orders, the main one being that T.J.
must enroll in a correspondence course with an outfit
in Utah called Western Corrections. The judge wrote
in the order:

> Next court date is 12/16/99. During the time
> (from now until then) the court has ordered you
> to complete a course of instruction administered
> by Western Corrections. The fee for the course
> must be paid in full by 9/30/99. There is a total
> due of $225. Upon receipt of the full amount, all
> the course materials will be mailed to you. Failure
> to complete the course and return to Western
> Corrections so that the envelope is postmarked
> no later than fourteen days prior to the above
> mentioned court date, will result in your program
> failure. If you follow these orders, your case will
> be dismissed by the court.

Both Sorias got off relatively easy for their crimes.
But this brush with the law and the deteriorating relationship with Tasha had a very negative effect on T.J.
Not only that, his father by now was using psychological warfare on him. He told T.J. that he had a brain
tumor. According to T.J., "[Dad] told me that he was
having trouble with ringing in his ears. He went to the
doctor and our family physician had X rays done and
said a tumor was growing in the middle of his brain. So
he told me that he only had so long to live before this
thing got so big that it killed him."

This story may have fooled T.J., but it was Tasha's
contention that his father had concocted the whole
brain-tumor thing to play upon T.J.'s guilt and fear of

being away from him. Tasha said, "Your dad never in his wildest dreams was going to die of a brain tumor." She believed that T.J. had rebelled against his father for the first time in his life and this was a ploy to bring him back into the fold.

Whatever the validity of the brain tumor story, that and the scrape with the law made T.J. leave Tasha and move up to Lake Tahoe and live with his father and Lupe once again. Perhaps he too hoped for a new start in the Tahoe region. But living under Tom Soria Sr.'s roof would mean more sexual exploitation at his father's hands. It would mean more procuring of young girls. And it would place T.J. dangerously close to his father's increasing lusts for violent rape.

It also had one more dire consequence for those around T.J. Soria. He became a part-time worker at the local Boys and Girls Club, where he had access to young girls and gained their trust.

EIGHT

"Krystal Light"

Nine-year-old Krystal Dawn Steadman of South Lake Tahoe was a golden girl. There was an absolute glow about her. Even Sonia Sunshine Klempner, her much older sister, was in awe of her. She said, "Krystal was beautiful. She was honest. She was healthy. She was spirited and sassy. She would light up a room the moment she walked in. All of her teachers became very fond of her. She was an incredible young lady who was good at soccer and choir. Me and my younger sister had an incredible relationship. She was so much more than a sister. Because I was so much older, she would always call me 'Mommy.' We were like best friends. She was my best girlfriend to go shopping with. We were very, very, very close. She would always love to play at Tahoe Valley in South Lake Tahoe, at the playground."

Krystal Steadman was in the fourth grade at Meyers Elementary School and was running for student body vice president in the year 2000. Doug Forte, the principal at Meyers Elementary School, said "[Krystal] was a sweet and energetic fourth grader who brought smiles to our lives."

Krystal was an accomplished flutist, gymnast and karate adherent. She seemed to have had no fear and embraced each new situation with gusto. Her sister said, "She was much more bold than I was. She wasn't shy at all. She'd take on new things and situations without worry."

Krystal was so self-possessed, in fact, that she competed for the title of Junior Miss Lake Tahoe in January 2000. There wasn't much that slowed her down.

It was remarkable that Krystal was such a well-adjusted and happy young girl. Things had not always been easy in the Steadman household. Originally living in southern California, there was intense bickering between Krystal's mother, Elizabeth, and her father, John. It had grown so bad by 1993, when Krystal was three years old, that Elizabeth said, "In 1993 I ran for safety from a violent situation from my husband. A restraining order was obtained to protect us. My goal from that time forward was to provide a good life for Krystal. I struggled to give her dancing lessons, singing lessons and acting lessons. She was involved in soccer, gymnastics and karate. I wanted her to grow up with every opportunity for playing and being happy to make up for all the bad things in my life.

"For a while [after leaving southern California], we lived in Hawaii. Krystal played on the beach and loved to make sand castles. Seeing her playing and happy made up for all the bad things in my life. She was my center. My 'Krystal Light.'

"Krystal went to church with me. We did so many things together. She was a happy, healthy child. She followed all the rules and checked in with me frequently when she went to play, especially after we moved to Meyers, a town near Lake Tahoe. She was in talent shows and a beauty contest and ran for vice president of her school. She was in a choir and absolutely loved it."

Larry Brown, Krystal's soccer coach, said of her, "Krystal was lots of fun to be with. She was like an energizer—so vivacious."

South Lake Tahoe Middle School student Tayah Del Vecchio, who was a friend of Krystal's, agreed. She said, "This one time, she came over to my house and we were playing with makeup and we came out with a bunch of eye shadow on. Like a lot! My mom laughed so hard."

Even Krystal's father, John Steadman, who now lived in Tennessee, had nothing but love and admiration for his daughter, even though his relationship with his ex-wife, Elizabeth, was as rocky as ever. Theirs had been a volatile relationship and she accused him of domestic violence. In 1994, when he was still living in southern California, he received divorce papers from her. John Steadman always hoped for some kind of reconciliation so that he could see his daughter, but Elizabeth was afraid of him and protective of Krystal. He later explained to a Minden, Nevada, *Record Courier* reporter, "I would try to see her, but her mother would tell me she'd gone to a party or was ill. I decided then that I was never going to be able to see my daughter again without a fight."

Steadman and his new girlfriend, Virginia, moved to Tennessee and bought a home. They added on a room especially for Krystal. He related, "I took an old window and made it into a bookshelf. I had a television with Surround Sound in there for her. And a wrought-iron bed. That room was mainly for her if she could come. Virginia's own children were grown and the home was just ours, with a room waiting for my little girl."

John Steadman retained a lawyer in Tennessee who helped him try and stay in touch with his daughter. But it was no easy task. Elizabeth and Krystal moved around a lot. First in southern California and then out to Hawaii. They did not keep John Steadman appraised of their moves. John, who was trying to get a court order to see Krystal at least once every six months, was certain that he would never see her again.

And then a breakthrough came in December 1999. New child-support papers arrived and they were addressed from the Lake Tahoe region of California. He finally had a concrete address. Even then his lawyer cautioned him, "John, she might be calling someone else 'Daddy' by now."

John Steadman decided to start out slowly. He sent Krystal presents and small notes until she would feel comfortable with him once again. He admitted they had a lot of lost time to make up for. But at least he was taking the first tentative steps for a reconciliation with his daughter.

If Krystal's relationship with her father was strained to the point of almost nonexistence, the same could not be said with her maternal grandparents, Leslie and Irene Bucknell. Leslie, her grandfather, was a retired aircraft instruments technician now living in Stewart, Florida. Krystal went to visit him for a couple of weeks, and just as in Hawaii, she had fun at the beach. Later, she made a trip to New York to visit her maternal aunt Karen for Christmas. Like everyone else, the relatives adored Krystal. She had such a zest for life.

Even more exciting for the young girl was a trip to the Caribbean with her grandparents. They had a wonderful time among the balmy islands and azure waters. She may have had a separated nuclear family, but she never lacked for love from a wider range of siblings and relatives.

But Krystal's very effervescence was about to lead to tragedy; because she was so bright and beautiful, she stood out in a crowd. In the year 2000, she came into the orbit of Thomas Soria Jr. Even worse, her mother now had a boyfriend who lived at the same apartment complex as the Sorias.

NINE

Terror in Apartment 22

By March 2000 part of the Soria apartment at Lake Park Apartments looked like Toys "R" Us. There were games, toys, dolls and stuffed animals lining a large walk-in closet. There were even more toys and games scattered around the computer room. All of it was meant to lure in and pacify young girls. T.J. was just as aware of what the items were for as the senior Soria was. He had no illusions about their allure for young girls.

Tom Soria Sr. fantasized about a blond-haired bank teller named Debbie Sloan who worked in a bank where he kept his money. He wrote down his fantasies in a journal and on computer files, and they were brutal in the extreme. He wrote: "I [will] destroy all that is feminine in her body with my knife. I cut her into bloody shreds. She asks why. Because someone like you would never give a guy like me a chance to have sex with you and do nasty things to your body and allow me to worship you. Because I'm in love with you. So this is the way I will have you."

Thomas Soria Sr.'s computer files had become an absolute catalog of his wild fantasies and desires. He had a text file that listed young girls' names and their ages and what he had done to them. Another text file related how he wanted to rape and brutally kill young women, especially blondes. There was desire and hatred all mixed up into one. He wanted blondes and he hated them for slights, real and imagined, that he had suffered over the years. He was aware of his Hispanic background and culture. He hated certain Anglos, which he called "whites," who had put him down in the past. Particularly women. If he had his way, some of them would "pay" in the most brutal fashion he knew how. He wrote, "I want to perform anal sex, analingus, lick their armpits and eat their shit. I want them to eat my shit, too." But more than anything, he wanted to cut them with a knife as he had sex.

The extent of his savagery was explicit in one computer text. He wrote, "I will slice off her cunt lips and make her taste them. I will brutally rape her cunt with my knife and tear up her vagina, cervix and uterus. I will brutally rape her little white ass with my nuts until her sphincter and rectum are all torn up and ripped beyond repair."

In one file, he wrote, "Lupe is gone. It makes me have bad thoughts. I want to plan how I'm going to rape a milky-white, blond-haired, blue-eyed kind in the forest. I will take revenge on the female species by seizing every opportunity to sexually exploit, sexually molest, savagely mouth fuck, brutally rape, brutally sodomize, whip, beat, torture, use as my personal toilet, and kill these beautiful stuck-up bitches."

In another file, he wrote, "I'll find a young white blond-haired blued-eyed girl. The kind of woman who would never be interested in me. I will beat the hell out of her until she's unconscious, then I can get naked and pull her pants and panties off, so I can see her pretty white butt. Then I want to sniff and lick and kiss her smelly ass. I will tell her limp body it will do everything that I want it to do."

Thomas Soria Sr. had come a long, long way from the boy who worshiped his mother and deplored the depredations of his stepbrother Ronny Mozingo.

Soria also kept some of his most virulent antagonisms on file about his feelings for Francine Soria and Lupe Soria. In some ways, he felt that they had emasculated him and he wanted revenge. If not on them, then on other women. He wanted to "degrade, embarrass, dehumanize women, while sexually torturing them. I want to fuck their filthy white bodies and have their slutty mouths do to me like I did with, Julia and Sara which I got intense sexual charge free of guilt or sorrow out of doing them."

As a bizarre justification for his actions, the senior Soria wrote a rambling text about his younger years. It concerned his own rape when he was only a child by stepbrother Ronny Mozingo. He wrote, "I was trained to be a man's bitch as a young boy." It also stated that he had performed oral sex on men later in life.

But young girls were his obsession now. He surfed kiddie-porn sites on the Internet, he subscribed to a child-pornography magazine.

As luck would have it, Krystal Steadman and her mom, Elizabeth, were spending the night of March 18, 2000, at Elizabeth's boyfriend's apartment in building 3 of the Lake Park Apartments. Dan Simmons (Elizabeth's boyfriend) was moving into a new apartment and Elizabeth and Krystal were there to help him pack.

When they awoke at 9:00 A.M. on March 19, there was no television for Krystal to watch, since it had already been taken to the new apartment. Feeling very antsy, Krystal asked, "When are we leaving?"

All three went down to a nearby Burger King and got some take-out food for breakfast. They brought it back to Dan's apartment and ate there. Then Krystal opened up the Sunday newspaper and read the comics, especially her favorite, "Peanuts." After 10:00 A.M., when it began to get warmer, Elizabeth allowed Krystal to go outside and play, with the admonition she was to check in once an hour.

Krystal returned at about 11:00 A.M. and said that she was playing with Sandi Taylor and Connie Stewart. She said she wanted to go play with them down in a field. Elizabeth answered that it was all right as long as the other girls went with her.

On that same morning of March 19, 2000, Thomas Soria Sr.'s lusts were in high gear. He had awakened early and had started writing more sexually explicit texts in his computer files. Right before breakfast, he told T.J., "Get me a girl."

T.J. was particularly grumpy that morning and not thrilled about this prospect. But it was something he would do just to keep Dad happy. As he said later, "[Dad] was kind of grumbly. And I was kind of grumbly. I didn't want to get up early. A little bit later, I got up, got dressed and went outside. I went out a few times and came back. Eventually I ran into some of the kids."

T.J. spotted Sandi Taylor, Connie Stewart and a new girl playing with them. The new girl was petite and blond. She fit exactly the description that his dad was looking for. He didn't know it at the time, but he was looking at Krystal Steadman.

T.J. kept an eye on them and remembered, "[The

blond girl] was among them and I'd never seen her before. They wanted me to play with them. Like following them around and stuff. We walked around the side of the complex and down to a field. They were looking for some other kids for some reason. We finally went back to the apartments and stopped off at a big tree. There's a big tree out in front of the complex. They went and climbed on it. It was their little clubhouse or something."

Eventually T.J. grew hungry and drove down to a local McDonald's for burgers and fries. When he came back, the kids, especially Krystal, pestered him for some French fries, but he shooed them away. He returned to apartment 22 and gave his dad a burger and fries. He also gave him the information that his dad wanted. T.J. said, "I might have a girl for you."

His father's reply was "Well, go bring her up."

At around 2:00 P.M. Krystal went back to Dan Simmons's apartment. They were all going to go have brunch at Caesar's Tahoe soon and Elizabeth told her daughter to be back in half an hour. T.J. went down into the parking lot and talked to the girls. Connie Stewart and Sandi Taylor knew him well. They both felt at ease with T.J. It wasn't long before Krystal Steadman trusted him as well. He began to give them rides on the running boards, of his father's 1989 Chevy Blazer. While the girls stood on the running boards, he drove slowly through the parking lot. It was just like a carnival ride in slow motion.

Meanwhile, his father was inside the apartment getting ready. According to one source, he pulled out some duct tape and a knife that he had swiped from T.J. on the previous Friday. Then he phoned Lupe and told her not to come home. She was down in Sacramento at the time and knew what that meant. She was to stay away because her husband was about to go into one of his "sessions."

After a period of riding around on the Chevy Blazer, Sandi and Connie had to leave, but Krystal stayed a little longer. She was beginning to get cold and ran up to the apartment of her mother's boyfriend to grab a coat. At six thousand feet, March afternoons could still be very chilly. With her coat on, she went back down to look for the other girls, but only T.J. was there now.

As he said later, "I waited on the back stairs of the building for Krystal to return. When she came, I said, 'I've got some candy for you upstairs if you want a piece.' She answered that she did and followed me upstairs. I introduced her to my dad, saying, 'This is my uncle Tom.' Then I said, 'I want to do some laundry,' and I left her alone there with my dad."

What happened next can only be pieced together by physical evidence collected after the fact and T.J.'s fragmented and ever-shifting story. But the evidence was graphic and compelling and depicted scenes of horror. Thomas Soria Sr. overpowered the nine-year-old girl, placed duct tape over her mouth and bound her wrists with duct tape as well. It's not clear where he took her next—either to the master bedroom or the bathtub. He pulled off her clothing, item by item, until she was completely naked. She fought back and scratched him, but she was no match for his size. Krystal was exactly as he had fantasized on the computer. He had a "petite, young blond" at his mercy. He inserted some kind of object with "strawlike" material into her vagina and anus. This was probably a household broom. Her struggles only excited him further. He digitally and orally molested Krystal's vagina. Then he pulled out his knife and began to cut her with nonfatal, torturing wounds on her arms and neck. He inserted his penis into her vagina and raped her. He also inserted his penis into her rectum. He beat her in the head so badly that it fractured her skull. Sometime during this brutal rape, he placed the knife to Krystal's throat and slashed her jugular vein.

In apartment 22 of the Lake Park Apartments, Krystal Steadman bled out her young life and died.

In some twisted way, perhaps not even perceived by himself, Thomas Soria Sr. had reenacted his own mother's brutal murder. He did this right down to the detail of placing a plastic sack over Krystal's face after he was done and not covering most of her body. Ronny Mozingo had placed a towel over Thomas Soria's mother's face after he was done brutalizing and murdering her. In some bizarre manner, Thomas Soria's sexual drives and those of his stepbrother Ronny Mozingo had finally converged in brutality and death. Thomas Soria Sr. had become the person he hated most.

Meanwhile, T.J. was living his own nightmare, and the first version of what he did would alter in many details from his later versions. He said, "I checked the laundry room and there was a free washer. Then I told the other kids I didn't want to play anymore and I was going home to rest. So I went home and I didn't see Krystal anywhere and my dad's door was shut to his bedroom. So I went in and sat down at my computer and played a game that I had going on for a bit. I played my game for a little bit until Krystal's mom showed up with a couple of the kids."

Two-thirty P.M. had come and gone and there were no signs of Krystal at Dan Simmons's apartment. At around 3:00 P.M. Elizabeth Steadman started getting concerned by the absence of her daughter. Krystal was usually very punctual, and besides they all were going to Caesar's Tahoe soon for brunch. Elizabeth walked out onto the second-story deck and began yelling for her daughter. There was no response. At this point, she was more miffed than worried, until she talked to Sandi Taylor and some children and learned that they had not seen Krystal around.

Elizabeth and Dan headed down the hill toward a deli on the corner, thinking that Krystal might have gone there to buy some candy. But on the way they ran into some children who said, "T.J. was chasing kids with his truck."

Elizabeth had no idea who T.J. was, but this was frightening news. She hurried back toward Sandi Taylor's apartment, with Dan in tow, to find out where T.J. lived.

Elizabeth Steadman knocked on the Sorias' apartment door with Sandi Taylor and Connie Stewart in tow. When the door opened, she saw a young man standing before her wearing blue jogging pants, a T-shirt and no shoes. It was T.J. and he said he'd just been taking a nap.

Sandi looked at him; T.J.'s face was flushed and he looked "very strange" in her words. She had never seen him like this before.

Elizabeth Steadman asked T.J. if he knew where Krystal was. T.J. said, "I saw her going down the street on her bike. Toward the mobile-home park."

At this point, Elizabeth believed him and went back to her apartment to get Dan and go look for Krystal in that direction. Then, according to T.J., he went back to the laundry room and saw another boy there that he barely knew. T.J. discovered that he didn't have enough quarters to put the clothes in the dryer. He made some comment to the other boy about this, gathered up the clothes and went back to his apartment.

Back at the apartment, T.J. related, he was now tired and wanted to take a nap. But he found he was too wide awake, so he decided to masturbate instead. Afterward, he said, "I cleaned myself up. It was on my hands and stomach and stuff. So I cleaned myself up and threw all the toilet paper in the trash can in the bathroom. And then I urinated. I went back to my room and laid down and kind of started to doze off a little bit. That's when I heard my dad go into the bathroom and flush the toilet a couple of times. I thought I heard shower water running. A little bit after that, I heard him go back into his room. A little later, Krystal's mom and her mom's boyfriend came to the door again."

Elizabeth Steadman was extremely agitated this time. T.J. remembered, "She said that she couldn't find Krystal anywhere. She wanted to look around the apartment. So I went ahead and let her take a look around into the kitchen and front room and stuff. And she glanced in my room and the bathroom. She wanted to go into my dad's room and I told her that my uncle was sleeping. I wasn't allowed to go in there when he was sleeping. She kind of persisted a little bit and I told her I just couldn't. She asked if it was okay if her boyfriend went in, since he was a man. And I told her I couldn't. I wasn't allowed to. And her boyfriend said, 'Just forget it. Let's go.' They went back outside and I told her I hoped that she would find her. She said that she would probably end up calling the police."

Elizabeth Steadman's version of what happened on her second visit to the Soria apartment was slightly different from T.J.'s. She recounted later, "Everything seemed to be quiet and calm and nothing seemed disturbed. The first bedroom (T. J.'s room) was open and I looked in there. I [searched] the kitchen and bathroom."

She listened for sounds of crying or voices. There was nothing.

Finally, she said, "I went down the hall to the back bedroom."

T.J. rushed in front of her and spread his arms. He said, "My uncle is sleeping in there and can't be disturbed."

Then he suddenly said, "Oh, I remember. She just went to the trailer park. That's where I saw her."

Elizabeth was determined to get into the bedroom with the closed door. But Dan was uncomfortable with the whole situation, and besides, if T.J. was telling the truth, they had better search in the trailer park before it got too late. He convinced Elizabeth to follow him and they left.

But before they left, T.J. said something to Dan that he thought was very odd. T.J. told him, "I know how you feel. I have a kid too."

Dan took one look at T.J. and thought that he looked very young to be having a child of his own.

After Elizabeth Steadman and her boyfriend left, T.J. would have various versions of what occurred next. In his first version, he recalled, "I went back in and laid down on the bed and kind of closed my door partway. And a little bit later, my dad ended up calling me from his bedroom. And one of the first things I noticed was there was a real strong smell in the bedroom. Something I had never smelled before. I didn't know what it was. He told me he needed me to do a favor for him. I saw that Krystal was there with a garbage bag over her head and down to her legs. She wasn't moving or anything. She was dead. I got worried and scared. He said that he needed me to get rid of her for him. And I saw that her clothes were on the floor at the foot of the bed.

"I was kind of shaky and nervous, and he told me to

open a box while he put her in it. So he kind of just stuffed her feet back in the bag and twirled it up and I held the box open and he set her in it. And he told me to put her clothes in another garbage bag. So I threw them in the bag and I noticed that her underwear looked like it was cut up or ripped or something. I threw everything in the bag and put the bag in the box. He handed me a roll of duct tape. He told me I should throw it away in the garbage can or something down in Carson [City]. He said he wanted me to take her and throw her off one of the cliffs or something . . . down the road on Fifty. Down to Carson.

"So he had me put the tape in the box and told me to go outside and make sure there was nobody around. So I went ahead and went out and looked, and he gave me the keys and he said, 'Thank you.' I went ahead and carried the box out to the front room and opened the door and he told me to get a soda for him when I came back. He gave me some Susan B. Anthonys and stuff and a five-dollar bill to pay for the gas.

"I carried the box down and had a lot of trouble getting it into the vehicle, 'cause it was real heavy. And a couple of people drove by."

T.J. also noticed a woman walking toward him in the parking lot. It was Maria Gonzales, a neighbor, whom he recognized. Very nervous and watchful, he nodded to her and she nodded back.

There were 101 places in the area to dispose a body. The backcountry was very rugged and forested with lots of small roads. But time was of the essence. Several people had seen Krystal go toward the Soria apartment and some had even seen T.J. walk out the door carrying a box. He had to dispose of her body soon. And his father had told him to throw Krystal's body down a cliff along Highway 50 near Carson City.

T.J., at this point, was through rebelling against his father's wishes.

T.J. headed east on Highway 50, up and over 7,300-foot Spooner Summit. At this elevation, it still looked like winter with snowbanks everywhere. He drove down the twisting eastern side, where the television series *Bonanza* had once been filmed. Only a few miles to the north, the "Cartwright Ranch" still brought in droves of tourists during the summertime. As T.J. dropped in elevation, the forest started to thin out and the canyon of Clear Creek on his right became more pronounced. Just where the forest started to end and the sagebrush began, T.J. pulled over onto a margin of the highway and stopped. It looked like his last good location for concealment. If he drove any farther, he would start getting into inhabited areas again. There were no houses here, just national forestland.

T.J. recounted later, "At one of the first turnouts after the wall stops (median-strip walls), I stopped and parked the vehicle and grabbed the bag of clothes and he had told me to throw them away in different spots. Her clothes and her. So I threw her clothes, out on the side of the mountain there. I was swinging the bag and it ripped and all the clothes flew out of it. All landing somewhere out there on the side. So I hopped back in the vehicle and drove off real quick. And I stopped at a few spots trying to find a place like he described, and I stopped alongside the mile marker or whatever halfway down [from the summit]. I continued along and finally found a spot that I thought would work for me. I drove over, pulled her out of the box. And I noticed that there was some sort of puddle inside the bag. But I went ahead and took the bag out. And I threw up a couple of times. I was real nervous and scared. I put the bag in the front floorboard, so I could throw it over quicker. And I was waiting for traffic to die down and that's when I noticed there was blood pouring out of the bag onto the rail board and the running board. And on the door frame a little bit. So when traffic looked finally clear, I pulled it out and went and threw it over the side. And that's when I noticed that there was another car that passed by and, like, the person was looking at me or something."

As luck would have it, Diantha Wilson, a woman who lived near Reno, was driving on Highway 50 at that moment. She had been on a trip to Placerville in California with her daughter to pick up a puppy for her husband and was returning to Nevada. As she rounded a curve, eastbound, she noticed a red-and-white SUV parked on the side of the road at a turnout. Recalling the incident later, she said, "[The boy] flung a bag of what appeared to me like a king-size pillowcase, grayish color, off the embankment. I slammed on my brakes because I wondered what was going on. That's because I have little kids and sometimes I'll put them in pillowcases or whatever and fling them around because they love it. That's what this looked like to me. Like there was a big dog or child or something in the bag. And as I hit my brakes, he looked. . . . We made eye contact for a moment. And as I went down the hill, I was pretty nervous because I thought he might follow me or something. . . . And my daughter, who's twelve, was very concerned he was going to follow us. We kept watching behind us all the way down to the Carson Nugget Casino."

After throwing Krystal's body down the mountain, T.J. was indeed heading for Carson City as well. But not after Diantha Wilson. He had to get rid of the blood that had spilled onto the floor mat and running board. He recalled, "I was walking back to the vehicle and I noticed I had blood on my hands and some on my shirt as well. So I grabbed some napkins out of the console and was trying to wipe it off the floorboard and everything. I felt sick again at the sight of it. I tried to clean it up, but I couldn't really get it cleaned. So I hopped back in and climbed across the passenger seat and started the vehicle and headed down to Carson. From there, I turned at the first streetlight at the Arco [station] and headed down toward the hills. I ended up over by the prison. I stopped at a turnout across from a church and I was trying to clean up the blood again and get it off the floor mat. And I couldn't. So I threw some dirt on it from the ground so nobody could see it.

"I drove back out to Fifty and to one of the Texacos and parked on the side there. I was hoping to find a car wash so I could wash off the vehicle. I went in the bathroom there at the Texaco and washed my hands and tried to wash my shirt off. After that, I drove right across the street to the Shell station and into the car wash there. I went inside and ordered the car wash and went through it, but after I was done, there was still blood on the running board. So I drove down that little back road that goes behind there and then down to the Arco that I passed earlier. I ordered some gas and continued to try and wipe up the blood. Then I threw a lot of the napkins in a trash can there at the Arco.

"After that, I decided I should try and find water at one of the service stations and try and wash it off. Finally I stopped at an Arco or something and threw the duct tape in one of the bins there. There was also a drop of blood on the floor mat. I couldn't really [clean it up], so I decided to just go ahead and come home."

Meanwhile, back at the Soria apartment, Thomas Soria Sr. was busy as well cleaning up. Exactly what he did was unclear. Whatever he did, it was enough to at least make it seem that nothing out of the ordinary had gone on in apartment 22. It wasn't perfect, but it would take more than a casual glance to notice that anything unusual had gone on in the bedroom or the bathroom.

As the sun set behind Mount Tallac to the west, Elizabeth Steadman was in a pure state of panic. Krystal couldn't be found anywhere. At 4:56 P.M. Elizabeth couldn't stand the suspense any longer. She phoned the Douglas County District Sheriff's Office at Stateline, Nevada. The office was only about a mile from the Sorias' apartment. The phone call was taken very seriously. A ten-year-old blond girl named Jaycee Lee Dugard had been snatched off the streets of South Lake Tahoe nine years before and never seen again. The Sheriff's office hoped they didn't have another Dugard case on their hands.

TEN

The Young Man
with Shaggy Hair

The first officers to contact T.J. Soria were Deputies
Craig Lowe and Sandy Cable of the Douglas County
Sheriff's office. As Douglas County detective Ted
Duzan recorded about this time frame:

> DCSO Case #00-1582T—On March 19, 2000, I
> was the on-call investigator for the Douglas
> County Sheriff's Office (DCSO). On that date at
> approximately 6:20 P.M., I was called at my resi-
> dence concerning the disappearance of a
> nine-year-old female, later identified as Krystal
> Dawn Steadman. (DOB: 08/25/90).
>
> Krystal Steadman was reported missing by her
> mother, on March 19, 2000 at 4:56 P.M. DCSO
> Deputies Sandy Cable and Craig Lowe responded
> to the Lake Park Apartments, the last place where
> Krystal was seen, to begin their search.
>
> During that investigation, information was
> learned that Krystal had been playing with other
> children in the Rabes Meadow and Lake Park

Apartments area. Krystal does not live in Douglas County and did not know anyone specifically at the apartment complex. Her mother was at the complex, visiting her boyfriend. It was also learned that Krystal and other children were in the company of an adult identified as Thomas Soria Junior who resides in the Lake Park Apartment complex.

The futile search for Krystal continued for several more hours. Her bicycle and jacket were found near Building #1, at different locations. Upon arriving to the Lake Park Apartments at approximately 7:00 P.M., I was notified via Sheriff's radio that Deputy Lowe had contacted the "suspect," Thomas Soria Jr., in the listed vehicle in the rear parking lot area of the Lake Park Apartments, Building #1. Upon Deputy Lowe's contact with Soria Junior, he was patted down for weapons.

Deputy Lowe introduced T.J. to Sergeant Tim Minister and I while he was sitting in the rear seat of his patrol car. T.J. agreed to accompany us to the Lake sub-station for a voluntary interview. He sat down between Detective Minister and Detective Ted Duzan. Duzan turned on a tape recorder and said, "It's March 19, 2000—7:24 P.M."

At this point Thomas Soria Jr. began the second version of what had occurred. It was filled with lies and deceptions and just enough truths to try and throw the police off track.

Duzan: Are you warm?
Soria: Yeah, I'm pretty much warm enough.
Duzan: God, you're young. How young are you?

Soria: Um, nineteen. I'm gonna be twenty.

Duzan: Thanks for coming down.

Soria: Yeah, no problem.

Duzan: Obviously, we have ourselves a situation here that we need cleared up.

Soria: Right.

Minister: We need to let you understand you're not under arrest.

Soria: Yeah, I understand that.

Minister: Did you come here voluntarily?

Soria: Yes, I did. I always like to help the community. That's what I've been trying to do since I got up here. I love it up here in Tahoe.

Minister: Where are you from?

Soria: Sacramento. But I was born in Carson City, though.

Duzan: So anyway, the problem that we have is this little girl. Do you know Krystal? My understanding is you were with her earlier today, giving her rides.

Soria: Um, yes. They were riding on the running boards, that's what it's called, of the truck, holding on to the doorhandle on the outside, and I figured I'd just give them a ride like right down the street a little bit, you know, in the complex. They like to have fun, so I figured I didn't see any harm in it. As long as they weren't moving around and stuff. Getting ready to fall or anything. Yesterday I gave two boys the same thing. So I figured I might as well go ahead and do it. I know it's not exactly the best thing to be doing. . . .

Duzan: At what time was that?

Soria: It was early this afternoon. Before twelve, probably.

Duzan: And then what happened?

Soria: Um, I went down and got a soda and came back and gotten some food and stuff and they're all like, "Give me some food, give me some food." And I'm like, "No, this is my food. I gotta eat something."

Minister: You went where?

Soria: McDonald's.

Minister: Which one?

Soria: The one at Ski Run Boulevard.

Duzan: Who was asking you for food?

Soria: Krystal was, and Sandi and that other girl. I think they were asking too. I told them, "You can't have any." And Krystal followed me, and I told her, "No, no, no," and shooed her away from my door. She ended up leaving and went back out and began playing with Sandi and that other girl.

Duzan: And that was where?

Soria: That was in the hallway right in front of my apartment.

Duzan: Okay. You live there by yourself?

Soria: Uh, no, with my mom and dad. So, what else do you need to know?

Duzan: You said you went out and got a soda. . . .

Soria: Yeah, I went down to Nik and Willies, got myself a soda, talked to the worker, Ken, there for a little bit. I've been talking to him since we're locals and stuff, and try to get to know as many people in the neighborhood as I can. Uh, plus with my job and all. I try to keep a positive attitude and influence on the community and stuff. I know my coworker Diana knows, and I have her phone number if you want to contact her later or something. Uh, yeah, I went down there and got the liter of soda and a couple of smokes and went home. Then they wanted a ride again, so I gave them a ride to where I park, you know, where I park the truck pretty much in the same spot every time. So after I parked the truck, they just went off and played. And Junior and this other boy tried to hop on the truck, but I just kept going. So I heard later that somebody said I was trying to run them over. I don't know where that came from. It's just something I heard, and . . .

Duzan: I hadn't heard that.

Soria: Yeah. Yeah. I don't know what that was about. I think the officer, Craig. I think somebody told him that. So, Sandi came up and told me. . . .

Duzan: Now, everybody calls you T.J. Is that right?

Soria: Mm-hm.

Duzan: What's your real name?

Soria: It's Thomas. It stands for Thomas junior, because my dad's name is the same as mine. So I just go by T.J. That's what I've always gone by.

Duzan: And what's your last name?

Soria: Soria.

Duzan: Okay. Now this little girl that's missing, what's the last time you saw her?

Soria: Um, it was sometime this afternoon. I was up in my house and she was running around on the bike, you know. And I seen her drop it off and run down the street.

Duzan: What time was that?

Soria: I don't remember. But it must have been around two or something like that. I don't remember.

Duzan: That was the last time you saw her?

Soria: Yeah. You know, I can't remember the exact time. I haven't been keeping track of time all day.

Duzan: Well, that's understandable. Now, the . . . is it a Bronco?

Soria: It's a Blazer.

Duzan: Okay. Who does it actually belong to?

Soria: That belongs to my dad.

Duzan: Have you been driving it all day?

Soria: Um, no. No. I've gone out two times, and then a third time was after this evening, you know, when I went out to drive because we had some words, me and him, and I was a little bit upset about it and I usually don't like to stick around, you know, because I don't want things to . . . I like to get out and cool off and mellow out. Driving sometimes . . . That's what I like to do. Other times, I've gone in the forest there, you know, and sat on the rocks. The kids have this place called Monkey Island. It's just a bunch of big rocks that they play at.

Duzan: So what time did you leave? What time did you and your dad have words?

Soria: It must have been around four o'clock or something like that. And then I left shortly thereafter. Four-thirty or something. I mean I just took off.

Duzan: Did Krystal go with you?

Soria: No, no. No, I didn't see her when I left. In fact, all the kids had gone in. And that was after her parents came up and looked around the place.

Duzan: For what?

Soria: Um, I guess for their personal selves. See if she was in there.

Duzan: So, she was missing before you even knew about it?

Soria: Yeah.

Duzan: Now, when you took your drive, where did you go?

Soria: I went driving out to Cave Rock. I drove around the area there. I drove up almost to the summit . . . Spooner Summit. I drove up there and spent a lot of time sitting around and looking at the trees and stuff. It's just like, what I like to do. It's part of the reason we like it up here so much.

Duzan: And that's understandable. Lake Tahoe is beautiful.

Soria: Yeah.

Duzan: Okay. What time did you get to the Cave Rock boat landing?

Soria: I didn't look at the time. It must have taken me twenty minutes or something.

Duzan: So, four-forty?

Soria: Yeah.

Duzan: How long did you stay in there?

Soria: Um, probably about ten or fifteen minutes. I sat there, looked at the lake. I took off and went up the road to the summit and there were a bunch of Zephyr Cove buses there. I guess where they're doing something. Construction or something. Where they keep all the signs and stuff. I went and sat up there, must have been an hour or something. I kind of dozed off a bit.

Duzan: Now, I understand you're the coordinator for the Boys and Girls Club?

Soria: I don't know if you'd call me the coordinator. I know on my time sheet it says Program

Aide. I guess I kind of coordinate things there. As well as my boss, Diana. She's the on-site boss. And Steve and Gary are my other bosses. So . . .

Duzan: Are you cold?

Soria: A little bit. My shirt's still a little bit wet.

Duzan: How come your shirt's wet?

Soria: Oh . . . while I was sitting there at Cave Rock, I—I got up and got out and um . . . you know, went down where it goes down into the water? Where they let the boats down.

Duzan: Mm-hm.

Soria: I went and was standing over there and stuff, and I got some mud on my shirt. So, I just thought, "Oh, I'll just dump it in the lake. Wash it off." So that's what I did. But it didn't quite dry as quick as I thought.

Duzan: Little chilly, huh?

Soria: Yeah. So now I'm freezing. I had the heat on like full blast on the way back.

Duzan: Yeah, the water's cold, I'm telling ya.

Soria: Yeah.

Duzan: So, do you have a room specifically at your dad's?

Soria: Yeah. Yeah, I have the room next to the living room.

Duzan: So you have no idea where Krystal is?

Soria: No, I don't.

Duzan: None?

Soria: No. Unfortunately. I wish I did.

Duzan: Do you drink beer at all?

Soria: Not really. I don't like the side effects of it. You know, the hangover and stuff. I occasionally drink, but that's about it.

Duzan: Ever been arrested on anything?

Soria: I was arrested down in Sacramento for some stuff that happened to me. I've had it cleared off my record since then. It was a real bad mistake and hanging around with the wrong people and such. I just got away from that and got my life back together.

Duzan: Good. Any tattoos or anything?'

Soria: No.

Minister: Where do you work, sir?

Soria: The Boys and Girls Club of South Lake Tahoe.

Duzan: Isn't it just in that room there at Kahle Drive?

Soria: Um, that's the site on the Nevada side. They have offices down behind the Terrible Herbst (gas station) and they have another location at the middle school up there.

Duzan: Is it full-time?

Soria: No, it's part-time.

Duzan: You going to school or anything?

Soria: No, I want to get my diploma. I want to finish my senior year, but that's it.

Minister: Do you head for work at a certain time?

Soria: Yeah, I get there at two-thirty and leave about six-thirty.

Minister: And what kind of things do you do?

Soria: We help the kids with their homework. Give them homework points for doing their homework. After two weeks, we give them trips or a party or whatever.

Minister: What age group?

Soria: Probably it goes anywhere from about two or three all the way up to twelve or thirteen.

Minister: Okay. How many kids are typically there?

Soria: Mmm . . . usually on a decent day it's about twenty or thirty. Sometimes it's less; sometimes we only get, like, fifteen kids in there. We've been trying to get more in there. Because we're trying to make it positive for them. Especially for those older boys . . . uh, that's why I tried to get an officer to come out there [to the club]. They're at the age where they can be influenced by gangs and such. I mean, I don't know what there is up here, but me and Diana have this philosophy to show them we're always there, you know, to support them and help them. If they need anything to talk about, we're there for them. Play on the computers and . . . one of the things I've been doing is playing a game called TaiPai . . . it's an old Chinese game, and I've been trying to get the kids to play that, you know, because it's real intellectual and it makes them think a lot, so I've been using that for their homework prize and stuff.

Minister: Did you go through a background check?

Soria: Yeah.

Minister: Processed and all that stuff?

Soria: Yeah, I had to go down to Al Tahoe [a section of South Lake Tahoe] and get fingerprinted and stuff.

Minister: Okay. What was the arrest for in California?

Soria: It was check fraud.

Minister: Okay. Have you ever been arrested for anything else?

Soria: No. I haven't.

Minister: Okay. We're talking about Krystal, right? What do you remember her wearing?

Soria: I thought I had seen her in some black pants and a white shirt.

Minister: Can you describe her for me?

Soria: Mmm . . . she's about this tall [*using his hands*] with dirty blond hair. It's about shoulder length. I don't know how old she is.

Minister: Does she wear glasses?

Soria: No.

Minister: Does she live down at Lake Park?

Soria: Yeah, as far as I know. I guess she lives in one of the buildings there. She was one of Sandi's friends. I was hanging out with the kids this weekend. We were doing stuff in the field. Walked Sandi's dog with her dad yesterday. Had a game over there at the tree and then I met Krystal today. Because Sandi was walking around with her and Connie Stewart.

Duzan: How old's Sandi and Connie?

Soria: Uh, I think Connie's about seven and Sandi's about, like, nine or something like that. As far as I know.

Duzan: Now, how did you meet them?

Soria: Through the club. And I'm good friends with the parents and stuff. I know her mom. I try to keep good relations with the parents and stuff.

Duzan: Now, earlier you told me that Krystal's mother had come by looking for her. Were you at home at the time?

Soria: Yes, I was. Uh, she had come by once with Sandi and . . . and I told her about how I had thought I had seen her running off, you know, down the street toward the trailer park, and

Nine-year-old Krystal Steadman was a Girl Scout who participated in gymnastics, karate, and choir.
(Photo courtesy of South Lake Tahoe Tribune)

The Douglas County Nevada Sheriff's Office distributed Missing Juvenile posters as soon as Krystal's mother reported her missing on March 19, 2000.
(Photo courtesy of Douglas County Justice Center)

Krystal Steadman was raped and murdered by Thomas Soria Sr.
in this Stateline, Nevada, apartment complex.
(Photo courtesy of Douglas County Justice Center)

T.J. Soria used his father's Ford Bronco to drive into the woods
and dispose of Krystal Steadman's body.
(Photo courtesy of Douglas County Justice Center)

On the morning of March 20, 2000, Douglas County Sheriff's Officers discovered the naked body of Krystal Steadman dumped by the side of the road on Highway 50. *(Photo Courtesy of Belinda Grant and Record Courier)*

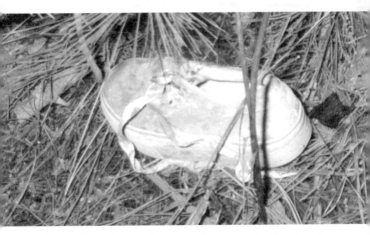

One of Krystal Steadman's shoes was discovered by Douglas County Sheriff's Officers in the woods near Spooner Summit, Nevada. *(Photo courtesy of Douglas County Justice Center)*

Thomas Soria Sr. led young girls into his apartment, #22, to fulfill his psychotic fantasies.
(Photo courtesy of Douglas County Justice Center)

Soria Sr. kept detailed files on this computer about how he wanted to sexually torture and murder women and young girls.
(Photo courtesy of Douglas County Justice Center)

This walk-in closet became Soria Sr.'s lair for planning rape and sexual torture. *(Photo courtesy of Douglas County Justice Center)*

Technicians for the Douglas County Sheriff's Office took apart the drains in the Soria apartment looking for blood that would match Krystal Steadman's. *(Photo courtesy of Douglas County Justice Center)*

Soria Sr. kept board games and toys to lure girls,
and even young boys, into his apartment.
(Photo courtesy of Douglas County Justice Center)

Soria Sr. kept dolls in his closet so that he could make
young girls feel at ease with him.
(Photo courtesy of Douglas County Justice Center)

Soria Sr. raped and sexually tortured Krystal Steadman on this bed.
(Photo courtesy of Douglas County Justice Center)

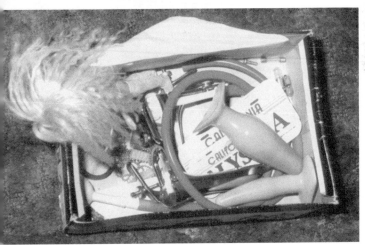

Soria Sr. kept sex toys and devices in this box at his apartment.
(Photo courtesy of Douglas County Justice Center)

After Soria Sr. was arrested, Douglas County Sheriff's Officers noticed scratch marks near his rib cage consistent with someone trying to fight off an attacker.
(Photo courtesy of Douglas County Justice Center)

Mugshots taken of Soria Sr. when he was arrested for the murder of Krystal Steadman.
(Photo courtesy of Douglas County Justice Center)

Last Name	First Name	Middle Name	Social Security No.
SORIA	THOMAS	ROBERT	563114004

of Birth	Skin Color	Ethnic Origin	Sex	Nationality	Eye Color	Height	Weight	Hai
7/61	BR	H	M	MX	BRO	507	145	81

Glasses? True   Beard? False   Mustache? True

T.J. Soria was sexually abused by his father from an early age. He was so far under his father's influence that he offered his own girlfriends to be sexual partners with his dad.
(Photo courtesy of Douglas County Justice Center)

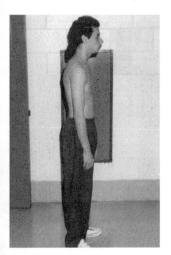

Side view of T.J. Soria at the time of his arrest in March 2000.
(Photo courtesy of Douglas County Justice Center)

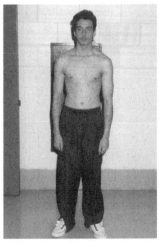

Frontal view of T.J. Soria at the time of his arrest.
(Photo courtesy of Douglas County Justice Center)

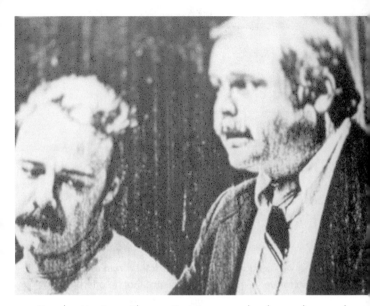

Douglas Mozingo, Thomas Soria's step uncle, shot twelve people in the Mother Lode Bar in Sacramento, California, during a wild rampage. *(Photo courtesy of Sacramento Superior Court)*

Ronny Mozingo, Thomas Soria Sr.'s step-brother, murdered Thomas's mother, Janey, by attaching a cord from her ankles to her throat. *(Photo courtesy of Sacramento Superior Court)*

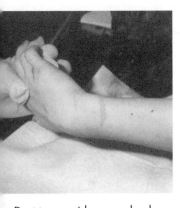

Duct tape residue was clearly evident on Krystal Steadman's wrist at the time of her autopsy.
(Photo courtesy of Douglas County Justice Center)

The bloody gray trash bag used by T.J. Soria to transport Krystal Steadman's body from the apartment to the Ford Bronco.
(Photo courtesy of Douglas County Justice Center)

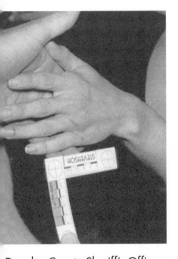

Douglas County Sheriff's Officers discovered several scratch marks on T.J. Soria's hands after the abduction of Krystal Steadman.
(Photo courtesy of Douglas County Justice Center)

Blood on the floor mat in Soria Sr.'s Ford Bronco matched that of Krystal Steadman.
(Photo courtesy of Douglas County Justice Center)

Senior Deputy District Attorney Thomas Perkins of Douglas County (on right) talks to Krystal Steadman's grandparents about Soria Sr.'s suicide. *(Photo courtesy of Jim Grant and* South Lake Tahoe Tribune*)*

Sonia Klempner, Krystal's older sister, cries on the stand at T.J. Soria's sentencing phase.
(Photo courtesy of Belinda Grant and Record Courier*)*

T.J. Soria at his arraignment for the abduction
of Krystal Steadman.
(Photo courtesy of Belinda Grant and Record Courier*)*

T.J. Soria (on left) and Thomas Soria Sr.(on right) at their respective
arraignment hearings for the murder of Krystal Steadman.
(Photo courtesy of Jim Grant and South Lake Tahoe Tribune*)*

T.J. Soria crying at his sentencing phase for which he would receive a life sentence without the possibility of parole.
(Photo courtesy of Belinda Grant and Record Courier*)*

Soria Sr. and his lawyer during the early stages of his trial.
(Photo courtesy of Belinda Grant and Record Courier*)*

Douglas County Sheriff Ron Pierini talks to the news media about the murder of Krystal Steadman and the arrest of T. J. Soria. *(Photo courtesy of Jim Grant and South Lake Tahoe Tribune)*

T. J. Soria and his lawyer during his sentencing phase for the abduction of Krystal Steadman. *(Photo courtesy of Belinda Grant and Record Courier)*

Douglas County Superior Court Judge David Gamble gives T. J. Soria a life sentence without the possibility of parole. *(Photo courtesy of Belinda Grant and Record Courier)*

A small wooden cross was placed on the spot alongside Highway 50 where Krystal Steadman's body was discovered. (Author's photo)

Krystal Steadman's cross looking down Clear Creek Canyon toward Carson City. (Author's photo)

Sonia Klempner dedicated a plaque to her sister at the spot where her body was found. It reads: "In memory of my sister Krystal Dawn Steadman. August 25, 1990 - March 19, 2000." (Author's photo)

she went and looked for her. She came back about ten minutes later and said she couldn't find her still. She had her husband with her and my uncle was sleeping at the time, so I was trying not to disturb him. And she said she was going to probably contact the police because she couldn't find her, so I says if you need anything to let me know. I'll be glad to help you in any way I can.

Minister: Well, did they ask to look in your house?

Soria: Yes, they did.

Duzan: Why do you think they did that?

Soria: Probably because they don't know me. And I've never met them before or seen their daughter before. So I guess that's why.

Minister: Were your parents home at the time?

Soria: Uh, my uncle . . . or my dad, was home and he was sleeping.

Minister: Who is your uncle?

Soria: Oh, no, no. My uncle . . . it's a slip of the tongue, I guess.

Minister: What?

Soria: Slip of the tongue. Uh, um, my—my dad was sleeping at the time.

Minister: Does your uncle live there?

Soria: No, he doesn't.

Minister: Okay. So, your mom and dad, do they work?

Soria: Not right now. My mom's working at the Horizon; she's going to be taking tomorrow off, I guess to visit my stepsister. She's just my stepmom, by the way. So I guess she's staying down there [in Sacramento] with her tonight.

Minister: Were they home the whole time today?

Soria: Um . . . my unc . . . my dad was, yes.

Minister: Why do you keep saying your uncle?

Soria: Because sometimes I just joke with people and tell them he's my uncle, you know. Something I have been doing lately. Sort of a joke on some of my friends. But, uh, yeah, he was asleep at the time.

Minister: Does he work nights?

Soria: Uh, no. He's not working currently. He's going to be getting unemployment on the Nevada side. He had something going with somebody at Tahoe Net, but the deal fell through. Working with computers. That's his specialty.

Minister: Would you mind telling me what you were arguing about today?

Soria: Um, just some stupid things about not cleaning up the house and stuff. You know, how the house was a mess, and I got all edgy and uptight and started yelling a little bit back at him and he went to his room. I sat there on the couch and then ended up leaving. There was the keys on the dining-room table.

Minister: Okay. Where did you go today?

Soria: Yeah, I went to Cave Rock and sat there for a while. And I got out and looked at the water and got my shirt dirty.

Minister: How'd you get dirty?

Soria: Um, the mud and stuff down there. . . .

Minister: Can you describe to me how you got it dirty?

Soria: I was sitting down on the ground at the water and stuff; so, since it's long (the shirt), it had gotten dirty from that. So I pulled it off and just kind of rinsed it off in the water and got all wet. So I wringed it out as best I could, but it's only drying out now.

Minister: Was it like mud or dirt?

Soria: Yeah, it was like dirty mud.

Minister: What part of Cave Rock?

Soria: I pulled down into the little parking area where people fish and such. I was down at the boat landing.

Minister: Oh, you were? And were you sitting, standing, laying . . . ?

Soria: I was just sitting on the ground.

Minister: On the paved ramp, or . . .

Soria: Uh, no, down lower . . . off on the side, down where the water comes up and meets the shore. . . .

Minister: Is there a muddy bank there? Is there rocks or what?

Soria: There's a lot of rocks and there was also some mud. . . . I was just looking off at the lake and the mountains and stuff. I just sat there. I like the sound of the water and the view of the mountains and stuff. It looks real nice when the sun sets.

Duzan: You said you went up to Spooner Summit. And you said something about snowmobiles and Zephyr Cove buses.

Soria: Yeah.

Duzan: And how long did you stay there?

Soria: Probably about an hour or two. Something like that.

Duzan: Just sitting there?

Soria: Yeah. I was just sitting there. I kind of dozed off a little bit, reclined the seat back and relaxed.

Duzan: How much snow's up there?

Soria: Probably about four or five inches, a half a foot. Something like that. It was thicker off in the forest. But a lot of it had receded back from the warmer weather we had.

Duzan: Now, if you were at the boat landing, stayed out there for ten or fifteen minutes, got back in the truck and went up to Spooner . . . why'd you do that?

Soria: Just because I decided I wasn't going to stay at Cave Rock.

Duzan: Now, your pants aren't wet, right?

Soria: No, no.

Duzan: And Krystal . . . did she wear anything in her hair that you recall?

Soria: Not that I noticed.

Duzan: Do you know what kind of shoes she was wearing?

Soria: All I know is, I thought they were white shoes.

Duzan: You said she was wearing dark-colored pants?

Soria: Yeah, they were like black.

Duzan: Stretch pants?

Soria: Um, they looked real nice. Like dress-type pants.

Duzan: Okay. So, did you ever get out of the Blazer at Spooner Summit?

Soria: Uh, like once.

Duzan: What did you do?

Soria: I just kind of looked around, walked around a tiny bit. Looked at the scenery. And it was just kind of cold and there was some precipitation coming down, so I says, "Oh, I'm just gonna get back in the truck and relax."

Duzan: Any of the people on the Zephyr Cove bus see you?

Soria: I don't think so because they were backed down a little bit farther.

Duzan: [Back at Cave Rock] How would your shirt get wet or muddy?

Soria: Um . . . because I—I took off my shoes and socks and pulled my pants up and went down to the water level and just kind of sat there. So there was some mud there from the water, along with the rocks. So I let my feet get wet before they started freezing and then pulled them out, and, uh, that's how I got muddy, from sitting down there.

Duzan: You don't use drugs at all?

Soria: No.

Duzan: Would you tell me if you did?

Soria: No.

Duzan: Good answer. A lot of people . . . uh, uh . . . The only thing we want to do right now is find Krystal.

Soria: Right.

Duzan: There's a mother that's without her child. And that's the only thing we care about at this point.

Soria: Mm-hmm. I worry about the kids, and they're not even mine.

Duzan: Well, you'd have to, I guess, with what you do.

Soria: Yeah, I mean . . . I'm very intelligent. I have a lot of computer skills that my dad's taught me. Because I've grown up with them since I was eight. I've always had a longing to help people. I've always wanted to help people and I kinda get to do that with the kids. I get to influence their behavior so they maybe grow up a little bit better. I never cuss around the kids, other than maybe a slip of the tongue once in a while. I'm trying to get another job to help with the elderly before I go to work with the kids. So I can get extra money and it's something I enjoy doing. I enjoy helping people. I've often considered one of the people who ride in the ambulances and doing that kind of work. You know I have a CPR card. I'm certified to do CPR on kids and adults.

Duzan: Good deal. Are you warm?

Soria: Yeah. Yeah, I'm warmer.

Duzan: Now, you talked about driving around [with Krystal], what side was she on?

Soria: She was on the passenger side.

Duzan: Where did you drive around?

Soria: From where the truck's parked down to the entrance.

Duzan: Do you get in fights a lot with your father?

Soria: Mmm . . . sometimes. Not too much. Usually we pretty much see eye to eye, you know. Sometimes we have an occasional argument. It's probably the stress of living with somebody.

Duzan: How long have you lived there with your dad?

Soria: Probably about since last March or May. So it's been just about a year.

Duzan: And was he up here first?

Soria: Yeah, yeah, they had moved up here first. They got up here, I believe, in January of '99.

Duzan: And why'd you come up here?

Soria: Because I missed my family. I lived with my dad all my life.

Minister: What did you do around lunch today?

Soria: That's when I was out there with the kids still. . . . We walked around and, uh, out to the tree at the entrance. That's where they have like a little club there . . . and they played around there and I kinda watched and they showed me how they climb up the tree real high. And some kids they haven't been getting along with for the last few days . . . started calling them profanities.

Duzan: Like?

Soria: Like 'you stupid bitches' . . . uh, 'butt faces,' things to that effect.

Minister: Who went out there with you?

Soria: The three girls. They were dragging me and pulling me by the arm. . . .

Duzan: What field?

Soria: The field right across the street . . . um, the Kahle Field, I guess you call it.

Minister: How far did you go out in that meadow?

Soria: Um, there's a little hill that we go sledding on right there. It's just a hill and most of the rest of the land's flat. And we just went to the side of the hill and looked around a little bit; then we started heading back. There were some ladybugs out there on the little sagebrush bushes and we looked at those real quick. And then we came back and that's when they were saying those things.

Minister: Okay. So after the meadow, what did you do?

Soria: Uh, we looked at the ladybugs and then we're heading back toward the apartments and . . . we walked back toward my building and I told them I had to go in. I had to see if my uncle, you know my dad, was up yet. And he wasn't, and I was waiting for him to get up so I could get some lunch . . . and [the other girls] were yelling all these things at me, like 'stupid' and they were hiding and I kind of ignored them 'cause I didn't want to get into their mess. . . . I was just trying to stay out of it, because in some ways I kind of take the attitude of what they do outside the club I can't really control. But some of the things they were saying kind of included me, so I told them, "You guys are only, like, nine and twelve years old and you don't even know what those words are. So you shouldn't be using them. I'm nineteen, almost twenty. I been around a lot longer than you guys have, so just cut this stuff out, 'cause you guys don't know what you're saying."

Duzan: Okay, let's get back to Krystal real quick.

Soria: Mm-hm.

Duzan: You said you saw her drop her bike over there by the trash can Dumpster.

Soria: No, I had seen her drop it off somewhere around the carports. . . . Then I seen her run off.

Duzan: She was running which way?

Soria: Toward the mobile-home parks.

Duzan: She have some friends down there?

Soria: I don't know. I just glanced out my window and saw her, and that was about it.

Duzan: Since you had a fight with your dad, have you talked to him or seen him?

Soria: Uh, no. I was just gonna go up and see him and I was gonna apologize to him.

Duzan: Is he your real dad?

Soria: Yes, he is.

Duzan: I have a problem with the uncle thing. I mean, I don't call my dad my uncle.

Soria: Oh, yeah. It was just a joke we were playing on . . . I have some friends who live upstairs. It was kind of like a joke I was playing on them. So . . . sometimes I just call him my uncle because he's in some ways more than a dad to me. You know, we're pretty close and I can talk to him like a friend as well. Sometimes I call him uncle because I guess, you know, that's what uncles are for. You talk to your uncle or you talk to your friends differently.

Duzan: Now, when Krystal's mom came to your apartment . . . she went in and looked around?

Soria: The first time Sandi and . . . brought her up and she told me that she couldn't find her and she was looking for her. I told her that I had seen her, what I had seen. And she says, "Okay, I'll go look down there." Then just her and her boyfriend came back, I think his name is Dave.

Duzan: Did they check your apartment thoroughly?

Soria: Um, she came in; she glanced around. She looked in the bathroom and in my room and looked in the front room and she wanted to look back where my uncle was sleeping. . . .

Duzan: Right. In that room you wouldn't let her look in.

Soria: Yeah, because he was sleeping, so . . .

Duzan: If you're a pillar of the community, so to speak, down there, why wouldn't she believe you?

Soria: Like I thought, I'd never met her before, and I was kind of thinking that she probably didn't know who I was, you know, and she wasn't trusting me. That's kinda what I thought.

Duzan: Um, you understand where we're sitting? You understand your position?

Soria: Yeah.

Duzan: You understand why we're here, totally?

Soria: Yeah, because I hang around with the kids all the time and I'm in a position to usually know what's going on and talk to them and hear things.

Duzan: And you're in a position to help us.

Soria: Right. Right.

Minister: Do you understand you're free to leave anytime?

Soria: Mm-hm.

Duzan: You can get up and leave at any time, but we hope you won't because you were seen with Krystal up and around the time that she hasn't been seen since. And her mom's just a wreck.

Soria: Oh, I'm sure.

Duzan: Like we would all be.

Soria: Yeah. Oh, yeah, yeah. I would be too.

Duzan: Okay, okay. So you go back home with a Pepsi . . . and there's Dad.

Soria: Yeah. We ate, sat down and ate, and then he started getting on my case about the place being dirty. And we got in that argument and right after that is when her mom came to the door. So he went right to bed because of what was said and everything. . . .

Duzan: Does he sleep strange hours?

Soria: Yeah. He stays up late sometimes and watches TV or whatever. . . .

Minister: Do you know where Krystal is now?

Soria: No, no, I don't.

Minister: When's the last time you saw her?

Soria: When I looked out my window and saw her running.

Minister: Running?

Soria: Like down toward the mobile homes. . . .

[*Break. Some time passes and the investigators dispatch deputies to the Sorias' apartment*].

Duzan: Obviously, you're cold.

Soria: Yeah, a little bit. Not too much anymore.

Duzan: Here's what I want to do . . . because other people have seen you in those clothes. I would like your clothes.

Minister: Ted?

Duzan: Just hang on.

Soria: All right.

Minister: I'll . . . Okay.

Duzan: Okay?

Soria: Okay.

Duzan: So what I'd like to do now is get you out of these and take you in here (another room) and get you dressed. . . .

[*After T.J. changed his clothing*].

Soria: I noticed there's a camera out there." (a newsman with a camera outside).

Duzan: It's getting crazy. The whole world's out there.

Soria: Oh, man . . . And, oh, I thought you were going to give me your shoes.

Duzan: You want them?

Soria: Well, they look pretty nice.

Duzan: Tell you what . . . Like a week after I had them [*points at shoe*], that broke.

Soria: Oh, jeez.

Duzan: And you pay a hundred and five dollars

for a pair of shoes . . . .So I'll never buy another pair of Nikes. I hate them.

Soria: Yeah.

Duzan: All I know is . . . we went down and talked to your dad and he says you guys didn't get into an argument today.

Soria: No, no, he—he might have . . . We're pretty private people. He might just have not wanted to speak about it.

Duzan: How old's your dad?

Soria: He's, uh, thirty-nine. I think that's what he is.

Duzan: Just a pup. And you're nineteen?

Soria: Nineteen.

Duzan: Christ. Just a pup. So . . . he didn't want to talk about it?

Soria: Yeah.

Duzan: He didn't mention it.

Soria: I rather doubt it, you know.

Duzan: Why?

Soria: Because, you know, when we get into arguments, we usually just don't like to tell people about it.

Duzan: His son is sitting at the police station . . . not under arrest, but his son's at the police station. And if we go talk to him, and he says no, that didn't happen, how does that make you look?

Soria: I guess not too good.

Duzan: Right. So if your dad says you weren't in an argument and you drove around for hours . . . for what? Do you know? In his Blazer. And there's a little girl missing.

Soria: I want to find her too. See her back safely.

Duzan: Yeah, but you see where we're coming

from. We've been doing this for thirty-plus
years. And almost everything you've told us is
crap. We've never heard anything like this before. You get in a fight with your dad; you
leave, drive around for hours, two different locations. One at Cave Rock and your shirt
mysteriously gets wet. You drive out to—

Soria: Mysteriously?

Duzan: Listen to me . . . all I'm trying to do is put
yourself in my shoes. That's all I'm trying to
do. I'm not trying to piss you off. But something's not right here. Something's not right.
You drive up; you sit in your truck for an hour
and a half at Spooner; you drive over and stay
ten or fifteen minutes at the boat landing at
Cave Rock; your shirt gets wet; you're freezing
your ass off; you're shaking like a leaf in here
. . . you're dry-mouthed; you're nervous—

Minister: You're really nervous.

Soria: I'm always nervous around cops.

Duzan: I asked you earlier if you smoked or if you
did any kind of narcotics. You said no. I asked
you would you tell me if you did. You said no.
That tells me that you do. So our concerns
are—

Minister: We've probably got fifty people amassed
now to go out and look for that child. Sooner
or later, we're gonna find that child. If there's
a possibility the child is still alive, even if somebody choked her or something . . . we've found
instances where twenty, thirty minutes later the
child will come back to life . . . but they're fairly
immobilized and they can die if somebody
doesn't get attention to them. If you know
where this person is, can you please help us?

Soria: I wish I did. I mean, I only know what I told you guys. You know, I care about the kids too. I don't want to ever see anything bad happen to them.

Minister: Thomas, your story is not making any sense. Nothing's making sense. If I had to guess, in my experience whether you know more than you're telling us, I would say that you know more than you're telling us. If there's a chance that that child is alive, what is the foremost thing we would want to do? We'd go out and find that child, correct?

Soria: Yeah, that's correct.

Minister: And as far as we know, you're the last person to be with that child, and we need your help.

Soria: Yeah, man, like I said, I saw her on her bike and that's all I saw.

Duzan: It's gotta be forty-five degrees up here. You go out to Cave Rock, where it's freezing-ass cold. You sit down by the water, pull your pant legs up, take your shoes and socks off. That water's got to be easily thirty-something degrees. You see how strange that is?

Soria: Well, I—

Minister: None of that makes sense. If I go out and get dirty, I'll just go home and change my shirt. Why would you wash your shirt there, knowing you're gonna freeze your ass off?

Soria: Well, well, I figured I was not going to be out too much. . . . I was planning to be in my vehicle, not out in the weather getting cold, but my shirt ended up soaking up more water than I thought it would. When I tried to wring it out, it got more wet. I didn't want to go home yet. . . .

Minister: Has that child been inside your vehicle?

Soria: No, no.

Minister: In the backseat?

Soria: No.

Minister: Did you take her into the meadow by yourself?

Soria: No.

Minister: Because we're talking to some people now who are telling us things.

Soria: Mm-hm.

Minister: Because your story's not adding up, Thomas. And I hate to be the one to tell you that, but it's not. It doesn't make any sense.

Soria: I don't know why it doesn't make any sense. I don't understand why you guys don't understand it. I'm a nature person. I love to be outdoors. I go out, I don't care if it's pouring buckets of snow. Because that's the kind of person I am, and—

Minister: Your dad said you guys never got into an argument. You're telling us you did. Something's going on there.

Soria: Like I told you, we're very private. We don't like to discuss our problems to anybody else, including cops. Nothing against you guys, it's just the way we are. We've always been a private family. We don't like to tell people what we're doing or where we're going. We just like to drive around, you know, not have somebody expecting us.

Minister: Well, we're sending search teams out into the meadow now. So we should know something pretty soon. Is there anything you want to tell us?

Soria: No. I've—I've told you guys pretty much everything.

Minister: Can't think of anything else?

Soria: No.

Minister: Did you harm that child?

Soria: No.

Minister: Did you do anything with her body?

Soria: No.

Duzan: You know what I don't understand is why a nineteen-year-old hangs out with nine- to twelve-year-old girls?

Soria: Um . . . I'm not real sociable, I guess in some ways. I have lots of friends, but I don't consider them real friends because I don't think I can trust them. Uh, the kids . . . I know them, I know I can trust them, and—

Duzan: More importantly, if I was sitting in your seat and somebody was asking me about the questions we're asking you . . . I'd be flying off the wall. You're not doing that. That's another thing that disturbs me.

Soria: I'm trying to help you guys. That's how I see it.

Duzan: Do you have a girlfriend?

Soria: No, not anymore.

Duzan: You've been up here a year. No girlfriend?

Soria: I've tried a few girls, but when I asked them, they weren't interested.

Duzan: What age group were you talking about?

Soria: Right around my age. Like eighteen or nineteen.

Duzan: So where do you think we should start looking for Krystal?

Soria: Maybe somebody grabbed her from the trailer park or something.

Duzan: Why do you think somebody would grab her from the trailer park?

Soria: For the same reason anybody kidnaps a kid. I mean, I don't know, and—

Duzan: I know, but it's hard from over here, man. I mean, you got a little girl out there and it's getting cold; she wants her mom; she's not dressed for the weather. And we have no idea where she is. We want to find her. We want to find her now. Not tomorrow.

Soria: Yeah, I know.

Minister: There's other things you're not telling us, though.

Duzan: We think you're being honest to a point. But you're cutting off some stuff that may significantly—

Minister: We're talking about the life of a child here.

Soria: Well, if you guys are implying that I did something, I think you guys are way out of line. . . .

Minister: Well, then, who else should we talk to?

Soria: I don't know. I mean, some of the people in the neighborhood, and—

Duzan: And we understand that. But the point is, some of the stuff you've already told us here isn't jiving with what people have told us out there. That's the problem we have here. You've been doing things that aren't what normal people would do.

Soria: I don't see what you mean.

Duzan: Well, do I need to recap? Cave Rock, walking outside in freezing-ass cold; down by the boat ramp, you're in freezing water . . . then you go to Spooner Summit, where the elevation's higher. It's colder. And you sat up there. You're doing weird things out there. And I have a missing girl. They're weird to me and everyone else that's involved in this. And that's what concerns me . . . Just so I understand, here's building one and here's the corner and here's your little Boys and Girls Club . . . Do you have an alarm code?

Soria: Yes, I do. I have my own code. Everybody has their own code, but I don't know if anybody knows the code besides me, and—

Duzan: Well, isn't that another strange thing? Her bike's here . . . Boys and Girls Club is here, which you have access to twenty-four hours a day. You know the alarm code. It's just one more thing.

Soria: I . . . You know, I don't think I want to answer questions anymore because I don't like the direction that you guys are leading this into. I see what you're trying to get at here. . . .

Duzan: We're trying to get at the truth. We're trying to find a little girl. Now, if you had nothing to do with this, point us in the right direction.

Soria: I don't know where to point. I mean . . .

Minister: Can I see your arm? What's that?

Soria: I don't know. I guess I hurt myself.

Duzan: Things aren't adding up. That's all we're saying. If you were the father . . . Which if you have a child someday and she disappears, you would totally understand. We've tried to appeal to your sense of humanity, and if we're off base here, then I'll be the first one to show up at your door and apologize. But you know what? There's some questions that really need to be answered. And if there's anything we need to know, you need to tell us now. Because later on, if things point back toward you, and there's things we find that implicate you, not only directly but circumstantially, you may not have another chance to help yourself. And you're okay with that? Are you gonna be okay if something does go sour and we come back and talk to you again?

Soria: I . . . That's all I have to say.

T.J. Soria was driven back home to his apartment. As for the clothing that he'd left at the Sheriff's office, one of his boots appeared upon closer inspection to have a small stain of blood near the toe. Soria's underwear appeared to have dried semen on the inside.

Because of the small amount of apparent blood and Thomas Soria Jr.'s inexplicable story of how he got wet, Detective Duzan decided to do a vehicle search of the Chevy Blazer. He wrote in his report, "Soria Senior gave consent to search his vehicle." The Blazer was impounded.

Events were happening elsewhere as well that did not bode well for the Sorias. On the drive to her home, Diantha Wilson remained disturbed by the sight of the boy throwing the "pillowcase" over the embankment. Once there, she discussed the matter with her husband and asked if she should call 911 and report the incident. His answer was "Well, call if you want to." She still wasn't convinced it was a good idea to phone the police until her twelve-year-old said, "Come on, Mom, call. It'll make you feel better."

At a little after 8:00 P.M. she did just that. Wilson phoned 911 and got a dispatcher named Liz on the line. Wilson's commentary went: "Ah, yes, Liz; ah, I have a concern, and I was driving down from Lake Tahoe today and I don't know if this is anything, but it just seems really strange. There was a guy parked on the side of the road on the first turnout as if you were going up to the lake. I was coming down the opposite way . . . and it seemed awfully strange to me, but he had like a king-size pillowcase-looking thing, but it was kind of full and round. And he flung it way over the side of the hill. And I thought, 'Oooh, that's weird.' And he looked at me as I drove by 'cause I looked right at him. And he looked at me and it really made me nervous, like 'cause I don't think he expected me to be coming down right then, 'cause there were no other cars. Then I just drove on, and I thought, 'Well, should I call?' It's just been eating at me. And he threw it, like there's not really an embankment there. There's like a little scenic turnout. And I thought at the time, 'Ooh, that's the size of my dog [in the pillowcase].' Then I thought, 'Well, that could be a small child [in there].' I mean, he was obviously trying to get rid of something."

The dispatcher replied, "Well, we can certainly check it out. I'm not sure whether we will tonight or not because of it being dark. It might be better to wait until morning. . . . Was he a white male?"

Diantha answered, "He was a white male. And he had brown hair. Dark brown hair, but not long. Kind of shaggy. That's all I could really see. If he walked up and kissed me, I couldn't point him out to you."

Liz said, "Oh, that's fine; that's fine. We'll let the sergeant know about it tonight and then I imagine that he'll pass it on for a patrol car to go up there and check it out in the morning."

Wilson felt a little foolish now for making the phone call. She said, "Yeah, it just seemed . . . I just . . ."

Liz said, "Oh, I don't blame you. I think it's a good idea that you called. You never know."

Perhaps Thomas Soria Jr. had assured his dad that he'd thoroughly cleaned the vehicle of any telltale signs of blood. He had certainly done his best at washing and scrubbing the vehicle. And the senior Soria might have been afraid to refuse the lawmen's request to search the Blazer. For whatever reason, he had let them impound it without a fight, perhaps hoping that nothing definitive could be found. But this was not the case. Detective Duzan's report went on to say of the vehicle search, "South Lake Tahoe Police Department evidence technician Shirley Shaw conducted a preliminary test on possible blood found on the passenger side running boards. It tested positive for human hemoglobin. Blood also appeared to be on the inside of the vehicle on the passenger side floorboard and the rear passenger side floorboard. The vehicle appeared to be partially cleaned. A search warrant was applied for [for] the 1989 Blazer. The vehicle was seized and transported to the Washoe County Crime Lab [in Reno, Nevada] for further testing."

Preliminary evidence was starting to stack up against the Sorias despite their best attempts to cover it up and wipe it clean. They had already cleaned up the bedroom as best they could and possibly dumped bloody liquid down the drains and toilet, had certainly done enough so that no law enforcement officer suspected that the senior Soria was involved in any crime. And as yet, the most profound evidence of all, Krystal's body, had not been found. For the Sorias, with any luck, a wild animal might eat her flesh and scatter the bones. The canyon she had been thrown into was the haunt of coyotes, bears and other scavenging animals. But luck was deserting the Sorias quickly as March 19 turned into March 20. The news of the missing girl hit the local airwaves and newspapers. And one of the key components to the missing girl finally made the rounds of the local law-enforcement officers. It was Diantha Wilson's phone call of something suspicious being thrown over the edge of Highway 50 the previous evening.

Detective Duzan's notes once again pick up the time-line: "At 8:25 A.M., March 20, 2000, I contacted Diantha Wilson who told me she had seen a vehicle similar or consistent with the suspect vehicle. D. Wilson told me she was driving westbound at about 5:00 P.M. when she saw a red and white two tone 'Bronco' parked along-side the W/B lane on Highway 50, Spooner Summit. D. Wilson said she could show me the exact location of where the suspect vehicle was parked the day before. D. Wilson also said she saw the suspect throw something over the edge, resembling a pillow case. D. Wilson described the suspect as a white with medium shaggy hair and wearing a white shirt."

Diantha Wilson and Detective Duzan, along with other law enforcement personnel, went out to the spot where Thomas Soria Jr. had parked the evening before. It was a chilly morning and snow was piled in drifts beneath the pine trees. Everyone's stomach clenched as they walked down the slope from the parking area. They all had suspicions of what they would find below the roadway.

They didn't have to walk far. Near a ripped black-gray oversize garbage bag was the nude body of Krystal Steadman. The wound to her neck had been so severe that her body appeared to have been spray-painted with blood. It was a sight that made the most hardened law enforcement agent feel like crying.

Detective Duzan's report picks up the narrative once again: "On this date at approximately 9:20 A.M., the body of a white female child believed to be Krystal Dawn Steadman was found between the eastbound lane of Highway 50 and Clear Creek Road, approximately two miles west of U.S. Highway 395. Subsequent investigation revealed that the child matched the description of Krystal Steadman and that she suffered a deep laceration on her neck."

It was time to make an arrest. Detective Duzan must have been biting his lip in anger remembering all the lies and deceptions that T.J. Soria had fed him the night before. But he controlled his anger as he and Tim Minister approached the Soria apartment with a little deception of their own. He later said, "At eleven A.M. Sergeant Tim Minister and I contacted Soria junior at building number two, apartment twenty-two. Sergeant Minister asked Soria junior if he could show us the last known location in the parking lot where he had seen Steadman. Soria junior agreed to voluntarily exit the apartment. Upon his approach to the exterior door overlooking the parking lot, Soria junior was arrested.

"Soria junior was transported to the Lake Tahoe substation. At eleven forty-eight A.M. I read Soria junior his rights as per Miranda. He invoked his right and refused to be interviewed. The interview was terminated and Soria junior was released to the jail staff."

ELEVEN

The Real Nevada CSI

After the arrest of T.J. Soria, a team of investigators began to go through the Sorias' apartment. So far, only T.J. had been arrested and he wasn't talking. Not yet. But the "Search and Seizure" warrants applied for by Detective Duzan and Sergeant Minister to the Tahoe Township Court, Douglas County, Nevada, showed exactly where the investigation was headed. Almost the entire Douglas County Sheriff's office was handling some aspect of this case. Young girls were not abducted and murdered in their county every day and the response was massive.

Sergeant Tim Minister's warrant read in part: "There is probable cause to believe that the crimes of murder, a felony in violation of NRS 200.010, 200.020 and 200.030 and kidnapping, a felony in violation of NRS 200.310, and sexual assault and sado-masochistic abuse of a child, a felony violation of NRS 200.310, and sexual assault and sado-masochistic abuse of a child, a felony violation of NRS 200.366, have been committed, and that additional evidence of said crimes will be found on or in a residence as follows: 134 Kahle Drive, Building #2, Apartment 22, Stateline, Nevada. The

apartment building is further described as a three
story, wood structure identified on the exterior by a
white sign indicating number two of four existing similar structures. Apartment 22 is located on the second
floor of the south wing of the building marked with a
number 22 sign on the door."

Unfortunately, there were some mistakes made by
the law enforcement officers in the initial stages of the
investigation. These can be chalked up to human error
and just plain bad luck. The nexus of the mistakes
would later be summed up by Deputy DA Kris Brown
of Douglas County. She wrote in a report, "They [the
officers] treated Soria Sr. with courtesy as an ill and
grieving father whose son had just been arrested for
murder. So they allowed him and his wife, Lupe, to remain in the apartment while they conducted the
search, and they searched for things only authorized in
the first search warrant. The computer, the garbage
bags compared with the ones found with Krystal's body,
the books that were found in the apartment, these were
the type of items that were found and taken from the
apartment at that time." This unfortunately gave
Thomas Soria Sr. a lot of time to clean the apartment
and dispose of incriminating items.

However, due to the evidence they were finding from
already seized items, the law enforcement officers
sought and got a second search warrant issued. It
stated, "You are therefore directed to search the above
described residence for evidence and information not
previously described to the court including the following: The entire premises as well as toys, games or dolls.
Indicia of the identity of any and all occupants of the
premises. Further, for photographs and video equipment, digital or analog, including cameras, exposed
and unexposed film, photographic paper, photo-

graphic negatives, developed photographs, and storage of photographic images on computer equipment including hard drives and diskettes. Further, for the collection of clothing and clothing fibers, paint, stain and other material used to cover wall, doors and wood work. Additionally, for blood, semen and other fluids and tissues, or traces thereof, dirt, debris, carpet and carpet fibers, materials used for torture, binding or stabbing the victim that may be found on around or within the entire premises."

When the officers went back to the Soria apartment the second time, they were in for a big surprise. As soon as they opened the door, they smelled the overpowering smell of bleach. The entire apartment had been scrubbed down by Thomas Soria Sr. and perhaps Lupe as well. Whether Thomas Soria knew it or not, bleach is one item that destroys DNA evidence.

This was a real eye-opener. For the first time, the officers started thinking of Thomas Soria Sr. as more than just an ill man and grieving father. They began looking at him as a suspect. The idea had to be entertained that T.J. had not abducted the girl and killed her somewhere in the wilderness. A theory began to take hold that Krystal had been murdered in this very apartment by either T. J., his father or a combination of the two of them acting in concert.

Thomas Soria Sr. and Lupe were summarily removed from the apartment so that they couldn't do any more tampering with evidence. Yet a third warrant now spelled out:

Evidence that she [Krystal Steadman] had been sexually assaulted and cleaned subsequent to having been sexually assaulted, but before she was killed. Evidence of a sexual assault with vegetable material, wood or other similar sexual devices was found in the victim's body. The pathologist who is conducting the post mortem examination has made preliminary findings that a serrated knife or similar implement was used on the victim.

Based on foregoing, affiant is informed, and believes, that the victim may have been sexually assaulted and then cleaned on the premises, and that evidence of blood, semen and other fluids and tissues may be found in the kitchen, bathroom, fixtures, wastewater pipes, wall material, shower curtain and other places in the apartment, that evidence of materials used for binding or stabbing her may be found there.

Evidence retrieved from the residence is currently being examined and analyzed by the Washoe County Crime Lab. It is hereby ordered that the premises should be secure and under the exclusive control of the Douglas County Sheriff's Office for a period of time not to exceed fifteen days or as otherwise ordered by the court upon future applications if necessary.

The Washoe County Crime Lab and Forensic Investigation Section is only one of two crime laboratories sanctioned in the state of Nevada. Like its counterpart in Las Vegas, glamorized by the popular CBS television program *CSI*, the Washoe lab in Reno provided services to local, state and federal law enforcement agencies. The Forensic Section is a full-service forensic laboratory, supervised by a captain and staffed by more than thirty individuals in sworn and civilian capacities. There are various sections within the lab, which included a Primary

Examination Section, Controlled Substance Section, DNA Section, Firearms and Toolmarks Section, Forensic Investigation Sect., Questioned Documents Section (for forgeries) and Toxicology Section.

The Krystal Steadman case fell under the auspices of the Primary Examination Section, DNA Section and Forensic Investigation Section. The Primary Examination Section was the first step on the link of investigation. Any examination that did not fall under the purview of a specific section wound up in the Primary Examination Section first. The staff members examined items for the presence of body fluids, usually semen, blood or saliva. Presumptive and confirming tests were performed on the sample. When a body fluid was found, it was forwarded to the DNA Section.

The Primary Examination Section also analyzed evidence for the presence of trace evidence such as hairs, fibers, paint and glass. Many of the recovered materials were very small and had to be compared with known materials to see if they showed a common source. This usually required a high-magnification microscope. One of the most conclusive examinations was a physical match. When an item was broken or torn, the pieces were reunited to see if they matched. This method was as important as fingerprints in some cases.

Also within the framework of the Krystal Steadman case, the Forensic Investigation Section came into play. This section dealt with crime scene processing, which included photography and field latent-fingerprint processing. The Forensic Investigation Section operated a computer terminal that was hooked up to the WIN/AFIS Network. This was an automated nationwide fingerprint identification system that compared and offered possible matches with known fingerprints of convicted offenders.

The Krystal Steadman case fell directly into the lap of one particular Washoe County Lab criminalist known for her years of expertise in the business—Renee Romero. She had a master's degree in biology and microbiology and was on the national committee that studied DNA testing. She'd personally worked on literally hundreds of crime cases. And despite her scientific bent, where the common image is one of a woman in a white lab coat with thick glasses and mousy demeanor, Romero had the good looks and self-confidence to actually fit in as one of the actresses on *CSI*.

In the initial stages of the Steadman case, Renee Romero received a wide range of items from the crime scene at the Soria apartment and from their Chevy Blazer. These included a bathtub drain flange, sink trap from the bathroom, one brown paper bag labeled "blood samples taken from metal lock," and stains from Soria junior's clothes, which included undershorts, pants, shirt and right boot. She also received a sample of red-brown staining on the forward end of the right-side running board from the Chevy Blazer, four tissue fragments collected from the right-hand of Krystal Steadman's fingernail scrapings, tissue fragment from her left-hand fingernail scraping, and a root-end hair found on her left elbow. In addition to all these, she obtained swabs from Krystal Steadman that included material from her left cheek, left and right pelvis, perirectal buttocks, right arm, perineum buttocks, oral, rectal, nasal and vaginal cavities.

The Douglas County detectives weren't relying on physical evidence alone but were conducting interviews as well. One young man named Christian Araballo, who lived in the Lake Park Apartments complex and knew T.J. Soria, had an interesting story to tell. He said that he had been in the laundry room at about 3:00 P.M.

on March 19 and had looked into a washer that had completed its cycle. The washer contained what he thought looked like young girl's clothing. He told police, "It didn't look like men's clothes. More like something a seven- or eight-year-old would wear. When I went there, he [T.J.] walked in nervously and opened the machine that I looked in, picked up the clothes and walked off. Then he said for no reason, 'I don't have any change to dry the clothes.'"

Araballo thought this was a strange comment to make and that T.J. was very furtive in his actions.

Maria Gonzales, who also lived in the Lake Park Apartments, had an interesting story to tell the police as well. On March 19 she had just gotten off her shift at Harrah's Casino and was walking back to her apartment. In the parking lot, she saw T.J. Soria, whom she knew, carrying a box toward his father's Chevy Blazer. The box looked heavy and T.J. was having trouble balancing it. She told police, "He was kind of holding it with his leg and the door of the open truck. As soon as he saw me, he just nodded to my face. Then some distance from there, I looked at him and he looked at me. I nodded and kept on going. He was holding the box with two hands and a knee. It seems like it was heavy. He was jockeying with it. It was moving like it wasn't settled. It was different than just an empty box. I turned my head around and it was like he was still looking at me."

As if all of this weren't enough, Sergeant Tim Minister requested a seizure of specific items in the Soria apartment. He wrote to the presiding judge in the case:

Based on training and experience, affiant is informed, and believes that persons referred to herein are pedophiles, who commit sexual misconduct with children, or who are preoccupied with the same, often keep journals and diaries, keepsakes and treasures from their experiences with children, which may be stored in digital form. These people who use computers to communicate with one another by the Internet, and it is known that they have bulletin board systems, chat rooms and email correspondence to communicate with other pedophiles about their sexual experiences with children. They use these forms of communication to validate and justify their actions, activities and feelings because of perceived anonymity and immediate feedback that the Internet provides.

Given the evidence that Krystal Steadman was bound and sexually assaulted, orally and vaginally, prior to death, and that there is evidence developed in the investigation of child pornography and exploitation of children in the premises . . . affiant is requesting a warrant to broaden the scope of the previously issued warrants to authorize a search of the video tapes and all forms of digital records seized in the execution of the search warrants for text files, or any other records contained therein, for evidence of pedophilia in any form, including but not limited to email transmissions, and journals, letters, diaries, records or plans of criminal and sexual activity.

In the execution of search warrants [in this case], investigators found photographs of children, an album containing child pornography, children's toys, and a play room for children. According to child witnesses, Thomas Soria Jr. took children from the apartment complex into the apartment to play with the toys.

And then he dropped a bombshell as far as Thomas Soria Sr. was concerned. He wrote, "Witnesses have told investigators that he [T.J.] lured children to their apartment in Sacramento for the sexual relations with Thomas Robert Soria Sr., which is also consistent with allegations made in the sexual assault against them in the matter of Donna Orlando."

This case was no longer just about T.J. Soria—it was now about the senior Soria as well. When the story had first hit the local newspapers about the abduction, rape and murder of Krystal Steadman by Thomas Soria Jr., Mrs. Orlando asked her daughter if she had had any sexual contact with the Sorias. At first she denied it. But when her mother asked again, it was a different story. What happened next was written down in another investigator's report. He was Investigator Mark Munoz of the Douglas County Sheriff's Office.

Munoz wrote:

Your affiant has been a deputy with the Douglas County Sheriff's Office since 1988 and promoted to the position of Investigator in 1995. He has investigated hundreds of felony cases. Many of these cases investigated were crimes against persons, including homicide, and sexual assaults involving both adults and children. Your affiant has thousands of hours of training in the area of criminal investigations.

On Thursday, March 23, 2000, I was assigned to meet with and interview Donna Orlando and her mother. (Referred to herein as Mom.) The interview was in regards to a sexual encounter between Donna Orlando and Thomas Soria Sr. The disclosure came because Mom had read about the arrest of Thomas Soria Jr. in the newspaper, knew

that Donna was a close friend of Jr., and that
Donna was a frequent visitor to Jr.'s and Sr.'s residence. It is noteworthy to mention that Donna's
father lives directly above Jr. and Sr.'s apartment.
Donna said "no," she had no contact with Sr. Sub-
sequently, Mom read the newspaper and read
that Jr. often referred to Sr. as "Uncle." The following day, after Mom picked up Donna from
school, Mom told Donna what she had read regarding uncle. Mom asked Donna if she had any
contact with uncle. Donna broke down and cried,
telling Mom, "yes." Mom called her husband and
Donna's father (herein referred to as Dad). They
decided they should report the alleged sexual
contact.

On March 23, 2000 at approximately 12:30 P.M.,
Mom contacted the Douglas County Sheriff's Office telephonically. This contact led to your
affiant interviewing Mom, Donna and Dad. The
interview took place between the hours of 4:00
P.M. and 7:15 P.M., March 23, 2000.

As a result of the interview and further investigation, your affiant believes that Jr. and Sr. getting
together in concert, led Donna Orlando into a situation where she was sexually assaulted by Sr.
during approximately the first two weeks in October 1999.

It is your affiant's belief that Jr. introduced
Donna Orlando to Sr. in approximately July,
1999. Sr. was introduced to Donna Orlando as
"Uncle Tom." Early on, Donna was told that Sr.
had tumors and if Sr. got upset that his tumors
would rupture, explode or the like, causing him
to die. Also, Donna came to know a person
known as Lupe, very well through her contact

with Jr. Lupe Soria is actually Sr.'s wife and Jr.'s stepmother.

Donna got to know Jr. like a brother and Lupe like a mother. She got to know Sr. as "Uncle Tom," Lupe's brother. Donna developed what she thought was a close relationship with all of the Sorias.

Donna Orlando made it known to Jr. that she liked him in a romantic way. She spoke to him in terms of having a date. Jr. actually encouraged Donna to go out with Uncle Tom instead, telling her he was a really good guy.

Contact between Donna and Sr. led to sexual discussion and ultimately an invitation from Sr. to Donna to have sexual intercourse. Sexual acts, specifically, digital and oral vaginal penetration, were committed by Sr. upon Donna during the first two weeks of October 1999. The acts occurred in the Soria's apartment. They occurred within the master bedroom between 4:00 P.M. and 6:10 P.M.

Donna Orlando described in detail the furnishings and interior of the master bedroom. During the interview Donna explained to your affiant that she was encouraged to have a relationship with Sr. by Jr. Also, that she was told not to get upset and that if he got upset he would die because his tumors would rupture or explode. It is believed that Jr. and Sr. gained the trust and friendship of Donna Orlando and Donna was led to feel pity for Sr.'s condition.

The situation with Donna Orlando was truly pathetic by now. Deputy District Attorney Alan Buttell, who was assigned to the case, would soon write to the judge,

"The victim [Donna Orlando] suffers from a congenital syndrome that leaves her in a physically frail condition. Your affiant recently learned that the minor victim in this case is suffering from a profound emotional distress and may be suicidal. Further, the victim has been suffering physically and emotionally over this case since its inception. She has recently lost a significant amount of weight because of her emotional state, and; recently she has been unable or unwilling to eat. She has vocalized suicidal intentions and it is submitted that her health is so fragile that it is in the interests of Justice and prudence to preserve her testimony."

The deputy DA's unspoken thoughts were that Donna Orlando better have her testimony videotaped and audiotaped because she might kill herself before a trial could commence. With that in mind, they proceeded to videotape and audiotape Orlando.

T.J. Soria was already in jail and as March 2000 moved toward its final days, a noose was growing ever tighter around Thomas Soria Sr. as well. He counted on T.J. keeping his mouth shut because of his total dependency on "Dad." But mounting evidence alone was placing the senior Soria right in the middle of this sordid business.

In some ways, T.J. Soria was now in the eye of the storm that swirled around the Tahoe Basin after the news of Krystal Steadman's rape and death hit the newspapers and airwaves. What everyone wanted to know was "How could such a monster be living in our midst?" And even more important, "How could the local Boys and Girls Club have hired him in the first place?"

TWELVE

"The Monster in our Midst"

The *Nevada Appeal* headline of March 21, 2000 stated YOUTH WORKER ARRESTED IN MISSING GIRL'S SLAYING. The body of the piece read, "Police arrested a part-time Boys and Girls Club worker within hours, Monday, after finding the body of a nine-year-old girl off of Highway 50 near Carson City. Thomas Soria Jr., 19, who worked for the Lake Tahoe Boys and Girls Club, was arrested about noon Monday after investigators connected him with the disappearance of Krystal Steadman."

The story went on to relate that Krystal Steadman had last been seen at the Lake Park Apartments around 2:00 P.M. on Sunday.

Douglas County Sheriff Ron Pierini told the reporter. "He [Soria] was seen talking with the girl before she disappeared and his vehicle was seen where the body was discovered."

Sonya Klempner (Krystal's older sister) was quoted as saying, "I can't believe this is happening. I feel horrible."

The school that Krystal had attended was particularly rocked by the news. The district administrator and

Meyers Elementary School staff offered to provide counseling to students, teachers and parents who needed it. Sally Williams, the director of the El Dorado County Department of Mental Health and Children's Services, told a *Nevada Appeal* reporter, "The game plan at this point is we're going to meet in the morning at Meyers School. I'll be there with a couple of members of my staff and counselors from Tahoe Youth and Family Services and the school psychologists. We'll go into the classroom and talk with the kids and basically let them talk. And we want to be available for teachers and if parents want to come in."

A pamphlet with information on how to deal with death and grief was given to all principals in the area.

Not only were students, family and friends dealing with the loss of Krystal Steadman, but the employees and staff of the Douglas County Sheriff's office were as well. This was not some large urban county where crimes like this occurred fairly often. Sheriff Ron Pierini told reporters, "The critical issue is to understand how terrible acts like this occur. They [the staff] will never understand how a predator will kill a young girl. They will be questioning, 'Why does this happen?' And they will not be able to relate to that. Added to the helpless feeling you have, they will be questioning themselves and asking, 'Why couldn't I have been there to stop it?' That's what they deal with. Even I, and the rest of the staff, we've often talked about this. It was a terrible thing and there's no rationale."

Because the investigation was still ongoing, the detectives most affected by the case could not take time off for counseling. But Sheriff Pierini said, "We will have a mandatory session for them to attend soon. Also, Jim Doornik is a psychologist in Carson City and they can see him up to five times free of charge. But the other thing is, history will tell you, employees think everything is okay. But down the road, they will have recurring problems, so it has to be monitored, and we will monitor the situation."

If the community in general was stunned and saddened by the brutal murder of Krystal Steadman, the local Boys and Girls Club was in an absolute state of shock. Cathy Blankenship, the executive director of the Western Nevada Boys and Girls Club, told the *Nevada Appeal* reporter, "We have an extensive screening process funded through a state grant and monitored by the Nevada legislature. But that doesn't always ensure you get the information you need concerning background checks." Blankenship went on to say that all branches worked autonomously and that employees were screened through local and FBI criminal records searches.

John Schroeder, the Pacific Region vice president of the Boys and Girls Clubs, said that clubs operated independently in their home states. He told a *Nevada Appeal* reporter, "We don't exercise any control, nationally or regionally, for the local clubs. Stuff like this is so rare. It just knocks the skids out from under you."

Schroeder noted that there were 2, 591 Boys and Girls Clubs nationally. He couldn't remember another instance like this one during his tenure.

Of course the club hardest hit by the news was the one that had hired T.J. Soria as a part-time worker. Steve Conroy, the executive director of the Tahoe Branch, told a *Tahoe Tribune* reporter that Thomas Soria Jr. had passed a background check, fingerprinting and reference check. There were no red flags that jumped out about him. You could not tell by looking at him or listening to him that he was different from any of the other part-time workers.

All of this made people wonder what was happening to their mountain community. Was it the influx of new people? The violence in television and movies? Or something else?

Addressing this issue, Kurt Hildebrand, editor of the *Nevada Appeal*, wrote, "Stories about violence in Nevada and California mining camps are as shocking as anything we have today. New York's Hell's Kitchen and Chicago gangland are just samples of the deadly periods America has known during its history. One Old West editor noted that it was too dangerous to go out on the streets without a sidearm. We are not at that point here. The fact is that the number of people living in Nevada has increased 1.7 million since I was a child in the 1960's. The 1960 census reported that there were 285,278 people living in the entire state. The state's population may hit 2 million in this year's census. The increase in the number of people increases the chance that one of those people will do something horrendous."

Before all the news of the Steadman case could die down, there was another abduction in South Lake Tahoe, which only fanned the flames that something was dreadfully wrong in the region. A woman who was the birth mother of a school-age child simply walked into Al Tahoe Elementary School and kidnapped her. Since she could prove she was the mother, she waltzed right out of the school building, even though she had no legal rights to the child.

Claire Fortier, the editor of the *Tahoe Tribune*, wrote about the dual shocks to the community: "In both cases, the parents of the two girls [Krystal Steadman and the other girl] did nothing wrong. The children weren't neglected, left with strangers or in strange situations or left in harm's way in any manner. That makes the tragedies even harder to absorb. Things like that don't happen here. That's the collective wisdom. It has been our collective small town mentality that has prevented more of these kinds of tragedies from happening. Even with the transient nature of this town, there is an overall feeling of community. We look out for each other, especially our children. So what went wrong? . . . The cold, hard facts may be that nothing went wrong. The responsibility of these tragedies should fall on the adults who are convicted of the crimes, not the community or institutions that have fostered a safe haven for its children for so many years. Lake Tahoe is a wonderful place to raise children. But that doesn't mean this community is immune to tragedy and the grief violence and depravation can foster."

Even before the revelations by Donna Orlando of sexual misconduct became common knowledge, T.J. Soria endured an arraignment at the Tahoe Township Court, presided over by Judge Steven McMorris. T.J. wore a borrowed shirt so that he wouldn't be photographed in jail clothing. All the local newspapers had reporters there, as did several television stations from Nevada and California. It wasn't quite a media zoo, but it came close, what with all the cameras and microphones. During the entire process, T.J. never glanced at the family and friends of Krystal Steadman sitting in the first rows of the courthouse. If he had, he would have seen Krystal's sister, Sonia, with a handkerchief to her face and crying constantly throughout the proceedings.

Instead, he kept his gaze on Judge McMorris and answered in a clear voice that he understood the proceedings against him. T.J was represented by local attorneys Tod Young and Mark Jackson, who had been appointed to represent him. Both lawyers contracted with Douglas County to provide criminal defense and had experience with death penalty cases.

The death penalty was a real option now against T.J. Soria. Deputy District Attorney Thomas Perkins, the new prosecuting attorney in the case, let it be known that he was leaning in that direction. District Attorney Scott Doyle of Douglas County told reporter Christy Chalmers of the *Record Courier* that a decision on pursuing the death penalty wouldn't be made until after the investigation was completed and all the information had been fully reviewed. He said, "The only thing we are doing now is taking steps procedurally to preserve our right to seek the death penalty. It is not a decision that is made rapidly."

At the end of the arraignment, Judge McMorris scheduled April 25 as the date for a preliminary hearing in the case.

Outside the courtroom, Sonia Klempner told reporters through a stream of tears, "My sister's death is an example of how you can teach a child all that is good and bad [in the world], but this kind of thing can still happen." Then she went on to say that Krystal's mother was taking the aftermath very hard and seeing a priest at Al Tahoe.

Sonia wasn't the only one talking about the case. By the following day, there was a local Web site on the Internet dedicated to the memory of Krystal Steadman. On the Web site, Jo Salisberry, founder of the Carson City Chapter of Compassionate Friends, a national organization for families who have lost children through death, said, "It changes your life completely. Even their little friends' lives. Your priorities change; you're put into a position you just don't want to be in."

About the memorials on the Web site, she said, "It's great that they are doing that. It helps them deal with grief and helps them heal." But then she added a note of caution: "The pain of the loss is not going to go away and it's always going to be there. Just a constant thing you learn to live with."

On the Web site, Krystal's cousin Debbie Connelly wrote, "I'll miss you, my little cousin. Wish we could have spent more time together."

Jane Conway, a friend of Krystal's who had also been in the Junior Miss Lake Tahoe Pageant, wrote, "I will always remember her dance, 'All Star,' at the pageant. That's what you are Krystal, an all star."

A poem by Krystal's aunt Karen and uncle Stan Gregorek stated:

> Mothers watch your children
> Keep them close to home
> For evil is out there lurking
> If they by chance should roam.
> It only takes a moment
> To lose someone so dear
> But it will take a lifetime
> To wipe away the tears.

There were messages not only about missing Krystal but anger as well at a system that seemed to have failed in regard to T.J. being hired by the local Boys and Girls Club.

Barbara Bentley wrote, "I think it's time that our so called 'system' take the time to make some drastic changes in the way it hires people to oversee and work with our most precious assets, our children."

Jo Ann C. wrote, "How is it that we aren't more aware of the hiring and employment procedures that put our children in the hands of an alleged murderer? When it comes to our kids, there is no such thing as too blatant, to annoying or too many questions."

If the Lake Tahoe residents were outraged by the present state of affairs concerning T.J. Soria, it was nothing compared to the anger they would soon feel when a new set of revelations about his father would rock the area the following week.

THIRTEEN

"He Deserves What He Gets."

By March 24, 2000, three-quarters of Douglas County's detectives were working on the Krystal Steadman case. According to some estimates, Sheriff Ron Pierini said, it would take them two weeks to process all the evidence. "We need to do this right. This is probably one of the most serious cases in the history of Douglas County. I've been here since 1976, and we haven't had anything like this."

Ellen Clark, MD, who performed the autopsy, noted in summary that "there was sexual penetration in the anal area and vegetable matter was found in the rectum. Also, above that, in colon, inside the rectal vault, it was clean as if an enema had been administered to her. Also, there had been penetration of the vagina and vegetable material was found in the vagina. Her throat was slashed several times. Some of the cuts just barely went through the skin, leaving a crease where the knife went. Others were deeper above her clavicle and under her chin. There's a group right at the base of the neck where there's two or three wounds that come together.

Finally there's a slash on the right side of her neck that severed an artery, eventually causing her death. Evidence shows that Krystal fought back. There are defensive wounds on both her hands."

Even though all this evidence was mounting and pointing toward involvement by Thomas Soria Sr., he still counted on one thing—T.J. keeping his mouth shut as he had always done in matters concerning his father. He knew he had an incredible hold over the boy. But just how far the bonds would stretch must have given him some uneasy nights since his son's arrest and incarceration. It was impossible to tell who the boy was taking to or what he was saying. Evidence was mute and might possibly point toward T.J. alone. But T.J.'s words would destroy him.

Physical evidence was damning to the Sorias, and Donna Orlando's testimony was also making its way into the system. Investigator Mark Munoz sent his report to the Tahoe Township Court: "Based upon your affiant's experience, training and belief, it is asserted that Thomas Soria Jr. and Thomas Soria Sr. engaged in a course of conduct wherein Thomas Soria Jr. encouraged, induced and procured Donna Orlando, knowing that Donna Orlando was mentally and physically incapable of resisting or understanding the nature of her conduct, for the purpose of positioning Thomas Soria Sr. to have sexual intercourse with Donna Orlando, and that in fact, acts committing a sexual assault were perpetrated on Donna Orlando by Thomas Soria Sr. Consequently it is asserted that Thomas Soria Sr. and Thomas Soria Jr., through his aiding and abetting, both committed the crime of sexual assault against a child under the age of sixteen years of age."

But the allegations that Donna Orlando had brought against Thomas Soria Sr. paled in comparison in what was now beginning to come to light in the Krystal Steadman case. Initially it had been thought that Thomas Soria Jr. alone had murdered Krystal Steadman. But as more and more evidence came in, the focus shifted from him to his father. One of the most telling clues came from criminalist Renee Romero. She discovered that the semen found inside Krystal Steadman's body had not come from T.J., but it corresponded to coming from a very close relative, such as his father.

Some of the most damning evidence arrived via Thomas Soria Sr.'s computer. This computer had been sent down to the high-tech crime lab at the Sacramento County Sheriff's Office. It was investigated by high-tech forensic expert Investigator Mannering.

First he copied the hard drive without turning the computer on by use of an instrument that could copy the hard drive without damaging it or deleting the original evidence. Using EnCase software, he was able to search through the hard drive and reestablish deleted files. Only their paths had been deleted. The files still existed in the hard drive because Thomas Soria Sr. had not overwritten them.

In his search, Investigator Mannering found some very compelling evidence. They concerned Thomas Soria Sr.'s wish to rape and sodomize a blond-haired, blue-eyed woman or girl. The files stated that he wanted to "sexually molest, savagely mouth fuck, brutally rape and brutally sodomize them."

The files went on, page after page, of how he wanted to rape and torture blond women and little girls. Some files mentioned Julie Drayton, Sara Stein and Debbie Sloan. A list of books was also cataloged that included a *Color Atlas of Child Sexual Abuse* and *Pediatric and Adolescent Gynecology*.

And Renee Romero's results on DNA testing reached the Douglas County judicial center. She wrote in her report, "Comparisons of DNA at 13 STR [short tandem repeat] loci showed in the reference standard from Thomas Robert Soria Sr. to be the same as the sperm fraction in the swabs from the vagina, rectum perirectal buttocks, perineum buttocks, right pelvis, left pelvis and right buttocks of Krystal Steadman. Based upon these results, Thomas Robert Soria Sr. is the source of this DNA." In other words, Thomas Soria Sr. had left his sperm on and in Krystal Steadman, not T.J. Soria as originally had been presumed.

Thomas Soria Sr. had enjoyed only nine days of freedom since his son had been arrested, but all of that was about to change. On March 29, 2001, Deputy District Attorney Thomas Perkins filed a criminal complaint with the Tahoe Township Justice Court #00-0352. It was the *State of Nevada* v. *Thomas Soria Sr.* The complaint stated, "[The State of Nevada] charges against Thomas Robert Soria Sr. the crimes of murder with the use of a deadly weapon, kidnapping and sexual assault of a child. . . . Soria Sr. did willfully, unlawfully and feloniously, with malice and aforethought, and without legal justification, kill a human being, to wit: Krystal Steadman, a child under the age of fourteen years, by means of child abuse and with the use of a deadly weapon, a knife or other sharp object . . . thereby inflicting mortal injuries, or aided and abetted, assisted and encouraged another person in the aforesaid manner, from which she died, all of which occurred in the Tahoe Township, County of Douglas, State of Nevada."

As to the charge of kidnapping, the document went on to say, "[He] took or seized Krystal Steadman with the intent to detain her against her will, kill her or perpetrate a sexual assault."

And finally about the sexual assault, it read, "[He] did willfully, and feloniously, subject a child under the age of fourteen years to sexual penetration against the child's will or under conditions to which the defendant knew or should have known that the child was mentally or physically incapable of resisting or understanding the action of the defendant's conduct."

Francine Soria got a very surprising request from the Sacramento office of the FBI to come and talk to them in the last days of March 2000. Since she had left Tom Soria, she had changed her last name and was living with a new boyfriend. The news of T.J.'s arrest had stunned her like everyone else, but she still didn't know about her ex-husband's criminal activities.

The FBI agent who questioned her did it with a non-confrontational, relaxed and conversational style. Fran was understandably anxious at first and her responses were punctuated by nervous laughter. And even though she was wary of the circumstances, she was co-operative and answered the questions to the best of her ability.

The agent started off with questions about her young life and about her meeting with Thomas Soria. Fran discussed their high-school romance, early marriage and the murder of Tom's mother and the effect it had on him. Then the FBI agent got into Tom's penchant for manipulation and how it might have affected her relationship with him. The agent said, "When little boys are molested or harmed when young, they grow up to be harmful people. Whereas, little girls, whether harmed sexually or physically, will harm themselves as adults. They will become prostitutes, drug addicts, sickly or reclusive. The reason I'm stating this is Tom was a very manipulative person. And he would do well with a passive person. Often when people are doing something wrong, they will try to get the person they are with to participate with them, even if the person doesn't know they are doing something wrong. Sometimes these people are part of the crime scenes. I'm not saying that took place with you. But if you think of anything, I want you to bring it out. I think you're a forthright, good person."

Fran's response to this was "Tom wasn't so much dominating as he was selfish. Everything was for him."

Then on more reflection, she stated, "He never hit me, never did anything really against my will. It was more like . . . persuasion. And at the time, you don't think it's manipulation. I thought about what you told me. And I never viewed it as manipulation. Selfishness, yes. Manipulation, no. But that's probably what it was."

The FBI agent asked her if Tom and T.J. had any knives or guns around the house. She said she wasn't aware of any. But it was a different story about computers. The agent asked where they kept the computers and Fran answered, "In the entertainment room. We had Prodigy. Then [Tom] built a computer for T.J. I didn't use it."

The agent said, "Kiddie porn has obviously been a big thing on the Internet. You ever known that to go on in the house?"

Fran answered, "No."

"And he had, like, fifteen porn movies?"

"Yeah."

"Did he have any bondage-type books?"

"I couldn't tell you."

"Was he secretive about these things?"

"I guess it was like, don't ask, don't tell."

Then the agent's questioning veered off into a different direction. He said that he had worked on a case in Lake Tahoe concerning a kidnapped girl named

Jaycee Lee Dugard. She had been abducted on her way to school on June 10, 1991.

Agent: I have a really hard question. And it's one that's been eating at me. On June 10, 1991, a little blond-haired girl was abducted in South Lake Tahoe. Her name is Jaycee Lee Dugard. She was on her way to a bus stop on the Pioneer Trail.

Fran: I remember the story.

Agent: The victim in this case (Krystal Steadman) physically in appearance is very similar to her and I don't know if Tom could have been a part of this abduction and I wanted to ask you. And that's why I've been asking a lot of questions about Tahoe.

Fran: Yeah.

Agent: And I told you I wouldn't hit you with anything. And T.J. with his hair down might look like a composite. . . . There were two passengers in a gray vehicle. And you said you had a Mercury Bobcat at the time. When did he get rid of that?

Fran: It was totaled in a wreck in 1980.

Agent: Then you said you had a Cutlass. How late did you have the Cutlass?

Fran: [*Long pause*] I couldn't tell you.

Agent: In '91 did you have the car?

Fran: [*Another long pause*] I'm trying hard to remember.

Agent: Since you remember the story, do you remember the artist's conception of the . . .

Fran: To tell you the truth, I don't remember. There was something about a man and woman.

Agent: Well, they're not entirely sure of the car description. And they're not entirely sure if the woman was a woman. Nothing to scare you. I'm not thinking about you, but the artist conception of the woman is very similar to you.

Fran: Oh, well, that's nice. Thanks for telling me.

Agent: Well, with T.J.'s hair . . .

Fran: [*Suddenly realizes the implication and gasps*] So, now I'm a suspect?

Agent: No, not at all. I wasn't telling you this because you're a suspect. I'm just trying to explore the possibility whether Tom could have done this. I mean, there's things here that raise my antenna a couple of notches. But nothing that says this is a done deal. . . . Was he (Tom) taking trips to Tahoe without you?

Fran: I'm not sure. I remember them going to Reno once by themselves.

Agent: Did T.J. wear his hair long?

Fran: Yeah, he was always wearing his hair long.

Agent: So how long was T.J.'s hair at the time?

Fran: Oh, like a ponytail.

Agent: When did the trips take place mostly to Tahoe? In the winter or summer?

Fran: Winter.

Agent: What about summer? Would they not go at all?

Fran: I remember a few.

Agent: Around June, July, August?

Fran: Yeah, I remember it was around T.J.'s birthday.

Agent: What day is that?

Fran: August ninth.

Agent: Have you always worn your hair long like that?

Fran: Yes. I don't like short hair.

[*Then the agent dropped an unexpected bombshell on her.*]

Agent: I don't think I mentioned Tom's in custody.

Fran: [*Rattled*] Ah, no. [*Starts crying*]

Agent: I'm sorry for not mentioning it.

Fran: That's something you were holding back?

Agent: No, no. We've been dealing with it so much, I just thought you knew.

Fran: Other than the first night when I heard the news [about T.J.], I've read and seen as little as I could. Just because . . . [*cries*]

Agent: Tom's in custody because of another girl. She's fifteen years old, but developmentally small in stature. If you took T.J. back to the age of ten or eleven, she would look similar to that.

Fran: [*Cries*]

Agent: Were there any clues in the house to make you think something was different [between Tom and T.J.]?

Fran: No, it was usually how I left it.

Agent: What kind of bed did Tom have?

Fran: A water bed. When we weren't getting along, I had a bed downstairs.

Agent: Did you ever go back into the bedroom when you weren't getting along?

Fran: The only thing I did was to carry clothes up and lay them on the bed.

Agent: What did the room look like?

Fran: There was a water bed. And a long gray dresser with a mirror on it.

Asked if she knew that Tom and T.J. were having sex under her own roof, Fran answered that she only suspected one time and then drove the thought from her mind as an aberration. As she had said,: I thought they just acted like the best of buds. I didn't suspect anything else. I thought Tom might have had a girlfriend at his job."

Finally Fran told the agent, "I'd never do anything to hurt anybody else. I consider myself a good person. I wouldn't hurt anybody."

The new revelation that T.J.'s father had been involved in the abduction, assault and murder of Krystal Steadman hit the Lake Tahoe and Carson Valley newspapers with all the impact of a freight train. That a father-and-son team had perpetrated these heinous crimes filled the residents with incredible anger and revulsion.

Sheriff Ron Pierini of Douglas County confirmed reports that California and Nevada officials were looking into other sexual-assault cases in the region that had either gone unsolved or unreported. He said, "All I can tell you is that California authorities are very interested in these two suspects and are working hand in hand with us."

Then he stated that the clothes Krystal Steadman had been wearing had finally been recovered beside Highway 50 about five miles from where her body had been discovered. They included a Tweety Bird shirt, black pants, green socks and lavender shoes. About the case in general, he told reporters, "We have up to ten investigators working exhaustive hours and they have done a superb job. They have been very meticulous and are doing what's right, taking their time to make sure everything's done legally. I'm comfortable we will have a successful prosecution with the evidence presented."

Even though a great deal of evidence had been recovered, the detectives were still searching for the murder weapon. They spent several unproductive hours scouring through a Dumpster at a gas station in Round Hill, not far from the Soria apartment, when an anonymous tip came in about its location.

All of this happened on the same day that a memorial service was held for Kyrstal Steadman in South Lake Tahoe. One of the persons who attended the service was eighty-year-old Don Bloom, a friend of the Steadman family. He had just driven over two hundred miles to be there, and when he learned of the father-son connection in the case, he told a *Tahoe Tribune* reporter, "I wanted to vomit. The abuse of children is just incomprehensible to me."

There was a new lawyer in the mix now, Michael Roeser representing Thomas Soria Sr. Just like his counterparts representing T.J. Soria, he knew that he had an uphill battle in a case as volatile as this one. He wasn't helped in the cause by the fact that much of the investigative details of the case were still being reported in the local newspapers.

Sheriff Pierini was just one official talking to the press, and he said, "It seems as if this was a very traumatic and terrible event for Krystal. Evidence supports the additional charges [of sexual assault]."

About all these comments swirling around in the newspapers and on the airwaves, T.J.'s lawyer Tod Young commented, "Mark Jackson and I intend to defend our client [T.J. Soria] in the courtroom and not the media."

There was, of course, no eyewitness to what had occurred in the Soria apartment when Krystal Steadman walked up the stairs on the afternoon of March 19,

2000, and disappeared behind the door of apartment 22. But forensic science had grown to such an extent that the scenario behind closed doors could be reconstructed with some exactitude. And putting those pieces together, bit by bit, was Renee Romero.

Before the end of the month, her detailed report about DNA testing was in the hands of the Sheriff's office and the district attorney. It read in part:

A partial DNA pattern was obtained from the sperm fraction from the left cheek swab [from Krystal Steadman]. Based upon these results, Thomas Soria Sr. can not be excluded from being the source of this DNA profile. Comparison of DNA profiles at 13 STR loci showed the DNA in the reference standard from Krystal Steadman to be the same as the DNA from the following samples: Stain #1—seat frame front passenger (Chevy Blazer). Stain #3—passenger door rocker panel. Crust from driver's door speaker grille. Stain from running board.

Also [there is a] dominant DNA profile from shirt, pants, and right boot. Epithelial fraction from swabs collected from the body of Krystal Steadman . . . Comparison of DNA profiles at 13 STR loci showed DNA in the reference standard from Thomas Soria Jr. to be the same as DNA in the stain from the red underwear [worn by Krystal Steadman] and the dominant DNA profiles from [her] pants and driver's armrest.

The results from the shirt stain show more than one source of DNA. Comparison of DNA profiles . . . contain the DNA from the source of Krystal Steadman, Thomas Robert Soria Sr. and Thomas Robert Soria Jr. Based upon these results, Krystal

Steadman, Thomas Robert Soria Sr. and Thomas Robert Soria Jr. are consistent with being the source of mixed DNA profile obtained from the shirt.

In effect, these results proved that Thomas Soria Sr. had raped Krystal Steadman, and for some reason, T.J. Soria's sperm was on her panties.

The piece of evidence about the shirt was particularly damaging to the Sorias. More than any of the others, it showed that they had both handled Krystal Steadman's shirt. One of them couldn't point to the other and say that he alone had perpetrated the crime. The mixture of DNA on her shirt plainly showed that there had been some kind of collusion between them once Krystal Steadman stepped past their apartment doorway on March 19, 2000.

On Wednesday, March 29, there was the unusual spectacle of both Sorias in the Tahoe Township Courthouse answering to various charges of molestation and rape of Donna Orlando. By now it was all over the newspapers and television how T.J. Soria had lured Donna into having sex with his "uncle" by saying the man had tumors and would die if he got upset. To the residents of the region, there seemed no bottom to the depths these two would stoop to obtain sex with children. In fact, the sheriff bolstered this notion by asking anyone with information about further sexual crimes by the Sorias to call the Douglas County Sheriff's Office.

Fran Soria was interviewed once again, this time by Investigator Rory Planeta of Nevada State. Investigator Planeta told her, "There's been some things that have come up between then and now that we've learned.

Tom senior kept a journal and had some interesting and pretty bizarre things."

Fran: For how long?

Planeta: I don't know. It's not dated. It just had some things in there that were related to your relationship with him. And some things that we're afraid happened during this case. Has Tom ever fixated on someone? Like stalking?

Fran: Not that I know of. But he probably wouldn't have told me anyway.

Planeta: There was this statement in the journal. . . . There was a sentence in there that bothered me. [He wrote] "With Fran I learned that I could rape any female against her will for my sexual pleasure and enjoy it without guilt or remorse."

Fran: [*Gasps*] Oh, that's nice! I guess it goes back to that selfish thing: "If you love me, you would do this for me."

Planeta: Did Tom have a brain tumor?

Fran: The last I heard, he did. The only thing I can tell you about what he told me is he was having upset stomachs and throwing up a lot. And really bad migraine headaches. He went to the doctor and they did testing and found the tumor. At that time, I believe they told him he only had five or six years.

Planeta: At what time?

Fran: Ah, before I divorced. So maybe '95. [*Nervous laugh*] I guess he should be dead now.

Investigator Planeta covered more of the old ground that had been gone over before concerning their marriage and T.J. Then they talked about how Thomas senior's lawyer had asked her if she would help them in his case. Fran told Investigator Planeta, "If he [Thomas Soria Sr.] did it, he deserves what he gets. I don't want to be involved with him anymore."

The steady drumbeat of the depredations by the Sorias in the newspapers only intensified as more and more information became known. On March 30, 2000, the *Nevada Appeal* quoted District Attorney Scott Doyle as saying, "Both participated in acts that culminated in the kidnapping, sexual assault and murder. Different acts were done by each, but the entire transaction included acts by both."

Sheriff Pierini went on to say, "Examination of trace evidence has linked Soria senior to the sexual assault and murder of Krystal Steadman." And then he added, "Investigators are looking into the possibility that the Sorias are responsible for other sexual assaults."

And finally the district attorney's office dropped the bomb. They said they were proceeding with documentation to seek the death penalty against both Thomas Soria Sr. and Thomas Soria Jr.

This was unprecedented in the state of Nevada. Since 1900, when Nevada outlawed unregulated hangings and began keeping records of those sentenced to die, there had never been a case where members of the same immediate family were put to death for a single crime.

Just to give an indication of how sentiment was running in the region on this issue, local talk-radio station 780 KOH ran a poll. The question they asked was "Should prosecutors seek the death penalty for the murder of Krystal Steadman?" The answer was 91.7 percent Yes and 8.3 percent No.

On top of all this, the media now discovered the link between the Sorias and the violent past of certain members of the Mozingo family in Sacramento. Suddenly these old cases were making news once again as well. A headline in the *Sacramento Bee* stated: SLAYING PROBE HAS NEW TWIST. SUSPECTS' FAMILY HAS VIOLENT PAST. Part of the article read, "Exactly how Soria Sr.'s life experiences and dysfunctional family connections will play out in the courtroom remains to be seen, but legal experts say that if the proceedings reach the death penalty stage they are sure to be used by defense attorneys to elicit sympathy for their client. 'If the evidence is substantial on his guilt, the defense will be desperate to find anything it can that could sway even a single juror on the issue of penalty,' said Michael S. Sands, one of Sacramento's leading criminal defense attorneys for more than three decades."

Michael Roeser, Thomas Soria Sr.'s defense attorney, may not have been desperate at this point, but he certainly wanted all the stories and comments to the press to cease, especially those emanating from law enforcement officials and the prosecutors. He wrote a brief to Judge McMorris explaining that his client could not get a fair trial in court if he was tried and convicted in the newspapers and on the radio and television. One of the statements he found most damaging was that by Sheriff Ron Pierini on March 29, 2000, to the *Record Courier* in which he said, "California and Nevada authorities are looking for more victims of the Sorias. All I can tell you is that California authorities are very interested in these two suspects and are working hand in hand with us. We want to get the word out, especially in the Sacramento area. There may be other victims out there."

Sheriff Pierini had the right to say what he did, and

all of it was true, but Roeser was worried about what went beyond the words. On some level, they, in effect, implied that there were more victims out there and the Sorias were at least serial child molesters, if not indeed serial child killers. In an area that still had not gotten over the kidnapping and disappearance of Jaycee Lee Dugard, it was like stirring up the embers of an uncontained forest fire.

In his brief, Roeser cited various stories from the local newspapers and television stations and their inflammatory effect upon a future jury pool. Judge McMorris agreed and put the gag order in effect. There would be no more "leaks" about evidence that the law enforcement officials were digging up.

Attorney Roeser won a small victory in this matter, but the battle had many fronts, and one of the most disturbing, as far as he and Thomas Soria Sr. were concerned, was the slow but sure defection of T.J. away from his father. As April 2000 progressed, it became evident that T.J. was no longer "Daddy's boy." If he didn't cut his strings with Dad, the terrible baggage his father possessed would drag them both down to destruction. It may have taken years of constant abuse and a murder to finally sever the hold that Thomas Soria Sr. had over his boy, but by late April, it seemed that the incredible powers he held over T.J. no longer worked.

FOURTEEN

"My Heart Breaks for You."

April was a time of maneuvering by all parties involved. By now attorneys Michael Roeser and John Springgate were sure that a severance was coming on the part of T.J. and his lawyers. Tod Young and Mark Jackson were no fools and they knew that T.J. stood his best chance having his trial separated from his father's.

There were several meetings now between the defense lawyers, Deputy DA Tom Perkins and the judge, all of them outside the public eye of newspaper reporters and news cameras. On April 22 all of the lawyers of both Sorias were in session before Judge McMorris as Tod Young argued that a preliminary hearing date should be postponed. He said that he and Mark Jackson were nowhere near digesting all the discovery evidence that was pouring in. There was a myriad of physical evidence reports, DNA reports and the allegations from various witnesses.

A heated argument erupted between the prosecutors and defense attorneys over the video testimony supplied by Donna Orlando. The defense attorneys were arguing that she should be there in person and a video was no substitute. But Deputy DA Perkins knew of her frail condition and demanded the video be used as evidence. After a long, hard day, the jockeying for position deteriorated over the point of using photocopies of transcripts versus certified copies, which cost a great deal more and demanded more time and preparation. By this point, Perkins had just about had it. He told the others, "I've never in my career objected to the use of a photocopy in lieu of a certified transcript. And I don't really like that kind of stipulation jammed down my throat!"

But the real bombshell came at the end of the meeting. Michael Roeser and John Springgate said that they would be asking Barry Scheck of O.J. Simpson Trial fame to give evidence on DNA testing. Just how this big-city lawyer would play in small-town Minden, Nevada, remained to be seen.

The inclusion of Barry Scheck was all well and fine for Thomas Soria Sr. and his lawyers. But DNA testing was not his biggest problem at the moment. T.J. Soria was. And on May 1, 2000, Soria senior's worst fears about the defection of his son came true. On that day, T.J. Soria cut a deal with the prosecutors. He would plead guilty to the charges of kidnapping and abetting a murder, and the death penalty would be taken off the table. There was just one stipulation—at Thomas Soria Sr.'s jury trial, T.J. would have to give evidence against his father.

With the DA Scott Doyle, Deputy DA Thomas Perkins, Tod Young and Mark Jackson present, Thomas Robert Soria Jr. agreed to the following: "My decision to plead guilty is based upon the plea agreement. As to the charges of murder in the first degree, the district attorney agrees not to file or pursue any other criminal charges or allegations arising out of this investigation. The DA will not seek the death penalty, will not file a notice of aggravating circumstances and will not make an allegation or seek sentencing enhancement for the use of a deadly weapon. As to the charge of kidnapping in the first degree, the DA will not make an allegation of substantial bodily harm. I will give full, fair and accurate and truthful information and I understand that the DA will not call me at the preliminary examination of charges against Thomas Soria Sr."

It was a somber and subdued Thomas Soria Sr. who sat through his preliminary hearing on May 9, 2000. He did little more than blink through the whole proceedings. His defense attorneys were much more vocal and argued that the prosecution had no murder weapon and no eyewitnesses. In fact, they said, there was little evidence against Thomas Soria except for some DNA from Krystal Steadman that was found in a vehicle driven by T.J. Soria and Soria senior's sperm on her body, which did not in itself link him to murder.

John Springgate said, "What we have heard is an utter fabrication of the evidence that any of these crimes relate to Mr. Soria senior."

The defense attorneys then went on to throw most of the blame of what had happened on Thomas Soria Jr. They said he had lured the young girl into the apartment, he had lied to Krystal's mother about her whereabouts and he had disposed of her body. Who was to say he hadn't murdered her as well and was now blaming it all on his father?

Judge Steven McMorris conceded that much of the evidence was circumstantial, but he argued that there was enough evidence for Thomas Soria Sr. to be bound over for a jury trial. He then said, "The word 'torture' comes to mind."

This immediately brought Roeser and Springgate out of their chairs with objections.

But Judge McMorris silenced them with the explanation, "In my opinion, there is evidence of torture." He cited a pasty substance on Krystal's cheeks and wrists consistent with a residue from duct tape. He also cited defensive wounds on her hands, bruises, two stab wounds on her back, cuts on the back of her head, seven stab wounds to the neck and a severed carotid artery.

On May 19, 2000, a very important meeting took place at the Douglas County Sheriff's Office with T.J. Soria as its main focus. Detective Tim Minister was there along with Deputy DA Tom Perkins and both of T.J.'s lawyers, Tod Young and Mark Jackson. There was also present one more man who specialized in this sort of interview, FBI Agent Jeff Rinek, out of the Sacramento, California, office. He was there not only to elicit clues to the Krystal Steadman crime but to delve deeply into T.J. Soria's entire life.

Before T.J. was brought into the room, Agent Rinek got into a discussion about the former Fran Soria with attorneys Tod Young and Mark Jackson. They recently had interviewed her, and they saw her in quite a different light from the way she had portrayed herself to the FBI agents in Sacramento and to Investigator Rory Planeta. Rinek asked them, "Does he [T.J.] have any feelings for Francine?"

Young responded, "He may tell you about the time Francine said to Tom, 'Look, I never wanted him anyway.' He was about seven then."

Then Jackson added, "Our feeling of Francine from our interview, [she's] a woman just trying to pass the buck. In other words, 'I'm a great mom.' Here's a woman that's not accepting responsibility for the way that T.J. was raised. 'I know nothing. I have no idea anything ever went on.'"

Young agreed by saying, "We probably heard that four or five different ways. 'None of this is my fault.'"

Then they brought T.J. into the room and FBI Agent Jeff Rinek set the ground rules. As he spoke, T.J. made almost no responses except to acknowledge Rinek by saying "Um-hm." It was a totally different T.J. who sat there as opposed to the very talkative young man who had lied his way through the interview with Detectives Duzan and Minister when the police were still looking for Krystal Steadman right after her abduction.

Rinek said, "I'm Jeff Rinek. Call me Jeff. The first thing I have to do is show you my picture ID. You got to promise not to laugh. I was a lot younger and happier. I've got twenty-eight months [left] and counting. We're here to talk about things with you. There have been all kinds of agreements made. Tod is here to look after you. I'm here not as an FBI agent, although I am an FBI agent. . . . I'm here to help Douglas County talk to you. We helped these guys down in Sacramento, and when they came down there, they told us they had never seen anything like this before. For some reason in Sacramento, and if you've lived in Sacramento you probably noticed from the media, there have been a lot of these things in Sacramento. And a lot of these things for some reason up and down the Sacramento Valley."

At this point, Tod Young jumped in. "Before we go much further, can I say a couple of things? You understand that we're being videotaped. And there has been an understanding to an agreement between the Douglas County District Attorney's Office and you through your lawyers, Mark and myself, to the parameters of this information and how it is going to be conducted and the potential uses of this interview. These are con-

tained in a letter from Thomas Perkins, Deputy District
Attorney, who is watching this interview via closed-cir-
cuit television, together with your attorney, Mark
Jackson, and they're in another room right now. If I object to a question, or something that I advise you not to
answer, what we'll do is just take a break. Then we'll go
outside and deal with that. Mr. Rinek is not going to
write a report out of this. He's going to indicate that he
did an interview for Douglas County. But he's not
going to write a detailed report. He's here to simply assist Douglas County. And there is no pending federal
investigation. There are no federal charges."

FBI Agent Rinek added, "Let me clarify that if I
could. This case was opened so that we could assist the
Douglas County Sheriff's Office in working this matter.
It's simply an administrative thing that enables us to
help. It's not any prosecutorial thing. And that is the
goal. Now, I know you've been in this room before.
And I know you had a hard time before. And I know
Tim [Minister] was here before. Okay. But it's different
now. You're through everything. This isn't an adver-
sarial . . . it's not belligerent. We're here to make things
right. And regardless of how you saw this before, well,
there you were fighting for your life. But now you've
saved your life. And now we're working for closure. Do
you know what closure is?"

T.J. responded, "To end the course of events that's
happening or something like that."

Rinek replied, "Right. To give knowledge. Because
knowledge leads to acceptance. I know there's things
that have been done that you think are wrong. And I
know that there's things that have been done that
you're not sure are wrong. Whether they're wrong or
whether they're right, when it's known what happened
and people get a chance to see everything, then that's

closure. It's not necessarily feeling better. It's more acceptance. And sometimes acceptance helps you get on with your life. There's a lot of people in this that have to get on with their lives. And don't think that sitting here talking to you about things we need to talk about is easy for us. For me to sit here and talk to you this way and the things we're going to get into, it takes a lot out of me. It will take me weeks to recover. Some people think I'll never be normal. T.J., I don't see you as a criminal. And Tim doesn't see you as a criminal. I see you as something else and we're going to talk about what I see you as. But I don't see you that way because I know you. I've seen a lot of other people like you who have been in this same chair, with the same problems. And I can't do it every time, but sometimes I can help. Sometimes I can help you. Sometimes I can help me.

"You know, people in this county are angry at you and they're angry at your dad. I'm sure that you've felt in the jail that the guards . . . some of the guards treat you nice and some of the guards are very, very bad toward you. And every time they're doing it, what they're showing is that they're angry and they don't approve of you.

"Well, human nature is to forgive. So when someone comes forward and says, 'I did something wrong and I just want people to know that I'm having a hard time living with this,' they forgive. Okay. Now I see you're getting upset. Tell me what's going on. What's happening?"

T.J. began crying and said, "I'm just upset about what has happened."

Rinek asked, "Are you upset about Krystal? Are you upset about your dad? Are you upset about you? Tell me. I mean, this is why we're here. Because I don't see you this way."

T.J. replied, "A little bit of everything." Then he kept on crying.

Rinek said, "In coming up to do the interview, a lot of people talked to me about you. And everybody saw you in a different way. But no one talked about you crying before. And you're crying now. And it's meaningful to me. And it's important for me to understand why because this is part of when you need to come to terms with this. What do you think it is? What are you thinking about?"

"Um, just the bad things I participated in with Krystal," T.J. answered.

"Okay, but that's good. That means you are a good person. T.J., I'm hoping that when you're done here today, you will understand more about yourself and that you'll be able to live with yourself. 'Cause you do want to live, don't you?"

"Yeah."

"You're nineteen years old. You got a whole life ahead of you. And even though you may not be where you want to be in your life, you're going to have the ability to learn, to read, to see things and who knows? Who knows? There's a lot of people out there that have been in jail for a long, long time and there are stories and movies about how they change and become different people. I'm going to use a term, and I'm going to throw it out now, and then I'm going to tell you a little about me. It's called 'compliant victim.' Have you ever heard that term before?"

"No," T.J. replied.

"Okay, I want you to remember that term because we're going to come back on it. I want you to understand who you're talking to. And this is going to be interactive. You can ask me any question you want. You can ask Tod any question you want. You can ask Tim. If you don't like his face, you tell him you don't like his face. I'm going to tell you honestly that one of the reasons I like Tim being in here is 'cause I honestly think I have more hair than he does. And this is good; he takes what little hair he has, he puffs it up and it looks like more. And even though he wears these nerd glasses, he's really not a bad guy. So I want you to feel free to . . . If you don't express yourself and if you don't tell us what's going to happen, this is kind of a great opportunity for you, for me, probably for Tim . . . to see if you have a gift you can give, T.J. You can tell us, maybe after today, how to prevent this. Maybe if we recognize something coming down the pike, we can prevent it and there doesn't have to be a T.J. crying over a Krystal being dead.

"And so you can give this. At the same time, when we talk about things, the knowledge, it gives closure. It gives acceptance. And it also gives us the knowledge in law enforcement not to let this happen again. What can we do not to let a T.J. be a victim? What can we do to go into the schools and look at kids that are being victimized and tell them they're being victimized?

"I've been in the FBI twenty-four years and I'm counting down every month. They don't like me. They think I'm nuts. They're a lot like my wife, but I've got a lot more time left with my wife. I have a son that almost died. And I didn't handle it well. And because I didn't handle it well, I have this desire to hate to see kids suffer. You're a kid too, T.J. And you're suffering. And my motivation for being here is as emotional as it is wanting to help in the investigation. If I walk out of here and you feel as if you know yourself a little better, then I'll feel really good. I've worked crimes against children for the last nine years. I've been very lucky. I've actually with my hands saved people. Children. And I've actually lifted dead children's bodies with my hands. And I'm telling you this is not something that's a job. It's something we live with and take home. It makes me react the way I'm acting now. So, I can sense the emotion because I feel it. Um, people think I'm a good interviewer and that's why Douglas County wanted me here. Well, there's another reason, honestly. I've talked to a lot of people that have done bad things that really aren't bad people. And my goal is 'Why did this person do this thing?' I come in here and I don't see you as a bad person. The people here in Douglas County that had to deal with Krystal's death and handle the body and the crime scene and look at the effects of the murder, they're not feeling as if they're capable of dealing with it because they care in their own way.

"I wasn't here. I'm not from here. I'm from Sacramento. And because of that, I don't have the anger. I don't have the emotional strings of having had to deal with her body and carry it up a hillside. So that's another reason I'm here. So, we need to establish some ground rules. Very important ground rules. First and most important, you have a relationship with Tod and Mark. And in that relationship you have discussed with them issues of your defense and issues concerning the strategy of your defense. You cannot tell me any of this, so I don't want to know what conversations you had with them. If they gave you direction, I don't want to know that. If there's something that's an outright lie, then you can speak to Tod alone and work it out. There's no secrets here about where I'm coming from. What I want to do with you, T.J., is start very young and I want you to work through your life. And I want to work through your knowledge of your father. And we're going to come to Krystal. And I want to talk about Krystal. As we go through this period in your life, there might be times when we're talking about a period of time where a crime might have occurred. If it's a crime that's not in Douglas

County and it's a crime that you haven't told your attorneys about, I don't want you to tell me any names. What I want you to do is stop the interview and tell Tod what it is. And then Tod will work it out with the prosecutor about making sure that you're not going to be exposed to any further prosecution.

"The goal here is not to hurt you. The goal here is to learn from you and if you can help yourself. When it comes to things about your father, I want you to tell me everything. It's very important. And I don't think your attorneys object to you telling everything about your father. One exception. If your father committed a crime and you participated in that crime with your father and you feel you have legal exposure for being prosecuted, then you need to tell your attorney so we can work that out. But eventually we need to flag those parts of our interview and come back to them at a time when things are worked out.

"So, this may be the last time that we meet. This may be the last time that you're being interviewed. But this, hopefully, is the most comprehensive time. And everything after this will be just kind of cleaning up. There are certain things that I'm going to ask from you without exception. And you got the right to ask me those same things without exception. The first thing is truth. T.J., what do you think is truth?"

T.J. answered, "Mmm, not lying."

"What is a lie?"

"When you tell something that isn't true."

"Right. Let's say we're sitting in this room and I say to you, 'Okay, T.J., what color are the walls in this room?' And you say to me, 'Oh, they're red.' Is that a lie?"

"Yes."

"Okay."

"Unless I'm color blind, maybe."

"Okay, let's say I say to you, 'T.J., what color are the walls in this room?' And you say, 'Yellow.' Are you lying?"

"Uh-huh."

"You are lying? They're yellow, aren't they?"

"They look white to me."

Tim Minister popped in and said, "You are color blind."

Rinek replied, "I must be seeing yellow. Well, whatever. Here's the important part about lying, since I screwed up the last part. If I say to you, 'T.J., describe the room we're in to me.' And you see that picture there, that's above your head, and there's a little medallion on it. And you go and you describe this room to me and you deliberately leave out that picture and medallion, that's a lie. So the key word here is, whole and complete. Nothing left to be guessed at. If you ask me a question, I will give you the whole, complete truth. If I ask you a question, I expect the same. Needless to say, I hope you're already doing that with Tod.

"Another question, and this plays into what we're doing today. Do you know what it means to be brave?"

"I think so."

"Tell me what it means to be brave?"

"To stand up to things and, um, not let it get you down."

"Okay. Let me give you a picture. Have you gone to the movies at all? Did you see *Saving Private Ryan?*"

"Yeah, I saw *Saving Private Ryan.*"

"That's quite a striking opening scene, right?"

"Um-hmm."

"And guys were being brave there?"

"Um-hmm."

"Okay, so let's say you're in that picture and you're running out of the boat. You're running up the beach and your best buddy in front of you gets wounded and he's laying there in the open. But you're protected behind a rock. So you know you can't be hurt where you are. But you also know that if he stays there he's either gonna die, bleed out or he's gonna be shot again."

"Uh-hmm."

"So there's two things here I want you to get. The first thing is if you're a carefree, reckless, I-don't-care kind of guy, you go there and rescue him; you bring him back; you did the right thing. But you had no fear doing it. That's not being brave. You did it because it had to be done. You felt it was right. But if you're hunkered down behind that rock and you're scared to death and the bullets are zinging around you and you know if you go out to get him that you may be killed too. But even though you're scared, you still go out and do the right thing and bring him back, that's bravery. So, being brave isn't easy. The only time it counts as bravery is if you're afraid to do it.

"You're going to have to be brave in this interview. There's going to be things you don't want to talk about that I may ask. And you have to make a decision to yourself. Are you going to be brave, even though you're scared, and talk about it? Or are you gonna not be brave and not talk about it? In which case, you're not giving the complete truth. So it all interacts. Does that make sense to you?"

"Yeah, it does."

"Okay, I want to start off with your childhood. But before we do, I want you to understand certain things. Eventually you're going to be doing all the talking. . . . Okay, children are very, very special people. One time I responded to a death of a little eight-year-old boy. I helped carry his body from a riverbank. And it really got to me. Much like you're reacting now. It got to me so much that I needed to get help. And I went and I asked the chaplain to . . . you know, I'm a mess. And he explained something to me that really, really has helped me get by. And maybe this will help you get by too. When we as investigators go to a homicide scene, instinctively we make two judgments. We can't help it. It happens. We look at the person that's been killed and the first thing we ask ourselves is 'How innocent is this person? Is this a drug dealer who was shot down in the middle of a drug deal? Or is this a child who was just enjoying life and didn't know that danger was on the horizon?' The second thing we ask ourselves is 'What value did this person have to society? Was this a person whose loss will not be missed or is this a person whose loss will be missed?' Now I see you glancing over at Tim. Do you want me to kick him out of here?"

"No, that's all right."

"Is he intimidating? Is he making faces at you?"

"No."

"Are you looking at his hair and trying to figure out how it got puffy?"

"No."

"Okay. It's the hardest thing in the world to go to. This is the thought process that these people had in Douglas County when they went and recovered Krystal. Children are special. And we know it instinctively. When you have a boy child, and that little boy is being abused, sexually or physically, or verbally or both, or you have a little girl that's being abused the same way, both children ask the same question. 'What did I do?' They look to the ones who care for them and they blame themselves for the way they're being treated. And it has a lasting effect on their lives. Little girls grow up to be prostitutes and drug users. They marry men that are abusive to them and hurt them. Little boys grow up and they hurt outside of themselves and they cause harm. But a weird thing happens. Their emotional maturity doesn't grow normally.

"Now, I'm not a licensed psychiatrist. I don't have certificates. I have training. But I'm not a professional. I believe all this from going from these types of crimes, and talking to hundreds of people, that this happens. I've been told this by experts who have done lectures. I see it all the time. With a little boy who is abused . . . you can tell the age of their abuse many times by looking at the age of their victims. Now, a little boy that grows up like this doesn't know it's wrong. He doesn't know he's being bad. He's only being him. And how can you be mad at that? How can anybody be mad at that? I mean, if there's a tree growing up on a hillside, and it has to grow slanted to get the sun, how can you blame the tree for wanting to get sun?

"That's the same way I look at children. And that's the same way I look at you. And it's very important that you understand that. The only thing that would cause me to judge you in a negative light would be if you're not truthful and you're not brave. Because this is your chance. Your attorneys have worked very hard to get you this chance. And they want you to do well and we want you to do well."

Then it began, the actual questioning taking T.J. Soria back into the darkest secrets of his past. Rinek asked T.J. about his first memory, and it was a sad one. T.J. said, "I remember having to leave some toys behind because the landlord asked us to move right away."

Then Rinek asked him about his early dreams. T.J. responded, "I remember running from Freddy Krueger. And he was chasing me with his claws and stuff."

"Did you ever have dreams about your father standing over you at night?"

"Not that I remember."

"Okay, first hard question. How old were you when you think your father began to have sex with you?"

"Umm, I'm not sure."

"What's your first recollection of it?"

"Probably going into his bedroom and laying on his bed."

"Now, why did you go to his room?"

"He wanted me to come in. I was six or seven."

"And in your memories, when you started having sex with your father, was it a lot?"

"Yeah."

"Did it hurt?"

"Yeah."

"Did you ask him to stop?"

"Um, I don't think so."

"Were you afraid of your father?"

"No, it was more, I love my dad."

"That's a good thing. It's good to love your dad. Everybody has problems. This is something that's going to hurt your dad too. There's no doubt about that. It's a no-win situation for everyone. You know, we don't walk out of this room feeling real happy-go-lucky, thinking, 'Oh, we had a great day today.' But we do feel good if we help you. So, after your dad called you in his room and he has sex with you and he hurts you, you had to be reacting to the pain."

"Um-hmm."

"How would he keep you doing what he wanted you to do when it hurt to do it?"

"I think he might have told me it might get better or something like that."

"Okay, here's a hard question. When is your first recollection of touching a kid in school?"

"Um, I don't believe I touched any kids in school."

"You'll be the first I've met."

"Uh, I do remember one of the kids in the neighborhood, though. . . ."

"How old were you when this happened?"

"It must have been right around the same age. . . ."

"So you think when your dad started touching you, you might have started touching someone else?"

"Um-hmm."

"And do you remember what you were touching?"

"Her butt."

"And when you were just touching it, did you reach under her dress?"

"Uh, she agreed to do it as well."

"How'd you talk her into that? Did you sell her a used car as well?"

"Um, I can't remember. . . . She pulled down her pants or whatever and bent over and spread her butt cheeks."

"Did you put your penis in her butt?"

"No, I didn't. I believe I just looked, you know."

"Didn't get closer?"

"I might have licked her."

"Well, what I'm getting at here is that a little boy, in our opinion and experience, doesn't normally talk a girl into pulling up her dress and bending over unless he's seen it before. Little boys have a tendency of redoing what is done to them. So if your father was having sex with you by putting his penis in your butt, it would seem logical to me that's what you were doing to her. So if your afraid I'm going to judge you because it did happen, I don't want you to be afraid of that. This is good. This is kind of like going down the road and recognizing the street signs. So, you remember she's bending over. You remember she's lifting up her dress. What then?"

"I can't remember exactly what happened. I do eventually remember her mom or somebody calling her from up the street. Our neighbor had a chimney and we were behind the bricks."

"Did you tell your dad about it?"

"Uh, yeah. I think I did."

"What did he say? Was he angry with you for doing this?"

"No. No, he wasn't."

"Did he encourage you to do it more?"

"I'm not sure."

"So how often were you going into your dad's room?"

"At least a few times a week."

"Okay. I'd like to talk about what your dad was doing with you. Because I think you remember because it was so often. Let me walk you through it—"

"There was one other occasion about that [other stuff]. With a couple of boys. One boy was one of my mom's relatives. They wanted to play with me and stuff. So we were on the side of the house and they showed me their penises and I showed 'em mine. And then one of them sucked on me and such. So that was something they initiated."

"Okay, another hard question. Are you sure they initiated it or could you have initiated it? If they initiated it, can you think of anyone that would have been abusing them?"

"Uh, I'm sure they initiated it. I was just . . . I was just too young to, you know, recognize anything."

"How old do you think you were at this time? What's your recollection of your age?"

"Um, might have been five or six."

"This happened after your father started sleeping with you?"

"Yeah, I'm pretty sure."

"Okay, let's talk about your dad. When your dad

would call you in his room . . . would you be dressed when you went in his room?"

"Yes."

"Would he take your clothes off?"

"Um, he'd have me take my clothes off."

"What did he say to you when you were in the room?"

"He'd have me get on the bed."

"Was he naked?"

"Yeah."

"Would he be on his stomach or his back?"

"On his back."

"And what about you?"

"I would be on my back too."

"And what would happen then?"

"I just remember we would talk and stuff."

"What was the first thing your dad would do?"

"Uh, he would have me suck him."

"Would he get erect?"

"Yeah."

"Would he ejaculate in your mouth?"

"Hmm, occasionally, yeah."

"How did you feel about this?"

"I'm not sure."

"What would he tell you about this?"

"Uh, that I was helping him or something."

"And what else would he have you do?"

"Lick his testicles or armpits. Sometimes his tits. And sometimes his butt."

"Did he ask you a lot about his butt? Did he want you to do a lot about his butt?"

"Kind of, yeah."

"Did he want you to focus on his butt?"

"Sometimes, yeah."

"Did he focus on your butt too?"

"Um, yeah."

"Do you see where we're going with this?"

"Um, back to the incident with the little girl. The one that I had pull up her dress."

"Right. Does it make sense?"

"Um-hmm."

"Okay. I want you to be careful. You're going to learn from this. And I want you to learn. But I don't want you to take what you're learning and start seeing your history in a different way. In other words, I don't want you to say, 'Well, because I was having sex with my father, I made this girl bend over and looked at her butt.' That's not what is right. You may understand now that that's why you did it. But when you talk about it, don't give me the benefit of your understanding. So I'm kind of creating somewhat of a double-edged sword. I'm kind of showing you things that help you being a person that can teach us better, but at the same time, it also gives you a better understanding of yourself. And you're going to be thinking, 'Oh, yeah, that's why.' I don't want the 'Oh, yeah, that's why' business. I just want the understanding. When this is all said and done and we're gone and you're going to think a lot about things you've heard here and things you've said here . . . you're going to start trying to understand. And I hope you do. I don't know if anything will ever bring you to peace. But hopefully, it will help. So, would he always have the same routine when he called you in his room?"

"Yeah, kind of."

"Why don't you run through the routine?"

"Uh, usually it would start out with him talking with me on the bed. Then he would have me do oral sex on him, you know . . . start off with his penis. Then I would usually either go down on his testicles or move up to his upper body. Then I would lick his butt."

"Would he explain to you exactly what he wanted you to do?"

"Yes. Sometimes he would do the same to me."

"He would lick your butt?"

"Yeah, or he would go down on me. Then he would, you know, fuck me."

"He would put his penis in your butt?"

"Yes."

"Is that what you're calling 'fucking me'?"

"Yes."

"Okay, do you know what that's called?"

"Uh-uh."

"Sodomy."

"Oh, yeah."

"Did it hurt?"

"Yeah."

"Did you bleed?"

"I don't think so. He used, like, K-Y jelly."

"Did your mom know any of this stuff was going on?"

"Probably."

"Why do you think she would have known?"

"Just 'cause we always went in there."

"She'd always see you go in the room together?"

"Yeah."

"Did she ever ask you what you were doing when you would go in?"

"No."

"Would he lock the door?"

"Yeah."

"So he locked the door so that no one else could come in?"

"Yeah."

"How long would he spend putting his penis up your butt?"

"Hmm, until he ejaculated."

"And then what would he do?"

"We'd get dressed and go back out of the room."

"Would he thank you?"

"Yeah, sometimes he would."

"Did he ever hit you during this time?"

"No."

"Did he ever hurt you by striking you or deliberately pinching or doing anything to cause pain?"

"Maybe sometime slapping my butt cheeks. Before [we did this] he would explain things to me. Like why we were doing it."

"So, you're lying on the bed. Would it be any specific time of the day?"

"Usually in the evening, since he worked days so much."

"Did it hurt every time he did this to you?"

"No, not every time."

"And how old do you think you were at the time?"

"Hmm, six or seven."

"Okay, T.J. The size of a man's penis and the size of a six-year-old's anal cavity . . . there's a big difference. I mean, for him to put his penis in you had to have been more pain than you ever realized in your life at that time."

"Um-hmm."

"Did he ever urinate on you?"

"Um, no."

"Did he ever do anything with your poops?"

"Um, sometimes. He wanted to eat it."

"Did he eat your poop?"

"Yeah."

"In front of you?"

"Yeah."

"What did you do?"

"I just watched."

"Did it make you sick?"

"Somewhat, yeah."

"Have you ever shared this with anyone?"

"No."

"So, I'm the first one you're telling?"

"Yes. I've talked to my attorney a little."

"They know about this?"

"Some of it."

"You know you're a victim. I mean, this is not a normal behavior for a father to do to his son. And the fact that you're sitting here where you are now, I can't say why or how, but I can tell you that what's happened to you in the past has contributed, in my opinion [to the crime]. My heart breaks for you because you never had a chance in life. So you're growing older and in elementary school. And your father continues his activity. Did it ever change?"

"Not until I got into junior high and stuff like that. I kind of avoided him somewhat."

"So at some point you either had to start dreading it or getting angry over it. Because it hurt you. Right? And every time he put his penis up your butt, didn't that hurt you?"

"It did for a while. But eventually it stopped hurting."

"Did you ever have an infection that you can remember?"

"I never had an infection."

"During this time, did you start interacting with other children like this? Don't give me their names. Just tell me, did you or did you not?"

"Other than the ones I told you about, no."

"And how would you focus your needs?"

"Uh, he would give me, like, magazines. Pornographic magazines."

"What would you do with them?"

"I would look at them and play with myself."

"Masturbate?"

"Yeah."

"Did you ever have a partner other than your father?"

"He had a friend that he told stuff to. I guess he liked the same things. They were in a room talking about setting something up, but it never happened."

"Okay. Maybe when we're done here at the interview, you can tell Tod and Mark the name of this friend. Because it's possible this friend is out there hurting children. So how does your mother work into this? Didn't you ever ask about Mom? What did he tell you about your mom?"

"As far as what?"

"The sexual activity. Was your dad having sex with your mom?"

"I'm not sure. I think so. I occasionally remember them going into the room and locking the door."

"How did you feel when your dad had sex with your mom?"

"Um, it didn't really matter."

"Did you feel that he should only have sex with you?"

"No."

"Did you think he loved you less?"

"No."

"Did you think if you didn't have sex with him, he wouldn't want to be your father anymore and not be your friend?"

"Um, maybe. I think I might have had some of those feelings."

"Did you ever ask him?"

"No."

"Was there anyone in your life that you wanted to go and tell that this was happening?"

"Mmm, no."

"So, when you graduate from elementary school to junior high school, you're getting around puberty. You're starting to develop your manhood. Pubic hair, underarm hair, whatever. Did things with your dad change?"

"Um, a little bit."

"How?"

"It wasn't quite as often. And he started allowing me to sodomize him."

"Is that something you wanted to do?"

"Um, yeah."

"And how often would this happen?"

"Not very often."

"Your dad has a real strong sexual need. I mean, he's with you as you're growing up many times a week. And not to mention with your mom. So if he slows down, where do you think he's going to get his sexual relief?"

"Mmm, I don't know. I know he would go out a lot. Go driving. I can remember him saying once or twice that he had relations with guys."

"Do you remember what kind of car he had at the time?"

"It was an Oldsmobile Cutlass Supreme."

"What color?"

"Green."

"And would you guys ever take family trips or anything like that?"

"Yes."

"Where did you go?"

"We came up to Tahoe. It was something we'd do every year. He had a condo on the grade here. Then one time we took a little trip up to Oregon. In the Oregon vortex and stuff."

"With your mom?"

"Um-hmm."

"How did your dad and mom get along on trips?"

"Not too bad. They argued a lot, though. She would yell at him a lot. They'd kind of get into screaming matches. Sometimes she'd yell at him about me."

"What about?"

"How she didn't ever want me and how she didn't love me and things like that. You know, 'He's *your* son.'"

"Did you ever think she might have said that because you and your dad were spending so much time together?"

"Um, maybe. She never liked us to go anywhere."

"She felt like a third wheel?"

"I guess. I don't know."

"Did she ever tell you the way she felt?"

"No."

"How do you feel about your mom?"

"I don't like her much."

"Why?"

"Because of all the mean things she said about me."

"When did she start saying those things?"

"When I was young."

"How young?"

"Seven or eight, I guess."

"What would she say?"

"Things like that. She never loved me. She never wanted me. She would never say 'em directly to me. But I would always hear them fighting out in the living room."

"Did your dad ever explain these fights to you?"

"Um, yeah, he did. I remember he used to say, 'She just doesn't love you.' Something like that."

"He would tell you that your mom didn't love you?"

"Um-hmm. He said he'd always be there for me."

"You believed him?"

"Yeah. He always was."

"Has your dad confided in you about things in his life when he was going out and getting other men? Did he ever talk to you about getting other women?"

"Um, a little bit."

"What would he tell you?"

"Just that he had sex with other men and they sucked him off until he ejaculated. He went ahead and got a prostitute."

"Did he start talking to you as you grew older about the things he enjoyed in sex?"

"Mmm, he kinda always did."

"What would he say?"

"Just as far as him liking butts a lot. Smelling and licking 'em."

"What about eating feces or eating poop?"

"Uh, yeah, he did talk about that some."

"What did he say?"

"He said he liked the flavor or something."

"Did he ever talk to you about having young girls?"

"Yeah, occasionally."

"What would he tell you?"

"That he liked the younger girls because they were tighter."

"Did he ever tell you who the young girls were?"

"I don't remember him doing anything with young girls at that time."

"So, all during this time when he's having sex with you, he's sodomizing you, he's eating your feces. Did he ever ask you to eat his feces?"

"Yeah."

"Did you?"

"Um, I tried once or twice. But it was always too nasty-tasting to me."

"Did he ever try and experiment with things that were outside your normal routine?"

"Like what?"

"Tying you up. Holding you down. Putting you in positions that were different?"

"Um, yeah. Yeah, he tied my arms up once with, like, a handkerchief or something like that."

"How old were you when he did this?"

"Elementary school."

"How often would he do this?"

"It only happened once or twice."

"Positioning you in certain positions?"

"He would sometimes lay me on my back and then get on top of me and have me suck him that way instead. Sometimes, like, a pillow under me."

"Did he ever put a pillow over your face?"

"Uh-hmm."

"Did he ever put his hands around your neck?"

"Uh-hmm."

"Did he ever ask you to dress a certain way?"

"No."

"T.J., did you think this was a normal life for a child?"

"Not completely, no."

"What did you think was abnormal?"

"Just all the sex and everything."

"So, you thought having sex with your father was not normal?"

"Yeah, somewhat. But he always told me that there were a lot of people who did it in the country."

"What made you think it was not normal to have sex with your father?"

"I guess it was because I never heard about anybody else doing it or anything."

"Did you ever ask your friends if they did it?"

"No. No, he had always told me to keep things a secret."

"Did he ever threaten you?"

"No."

"Did you ever try and have relationships with any of your peers at school?"

"Um, females."

"How old were you when you tried?"

"Like, in the fourth or fifth grade."

"What was in your mind of what you wanted to do with her?"

"Um, to have sex with her."

"Tell me what you mean by sex."

"Lick her, her vagina, and penetrate her and things like that."

"Penetrate her vagina or penetrate her anus?"

"Both."

"Did you want her to suck on you?"

"Yeah."

"Did you get that far with her?"

"No, I never did."

"How far did you get with her?"

"Mmm, she pecked me on the cheek. A kiss on my cheek one time. That's about it. I never pushed anything."

"Anybody else that you tried to have relations with at school?"

"Not in elementary school. In junior high, I tried to meet girls and stuff."

"A lot of times, it's very common to see boys and girls that are molested, sexually molested, act out at a very early age; where they're acting upon others what's done to them, and what I'm getting at is to try and determine if you tried to act out on others what your dad was doing to you. I mean, if you think about that, can you think of any instances we haven't talked about?"

"Uh, no . . . I wasn't real popular in junior high. I got along with people, but girls never looked at me that way. I guess they thought I was weird or something."

"So in junior high, when you start reaching puberty, your relationship with your father changes. For the better or worse in your opinion?"

"For the better."

"How?"

"I started being more evasive toward having sex with him and stuff. By not being around him or something like that."

"Hard question. Is it possible that your father was no longer interested in you because you were showing signs of being an adult?"

"Mmm, I don't know."

"Did you have a sexual relationship with your father all the way up through the years until now?"

"Yeah. It's been less. A lot less frequent in the [last] years, though."

"Okay. You keep looking at Tim [Minister]. Do you like him?"

"No."

At that point it, was almost noon and they took a break for food. Agent Rinek made a joke about breaking bread together and tweaked T.J.'s attorney by saying, "Unless you want to make a lawyerly agreement about breaking bread."

Then in an attempt to keep the mood light during lunch, Agent Rinek turned toward T.J. and said about his lawyer Tod Young, "You know, I used to work on the Unabomber cases. He [Tod] looks like the Unabomber."

But Young shot back, "I certainly look better than Tim [Minister], though."

T.J. laughed at this and said, "Yeah."

After a break Agent Rinek got into the episode with T.J. and Carla in Reno. This swerved into the Lake Tahoe area and the case about Jaycee Lee Dugard. Rinek said, "It's something that bothers me. On June 10, 1991, there was an eleven-year-old girl with blond hair that was taken from South Lake Tahoe. She lived right off the road your dad would drive to and fro. The car was seen with a similar description to the car you described your dad as having. The artist's conception is similar to your mother, Francine. The question is, has your dad ever talked to you about it?"

T.J. answered, "No."

"Do you have any idea if your dad could have done this?"

"No, I don't. I mean, he might have. I don't know."

"Okay, do you think he's capable of that type of abduction?"

"Considering what's happened and all, yes."

"Um, let's talk about your mom, Francine. A lot of things happened to her, that your father has done. Do you think this is true or false?"

"I don't know."

"Did your father ever talk about things he would do to her?"

"No."

"'Cause he did a lot of stuff to her. Did your mom ever tell you about it?"

"No."

"Do you think they were having a normal marital relationship?"

"Probably not. They argued a lot."

"Do you call her your mom or do you call her Francine?"

"I guess Francine. Or Fran."

"And did you start calling her Fran because your dad wanted you to call her Fran or because you just didn't like her enough to call her mom?"

"Just because I didn't like her enough to call her mom."

"Did she ever hurt you?"

"In what way?"

"Did she ever hit you?"

"No."

"Did she ever sexually abuse you?"

"No."

"Did she ever verbally abuse you?"

"Not in person. She would always, you know, say things to my dad about me. 'He's a fucking bastard.' You know, shit like that."

Then they started talking about the murder of his grandmother, Janey Mozingo. T.J. cried for himself and for his father as well.

"Okay, regardless of all the crap . . . if you didn't tell me you cared about your dad, I'd think there was something wrong with you. You know. I mean, I didn't get along with my parents, but I still love them. You got along with your dad, so if you didn't love him, it wouldn't fit in. I do expect it. It's a sign of a good person. Crying to me shows that you care about something. I just want to be sure I know what it is. I need you to tell me what it is."

"I cry 'cause, you know, I didn't get to know her [Janey Mozingo]. And he always told me what a good person she was."

"Have you drawn any parallels between the murder of your grandmother and Krystal?"

"No, I haven't."

"Have you thought that the things you're crying about relating to your grandmother are the same things people are going to cry about when they think of Krystal?"

"I did just now before you mentioned it."

"That's a heavy thought, huh? That's why it's important to get everything out and resolve everything we can resolve. And that's why you're important. Because you can help shed light on this. Did he ever talk about his life with her? Give you any indication that she was a great mom, she cooked great cookies, whatever?"

"Um, he said she always supported him and always helped him through school and tried to bring him up good."

"Do you think your dad had been molested as a child?"

"I don't know."

"Do you think your dad's been a good dad to you? Forgetting the sex stuff, do you think he's been a good dad?"

"Yeah."

"Is he your friend?"

"Yeah."

"He cares about you?"

"Um-hmm."

"You care about him?"

"Um-hmm. I mean, everybody's always seen what a good kid I am and that's 'cause of the way he brought me up."

"A lot of people would say that you're not a good kid. You know that, right?"

"Um-hmm."

"And a lot of people would say that your dad really didn't bring you up that well. That your dad brought you up for his own benefit."

At this point, they took a long break, and while T.J. was out of the room, Tim Minister brought Agent

Rinek up to speed on a couple of interesting aspects. One was that they had just found an enema bag in the apartment that they were sure had been used by Soria senior on T.J. The other was even more unexpected. Minister said, "There's been a lot of religious stuff going on. He [Thomas Soria Sr.] reads the Bible a lot. I think they both did in the past. When I went in and interviewed Dad, he was just sitting there clutching the Bible. So I'm just curious how he was raised in a religious sense. And how far that has affected his belief system and that kind of stuff."

When T.J. came back in after lunch, Agent Rinek and T.J. talked about Rinek's son for a while and then moved on to the question of religion that Tim Minister had suggested. Agent Rinek asked T.J., "How's your religion? People have noticed that your dad seems pretty religious. Did you have a lot of religion growing up?"

"Uh, no. We were never religious when I was growing up. Actually, [he lost] his religion after his mom died. [Later], when he and Lupe had some trouble, he found God and then during my time with Tasha, seeing the bad that was happening, I found God. And have stuck with Him."

"So, you personally have a God now?"

"Um-hmm."

"Did your dad make you go to church and stuff?"

"No, we never went to church or anything."

"So, the religion in your lives is fairly recent?"

"Yes."

"Is Lupe religious?"

"Yeah, she is."

"Do you think he's getting it from her?"

"Yeah. I think she helped him a lot."

"Now, let me ask you the million-dollar question. Lupe's married to your dad, right?"

"Um-hmm."

"So, she's his wife. And many of us here are married. Now, is your dad doing the religious thing to please Lupe so she leaves him alone or because he's religious?"

"Because he's religious. She understood that when they got together that he wasn't religious and she accepted that."

"Okay. Did your dad ever record your sex together? Either in the form of pictures, like [with] cameras, or videotape?"

"When I was older. Once or twice."

"Did he videotape you actually having sex?"

"Yeah."

"How did you feel about that?"

"It really didn't bother me."

"Did you ask what he intended to do with the video?"

"No. In fact, we ended up erasing it. Uh, later on me and Lupe, the three of us, [were in the video]."

"Do you know if your dad ever videotaped Francine?"

"I don't believe so. But I know he had taken some pictures of her. She was lying on the water bed."

"Was she nude?"

"Yeah."

"Did you look at them?"

"Yeah."

"Was it scary?"

"In some ways, yes; yes, it was."

"Okay. I guess when law enforcement was going through your stuff, they found an enema bag. Did you guys use the enema at all for sexual purposes?"

"Mmm, I remember seeing it when I was younger. I don't ever remember using one."

"Okay. You're doing, fine, T.J. I'd love you to ask questions if you want to."

"No, I don't ask a lot of questions normally."

"Well, you should. You never asked your dad questions when he was doing this stuff to you. And you could've and you should've. I'm not your dad. I'm not looking at you the way your dad looks at you. I'm a person who's never met you before. I feel bad for you. I feel that you've been deprived of your past as well as your future. I see you as a victim of your dad. It doesn't mean your dad's a bad person. It means that your dad may also be a victim. I feel bad for you. And so I don't want to contribute to your victimization by having you sit there and have a question and always dart your eyes over at this guy [Tim Minister]. You know he's not a bad guy. And there's no reason for you to be afraid of him."

Then they got into T.J.'s first girlfriend, Carla, in Reno and the business about calling his dad "Uncle."

Rinek asked, "When did that start?"

T.J. answered, "Up in Tahoe. About six or seven months ago."

"Why did you start calling him 'uncle'?"

"Um, he felt that to get together with younger girls, it wouldn't help if he was my dad. We feared they might kind of find it strange and awkward that he was my dad. It was to try and make the girls feel more comfortable with him."

Then Agent Rinek asked, "How am I doing so far? Are you okay?"

"I'm all right."

"You'll tell me if I piss you off."

"Yeah. I'm pretty hard to piss off. I'm mellow."

"Well, you know if we walk out of here and you feel some relief having gotten everything out . . . it's important to me that it helps you realize things. It helps you come to terms with the terrible thing that's happened. And helps you get on with your life. Because, T.J., you're just nineteen, and you're in manhood, but I see a child. And I feel bad. And in some way, if your life goes on in a better way because we've been so honest and forthright and done the brave thing here, then I feel good. I go home either way. But I go home a lot nicer and feeling better if I feel like I did something good. [Soon] we're going to talk about Krystal. It's going to be a really, really hard time. The hardest time. We have to be the bravest. I'm going to ask you to look at pictures. And it's going to be a hard time. But when it's over, what I'm hoping for is that we will understand. And we're building toward that now. It's trying to understand how it got to the point that it got to."

Agent Rinek asked him some questions about when his mom, Fran, left and his time with Tasha. Then it was time to confront the demons of the abduction and murder of Krystal Steadman. Agent Rinek asked him, "Are you ready for the hardest ride?"

"Yeah."

"Why don't we start off with you telling us completely as you can what happened?"

T.J. explained that his dad had awakened early and asked him to bring one of the kids upstairs. He had gone down to the parking lot and seen Krystal with the other girls he knew. He zeroed in on her because she was blond and small and he knew his dad liked that. He told of bringing her upstairs, of his dad taking her into the bedroom and of himself returning to his own room to masturbate. He covered the whole story, from Krystal's mom coming to the apartment to his dad asking him to get rid of Krystal's body, plus that whole process up to the time he was questioned at the Lake Tahoe Sheriff's substation.

After T.J. was through, Agent Rinek said, "Okay. Let's go back and start over. And this time I'll drive. It's Sunday morning. You're sleeping and your dad wakes you up to go out and get him a girl. So you went outside to see the kids playing and you were playing with them. You've spent a lot of time with some of these kids. You [didn't] hang out with high-school kids [at the apartment complex]. You hung with young kids. Did your dad specify a boy or girl?"

"No, he didn't."

"Do you know what a fantasy is?"

"Yes."

"When you think about sex and you're masturbating, what's going through your mind? Do you fantasize yourself with a woman?"

"Yeah. You know, like the girls from *Baywatch* or something like that."

"So, T.J., are you saying you have no sexual interest in children?"

"No, I don't."

"Okay. So you offer Krystal some candy and she comes up to the apartment."

"Yeah. I got the candy jar. She said she wanted a sucker. So I gave her a sucker. And then that's when my dad came out. He acted like he was surprised to see her in the house. And he came up and that's when I introduced them. And he said hi and asked how she was doing and stuff. And that's when I said I had to go get my clothes."

"Did he give you a thumbs-up or some kind of acknowledgment?"

"No, not really."

"Did you feel good that you had done something for him that he wanted you to do?"

"Kinda, yeah."

"So you knew when you brought Krystal up, that you felt good because you had given your father what he wanted."

"Yeah. Um, he seemed real happy."

"How long were you gone when you went out?"

"Um, must have been five minutes. When I went back, I found the house seemed empty in the front and his door was shut."

"His door was shut. Did you listen?"

"No, I didn't."

"And what did you do next?"

"That's when I went and sat down at my computer and played a game. I sat there for fifteen minutes to a half hour before her mom came to the door."

"What'd she say to you?"

"That's when she asked if I had seen Krystal or not. And I just told her I thought I had seen her running down the street or riding her bike down the street."

"But you knew she was in the back room with your dad?"

"I was fairly certain."

"Okay. Her mom leaves and you close the door. What happens next?"

"Um, that's when I went in and played on my computer a little bit more. And then I finally gathered my clothes and took them to the laundry room. Then I came back and laid down and was having trouble sleeping. Then I masturbated. And then I fell asleep. Not heavy . . . I thought I heard some shower water running. Then a little bit later, I heard him go back into the bedroom. [After that] her mom came to the door for the second time. That's when she looked around. I told her she couldn't go into his room and she left. So I thought if something was going on, I wanted to try and protect my dad. [I went] and laid back down for a little bit. The next thing I remember was him calling me—"

Agent Rinek broke in at this part. He said, "I'm not challenging you. I'm personally having a difficult time with some of the things you're saying. Because I've been to murder and homicide scenes before. And I know from seeing some of the injuries on Krystal that there was a lot of blood. An awful lot of blood. But there's very little blood in your dad's bedroom. So, in my opinion, Krystal's bleeding would have to be in the bathroom. And you say you went into the bathroom. What I'm getting at T.J. . . . you have survived. And part of any resolution is to be completely candid. To show the courage and being brave and talk about it. Because I'm having a hard time with some of the things you're saying. Now you're a kid, in my opinion. And you're acting like every kid does. You're scared to death. I can see you shaking. You're clearing your throat every ten seconds. I can tell you're not telling me the truth, 'cause you won't look at me. So . . . you go into your dad's room. What's the first thing that hits you?"

"The smell."

"And what does it smell like?"

"It's nothing I ever smelled before. Just real strong. I don't know. I'd never smelled anything like that before. I did see Krystal on the bed. She's kind of on her back. Her legs are up kind of a little bit. With the bag around her. I guess it was pulled over her head. [My dad] was at the door waiting for me. He was dressed at that point. I was kinda in shock."

"Okay. Have you ever seen the pictures of Krystal after she was dead? [Do you] want to see 'em?"

"Not really."

"I think it's important. Because [you're] describing no blood. And it's important [you] see the damage. I'm talking about blood in the bathroom. I'm talking about blood in your dad's room. I'm talking about the smell. You don't smell that much of a smell without a significant amount of substance. Now, I don't know what that smell comes from. I'm guessing, and my guess is blood. The girl lost all of her blood. And whoever killed her made sure that her blood was completely gone. And that's why she died. That's the one reason she died. This is a nine-year-old girl with a thirst for life. Who did nothing to your father. Nothing to you. This girl came up to your apartment in the spirit of friendship and playing like any innocent child would. And she died. Now, I don't know whether you participated in this or not. But I believe you've been truthful up to a point. And I think you're very, very afraid. And I think you're afraid to tell us what you think we'll judge you over. And I'm telling you, T.J., more important than your fear is knowledge because it's going to challenge you. We're not going to say, 'Well, T.J., that's impossible.' But I'm just having a hard time with what you're saying without being able to back it up. Your dad has protected you like a loving parent. Nothing you tell us about this is going to change what exists for you. But this is for us, for me, the closure, as well as for the family, and I believe you too. You know, you and Krystal have a little bit in common. Because I believe you're both children. And the same fear and the same naïveté that brought her up to your apartment is working against you.

"There's forensic evidence which contradicts what you're saying. T.J., the truth is everything. For you, in my opinion, it's salvation. I know that what you told us, but it's impossible that what you're portraying to us existed. I'm not saying this to piss you off. I'm not calling you a liar. What I'm saying to you is, I think you're very, very frightened. And I think you're a young person trying to come to grips with a very, very hard thing. Forensically speaking, T.J., it's a lot of people's opinion that what happened to Krystal could not have happened without you knowing about it. Now, it's okay. So let me give you an example of where I think you're at. And maybe you can relate to it.

"In West Sacramento a little girl was playing with her friends. And she fell into a silo and died. And her friends came out of the silo and out of the rice mill and told the authorities someone took her. So the [authorities] mobilized all these people. And for a week, the FBI, and the local police, we searched for this guy. We brought in numerous people and interviewed them. We just really pushed hard on it. But when we took the timeline and we looked at the facts, it was our opinion that this girl still had to be there. And we went back a third time and asked a fireman to search in this silo. He was angry 'cause he had done it twice already. On the third time, they used a brighter light. And down in the bottom of the silo, they could see this little girl's body. Now, I was participating in the interview with her two friends. Two boys. And when we told them we had found her and we knew what had happened, they both just broke down. And they both said they were just afraid. They shouldn't have been where they were supposed to have been. They shouldn't have let her fall. Her one friend began writing a letter of apology to her. And in the letter of apology, he said he wished he was dead. And he started drawing himself dead. It was heartbreaking. But we ended up taking this boy and trying to do everything we could to help him. And in his letter, he said she was his friend. He had let her down. It's an example of a person telling the truth.

"Courage and bravery is the truth, and we talked about that in the beginning. So I'm going to challenge you to what you're saying, in my opinion, is implausible. I promised I wouldn't hold anything back from you. So let's go back."

"Okay. After I ejaculated . . . I cleaned myself up in the bathroom and then went back to bed after I urinated. I dozed off and I awoke to hear my dad's door open from his bedroom. I then heard him go into the bathroom, and after a little bit, he flushed the toilet a couple of times. And then I heard the shower running. After a little bit, he emerged from the bathroom and went back into his room. I heard the door close. I dozed a little bit, but not much more. Then I heard the door knocking. I got dressed. I went to the door and it was Krystal's mom again with her boyfriend. After that, she came inside and looked around. I did not let her go into his bedroom. I told her he was sleeping. They ended up leaving. I went back to bed and closed my door. Eventually my dad called me into his bedroom. After that, I went in and smelled the smell. And I looked around kinda wondering what it was. Puzzled. It was very strong. I saw Krystal on the bed in the bag. He told me he needed me to do a favor and get rid of her body for him. After that, he wanted to put her clothes into the bag. He had me hold the bag . . . the box open first to put her body in while he stuffed her legs back in the bag. I put the clothes inside the bag and noticed that they were shredded or ripped or something like that. He told me to go and look outside. Uh, at that point, I went and got my laundry out of the laundry room. There was some other kid in there. A boy. I pulled my clothes out because I didn't have enough quarters to do the dry cycle."

"Okay. Let's go back. The smell that you smelled when you went to his room. You hadn't smelled it before. I mean, it was so strong in that room, but yet it wasn't in the apartment. That's a problem with me. You walked into the room and you see her on the bed in a plastic bag. From the bottom of the bag, you can see her feet. Did your dad say she was dead?"

"No, he didn't."

"What did he say about her?"

"He just said that he needed me to get rid of her."

"Did you ask him if she was dead?"

"No, I didn't."

"Did you ask him what happened?"

"No, I didn't."

"You didn't ask him anything about a dead girl on his bed? A nine-year-old dead girl on his bed and you don't ask him anything?"

"No. I was very much in shock. It was very scary at the time. I was shaky. I was nervous. I didn't know what to make of it. I didn't know he could do such a thing."

"And you were willing to get rid of the body for him?"

"Yes."

"So based on what you're saying, until you got rid of the body, you didn't do anything wrong?"

"Yes."

"I'm not going to put these [pictures] in your face. Look at them from a distance. We'll look at them together. That's what she looked like down on the hill. After you threw her down. This is what people had to encounter. You gonna be sick?"

"I will if I continue to look at this."

"Well, we're not done. I want to show you another

picture. I want to show you a picture of her wounds. And the reason I want to show you this picture is because there is so much blood that came from these wounds that it's hard for me to accept that you didn't know. Okay? This little girl did not ask for this. Let's talk about these wounds. This is a slash with a knife. There's at least two slashes with a knife. And then whoever killed her stuck it in her throat and started sawing away.

"We owe it to her. You owe it to her. Your dad owes it to her. Everyone owes it to this little girl for the truth to be known. They are analyzing trace evidence from her. All the tests are not done. Your semen has been located on her panties. Is there a reason why evidence of you would be under her fingernails? This little girl put up some kind of fight for her life, just like you're fighting us now because that's what's inside you. She's fighting for her life. Trying to survive. And you're calmly sleeping in the next room? Sandi Taylor comes to the door and you answer it and you're wild-eyed. Your wide-eyed and very flushed. As if something that's against your whole person is wrong.

"I think that you care. I believe that you care. If you care, please don't let this go on. Let us know what happened to this little girl. She has a bang on her head that literally fractured her skull. That makes a lot of noise. A wound such as this . . . She would have been gulping as her life was slipping away.

"There's certain things we believe. There's forensic science that can re-create to some degree of reliability what happens in a crime. Your father, in order to get the items he needed to commit this, was in and out of his room at least more than once. And that's not what you describe had to be in the apartment. All we're asking of you, all the girl is asking of you, is to tell what happened to her.

"We're not saying that you did this. What we're saying is you know. And all we're looking for is the closure for her and her family. For us. Most importantly, for you. To give you an opportunity. I can't make you take the opportunity. But if you don't take this opportunity now, we all go home and that's all. You have to live with this. You're shaking. You're crying. You were crying the moment you came in here. You have to make an adult choice. Whether you're going to show courage and be forthright with us and explain to us what happened here. We need, we want, we have to have an explanation. And I'm asking you to do that for us. What you're saying to us, T.J., cannot be. Do you understand what I'm saying to you?"

"I understand what you're saying. I just don't think you're correct. I—I—I had forgotten there was duct tape in the bottom of that box. I assume that was used on her."

"So you're saying to me and to everyone in this room that Krystal comes into your apartment. Your father does all of this. That semen, your semen, is on her panties and his semen is on her. That she was hit on her head sufficient to crack her skull. That she was stabbed and cut on her throat enough times to cause her death from lack of blood. That your father puts her in a plastic bag and is able to clean all of this up before you wake up. Is that what you're telling me?"

"As best I know how. Yes."

"Let's just say . . . What do you think will happen to you if you were there? What do you think should happen to your father?"

"I guess he goes to prison for the rest of his life."

"A lot of people want him put to death. What do you think about that?"

"It upsets me some. I don't want to be cruel. I guess he would deserve it."

"What do you deserve?"

"I think I deserve to start my life over after some time in the prison."

"Are you afraid if you tell us more than you've told us that you won't have that opportunity?"

"There's nothing more that I can tell you about. Think for a minute. How do you know he didn't plan to do this to her? Maybe what he needed was in the bedroom already. And while I was out with the kids, he was waiting for me to bring [someone] up."

"That's a lucid, logical thought. But I don't think it applies. I don't think your father intended to murder this girl. I'm not sure. I wasn't there. You are the only one that was there, and she can't tell her story. But I do know your father asked you to bring a girl. I do know that when your father was in his room with a nine-year-old girl he was planning to have sex with her. And that's something clearly against the law. And I know that when you brought her up, it was your opinion that's what he intended to do. And you're telling me that a nineteen-year-old person, such as yourself, will consent to disposing of a body, that he had nothing to with in the murder. Getting caught, having all the evidence of the blood from that body over his vehicle and over him, and do that consensually. Does that make sense?

"And you're telling me with all the blood in our bodies, when all that blood bleeds out, either in a bedroom or a bathroom, that there's no residue. You're telling me there's all this smell, but there's nothing causing it? You're telling me there's quarts of blood in a room and you couldn't figure out what the smell was?

"What I'm saying is, T.J., you have a responsibility here. But part of the responsibility is helping us understand what happened. Helping us understand what happened to this child. She was a child. She never hurt you. She never hurt your dad. She came up thinking she was getting candy. You led her to believe she was getting candy. She came up to have fun. To have a good time. And she's dead. And she's just not dead. She was brutalized. She was tortured. She was sexually assaulted. She was sodomized."

T.J. cried out in pain. "Stop!"

But Agent Rinek wouldn't stop. "I'm very happy that you're alive. But she's not. And I'm asking you to help her, T.J. Please! Because to help her helps you get through this. Are you going to go through the rest of your life knowing that this beautiful little girl came up and became an object of torture for your father? Is that what you want to go through the rest of your life? You talk about wanting to get out. Wanting to start over. How can you do this when this is sitting in your soul?

"What's hard is what's hard. That's courage. You're afraid. It hurts. It hurts us. We're not here because we're looking for a good time. We're here to help you. To help her. To help us. We want to deal with this. T.J., you've got a future. You are nineteen years old. Regardless of where your life takes you, either in the court system or outside the court system, you have this in your soul. You carry her in your soul. Okay? It's gonna always pull you down. You're never going to be able to rise to any kind of happiness until you deal with this. T.J., I can see it. It's too much for you to hold in. We're not here to judge you. We're not going to tell you you're a bad person. I can already tell that from the way you've lived. And you know what this girl went through, because you went through it. The only difference between her and you is that she's dead.

"The girl was nine years old. She never had a clue. And when she's bound with duct tape and a knife is being inserted into her throat and she's watching her life leak away, what do you think she's thinking? If you could give this girl something, what would you give her?"

"I don't know."

"T.J., she's dead. If I could, I'd bring her back to life. If I could give you the power to bring her back to life, I would. But we can't. But we can do something for her. We can let the truth be known. And not let her go on in the future wondering what happened. How do we stop this from happening again? That's all we're asking you for. Now I'm going to go home at some point. We're all going to go home at some point. I'm going to go home feeling as if I tried as hard as I could to help you through this. You can take my help or you can refuse it. It's totally up to you.

"You know the logic of what you're telling us is illogical. It's impossible for me to believe all this could have happened. Look [at the photos]. Look at this! We're talking cuts and scrapes and bruises. We're talking about a bashed-in head. This is where she got hit in the face. Look at her! I'm not saying that you did this to her. But I believe you saw it. There are people who are called compliant victims. People that are there when crimes are committed and they were afraid to stop them. They were afraid to act. Your father is not here. There's sides of your father that are wonderful and that you loved. But there's a side of your father that's very bad. And unfortunately, you led her to the bad side and she's dead because of it. The only thing we can do now is talk about it and make it right.

"I mean, you say you're finding God. How can you go

to heaven? . . . How can you live your life knowing God is looking down on you with this opportunity and you're not taking it? I mean what does it take? What can I do to convince you how much better you'll feel? All it's going to do is bring closure for her. And these pictures won't have to be studied anymore to figure out how it happened. We won't have to sit here and go over this cut by cut. Knife wound by knife wound. Are you aware of your father's things on the computer? He talks about doing this stuff. He got fired from the Lottery and prosecuted because he was calling women and saying, 'I want to fuck you up the ass. I want to make you hurt. I want you to suffer. I'm going to beat on your head. I'm going to cut your throat.' That's what he did to her. She's not even an adult. She had no ability to defend herself. She's completely innocent. This girl paid for her life for a piece of candy because she believed in you and liked you."

T.J., crying, said, "You don't think I feel very bad for that?"

Rinek answered, "I know you do. I know you do."

"I still think that if I would have let her mom in, that she may be alive today. And I didn't. I'm going to live with that for the rest of my fucking life!"

Agent Rinek replied, "But you don't have to. You just told us something we didn't know. Why live with this yourself, T.J.? How can we help you if you don't ask for it?"

"I told you all I know."

"You just told us something we didn't know. Do you think she was still alive when her mom came by the first time?"

"I don't know. Maybe."

"Why are you saying it then?"

"Because it's a possibility."

"Why do you think that's a possibility? You have to have a reason for believing that. Are you saying you think you could have saved her life and you didn't? Are you saying she's dead because of you? Do you think your knife killed her?"

"I don't know."

"What did your knife look like?"

"It was black and had a blade about this long and part of it was serrated."

"That's similar to a description of a knife the pathologist thinks could have killed this little girl. T.J., you've given us two things here that are very important. You believe you could have saved her life, so you're blaming yourself that she's dead. And now you're saying that your dad took your knife. How do you think Krystal died? You saw a lot of blood. Look, I don't blame you. You never had a chance. Your father never let you have a chance. This girl had a chance. And now she has nothing. And her last breath was a dying one. And she was tortured. And she died in pain. She did not die peacefully.

"And now you show this remorse. You act this way. But you drive down the road and you throw her off a cliff. She rolls many hundred yards. And she ends up a pile of flesh. And that's what people see. But I don't see you that way. Believe it or not, in our discussion today, you've said things to me that make me feel that even though you have some problems, that you're not a monster like your father. You were a witness. All we're asking is for you to tell us. It's not like the first night here [and you're thinking], 'Oh, my God, I'll die. They're going to put me to death.' It's not that way. All we want to know is the truth.

"I came from Sacramento because I don't believe you are what your father is. I can only justify [this trip] by knowing what happened to this girl and hearing you describe it. I think it's going to rip you apart. But I think you'll feel better. I don't think you enjoy death. I think you do enjoy children. I think deep down inside you are a child still. And you're scared. You're with strange people in a strange place. You're trying to figure out what the hell is going on.

"Your father caused you to be here. And telling us what happened that day might expose your father for what he is. But T.J., we already know. It's no secret. Your father's killed a girl. I don't know if he's killed more people. You think your father was having sex with her in that room?"

"I don't know."

"You do know! You do know! You know what he likes. You know he did it to her. There's forensic evidence that indicates he did it to her. You hold the key. You hold the gift. You can give that gift now. You can give that gift to yourself. You can give that gift to Krystal. There's a reason you believe she was alive when her mom came by. I can see it in you. It strikes you like a dagger. Now, when her mom came by the second time, was it too late?"

"I don't know."

"You go into your father's room and Krystal's there on the bed, dead. In a plastic bag. Is that showing respect for the dead? He threw her away like a piece of trash. And you were the garbageman. You took her like trash and threw her over the ledge like people dump their household goods. There's nothing I can do to remove that responsibility from you. I can't believe you slept through it. Not when you're telling me you're at the door with her mom and you're thinking you could have saved her life. If Krystal could say something to you today, what do you think she'd say?"

"Help her."

"You're crying. Your lips are quivering. If she could come down in spirit and talk to you, what do you think she'd ask you to do?"

[*Crying*] "Tell the truth."

"So she'd walk out of this room thinking, 'Oh, he slept through the whole time I was killed.' When someone else comes to the door and sees you in a state that they don't normally see you in. Those are clues to us. We follow up on clues. But we don't like those clues anymore. We know there was involvement. But we need closure of your eyes and your ears. When you leave this room, if you leave with what you know, it will only get worse. You've had a bad break in life. You've never had a chance. Are you going to give this girl a chance to at least have her death resolved? I'm getting tired. It's up to you, T.J.

"He ripped her neck open, possibly with your knife. There's a lot of blood that's missing. We think there was blood in the bathtub drain. He would have had to drag her over there. But you described dad as a frail guy. This little girl's hands indicate that she tried to defend herself. She fought for her life. That makes noise. That indicated struggle. If she was killed on the bed, the bed would be saturated with her blood. If she was taken to the bathroom, there would be banging and dull thuds. And there'd be that sound of water as her blood is being washed down the drain.

"I'm going to ask you a hypothetical question. Let's say you're in your room. You're trying to fall asleep, but you can't. And let's say you hear screaming and banging coming from your dad's room . . . I think your father has you so far under his control that all your life you've gotten used to doing what he asked you to do and seeking his approval. I don't think you would have gone against him. Explain to me how your semen ends up on her panties?"

"I don't know. I don't know forensics."

"Forget forensics. Your semen is on her panties. Did you ejaculate over the toilet?"

"No."

"Did you use her panties to clean up the toilet?"

"No."

"Did you ever see her panties at any time when she was in the apartment?"

"Only when I put them in the bag."

"Did your father come in and have oral sex with you and catch your ejaculate and put it on her panties?"

"No."

"So how does it get there?"

"I don't know. I wiped it off with toilet paper."

"You have semen on your hands; you wiped it off with toilet paper, which is absorbent. Not to mention a half hour of air time for it to dry. But it's on her panties."

Then Tim Minister popped in. "You had some marks on your arms. Do you remember how you got those?"

"No, I don't exactly remember."

"Do you know if anything else was taken from the house? Like a broom?"

"No, I don't know."

"Was it a plastic [broom] or was it the old-fashioned straw kind?"

"It was like the old-fashioned straw."

Finally Agent Rinek said, "Okay, I'm going to state to you my opinion. I think you were there. I think the scratches on your side came from the little girl fighting. I think your semen is on her panties because you were there with your dad. Your history is that your dad and you have shared every woman in your lives. I think that you may not have participated in her murder. I don't think you really intended that. I think you believed that she did consent to having sex with you guys. And that the murder was probably not intended by you. But what you're asking me to believe after twenty-four years of being in law enforcement, I just can't. And I just want you to know that when I leave here tonight, that's what I'm going to believe. And you're going to have a difficult time getting on with your life when you still hold all of that inside of you regardless of your culpability. Whether you share it with Tod and Mark, or whoever you share it with, I think it's going to haunt you for the rest of your life until you deal with it. And I just want you to know that. Because I'm done. I'm not going to ask you any more questions. I don't think you've told me the truth. And I don't know what the reason is. I have suspicions, but I don't know. I hope you well for the rest of your life. I hope that you find resolution with this."

T.J. Soria's final words to Agent Jeff Rinek were "I have as best I can."

Following the analogy that Agent Rinek had made about courage and *Saving Private Ryan*, T.J. Soria cowered behind the rock on the beach and could not step out into the open, even to save himself.

FIFTEEN

"I Will Hold This Burden on My Shoulders."

While Thomas Soria Sr. waited for his day in court, T.J. Soria's day of reckoning came on July 24, 2000. He sat with his attorneys before Judge David R. Gamble at the courthouse in Minden, Nevada, to receive sentencing for his crimes. At stake was whether he would get the possibility of parole or never see the outside of a prison again. The courtroom was packed with Krystal Steadman's friends and family and just the plain curious. There was an electric atmosphere in the small courthouse on Eighth Street.

Krystal Steadman's mother, Elizabeth, was still so upset by the death of her daughter that she was not able to attend in person. Instead, she sent a letter that was read by Deputy DA Buttell. It stated:

For me, Krystal Steadman's mother, the loss of my daughter was a devastating blow. My life revolved around Krystal."

Elizabeth wrote of how she and Krystal had run from a bad situation with her ex-husband; from that time forward her goal had been to create a safe environment for Krystal. She said that she had done everything to promote Krystal's education and happiness. Elizabeth spoke of how Krystal loved to sing in the choir. Then she added, "T.J. Soria and his father took her voice away. When T.J. kidnapped Krystal, he took my life away too."

Elizabeth wrote that T.J. knew Krystal would be killed after his father raped and tortured the girl. Then she spoke of how her life had been turned upside down. She had worked as a housekeeper for a man in South Lake Tahoe. But once the murder occurred, the man let her go because he had loved Krystal so much, and Elizabeth's presence was a tragic reminder of her loss. Her letter went on to say, "I have been in a state of shock and my life in chaos. I am no longer able to sleep. Closing my eyes only brings visions of the horrific and immense terror my little girl must have felt. I hear her uncontrollable sobs and then there is silence."

Elizabeth Steadman railed at the complete disregard the Sorias had shown for Krystal's life. She characterized their scheme as cold, vicious and premeditated, noting how they attempted to sanitize and wipe out all traces of her existence. She told how Krystal's life had been stolen from her, her family and the whole world. Everything that Krystal could have been, disappeared.

Elizabeth wrote, "Judge Gamble, I can only pray that you see fit to ensure other parents that this will never happen again to another child. T.J. Soria should *never ever* be allowed to see anything other than the inside of a prison for the remainder of his life, and that, Judge Gamble, is far more than my little girl will ever see."

Just as angry and compelling in her arguments for no possibility of parole was Krystal's sister, Sonia Klempner. Asked by Thomas Perkins how the crime had affected her, she said, "Horribly."

Then she went on to say, "I used to be a resident of Sparks, Nevada, and once this tragedy happened on Highway Fifty, I can't drive down that highway anymore. Since the nineteenth of March when I first heard of the news, I came rushing over and have not been able to drive home since. I obviously had a nice apartment with a lease. I had to break my lease early. I didn't have a place to live here in South Lake Tahoe to be with my family, so I, too, was staying with my girlfriend or living at hotels until I just finally got settled down, I believe in June. But my whole life has just been a financial mess.

"Working—I can't work such as I used to and I cannot drive down Highway Fifty. The memories of the night of the nineteenth, driving up here, the horrible memories out there searching for her and then, of course, the horrible memory of the next morning when we got the phone call that they found her."

Prosecutor Thomas Perkins asked, "Do you have some new fears because of what happened to your sister?"

Klempner answered, "Anytime I am given a hug, anytime I'm kind of in a situation that any person on television or any person walking down the street resembles Soria or his father, I get so disgusted that my entire train of thought is impossible. I just have these horrible, horrible, horrible visions of what they did to my sister. How they murdered her."

Q.—Do you have any anger at this man? [*Pointing at T.J. Soria*]

A.—Oh, yeah, yeah!

Q.—Tell the judge about that. Are you able to manage that, or is it something you are having to live with right now?

A.—Oh, it's something that I just have to live with.

Q.—Have you seen the way [this] crime affected other people around Krystal, like her friends and your mother and all like that?

A.—Some of her girlfriends, her little eight- and nine-year-old friends, have to seek counseling. One of her best friends was going to try to make it here to testify. She is seeking counseling at that young age because of the fear.

Q.—Do you feel like you've heard anything today that diminishes his responsibility for the loss of your sister?

A.—I do not believe I have seen anything today that diminishes it. What are you referring to? I don't quite understand.

Q.—I was talking about him and what he did. How do you feel about what he did to your sister?

A.—Nothing surprised me. I'm horribly angry at him and I feel that he's completely responsible, if not more so because he had her life in his hands. He is the one that chose her out of everybody else. Even in that audiotape, he said he made choices of his own. That day he could have told his father that he didn't find anybody. I feel that he's very responsible.

Q.—Sonia, will you tell the judge what you think

his sentence should be? You know, what the range of possibilities are?

A.—Well, if the range of possibilities is a maximum, if the maximum is going to be life in prison without the possibility of parole, that's not good enough for me. I don't really understand why the plea bargain happened. The possibility of parole based upon a plea bargain—for me and my family and friends are just absolutely destroyed by this. It's not ever going to be good enough, obviously. If life in prison without the possibility of parole is absolutely the maximum that we're offered, then we want the maximum, although it will never be enough.

As compelling as Elizabeth Steadman's and Sonia Klempner's statements were about T.J. Soria's guilt, defense attorney Tod Young's were just as cogent and heartfelt in the opposite direction. He said, "Your Honor, I don't have any great wisdom in the case and I wish that I did. This is a day and an hour that I have considered for months and what I would say to you when we reached this point. . . . The hierarchy of responsibility, how Mr. Soria junior, T.J., fits into that hierarchy of responsibility and how to fashion an appropriate sentence to particularize the responsibility, fits into the offense and who he is. So let me start with the first point of that, the hierarchy of responsibility. The death of this little girl is heartbreaking for everyone who has sat in this room, including Mr. Jackson and myself, and including T.J.

"The way this came about is through the sheer overwhelming dominance of Mr. Soria senior over his son. I want to tell you, Your Honor, that through these last few months that I have spoken about a minute ago . . . I live in this community, and I go to the grocery stores here and buy my gas here. I go to social events here. Many times, people that I know and complete strangers will come up to me and say things like: 'I hope they kill your client!' 'I hope that you lose your case.' 'How can you represent someone so horrible?'

"I understand these feelings. I am thankful I haven't had to share the feelings of Krystal's family personally for any member of my family, but I think I understand their anger and their rage. It's very much like [FBI Agent Rinek] saying to T.J. on the audiotape, 'There are a lot of people in this community that are mad at you.' I think my response to some of those people has been 'I understand your anger.' When they say to me, 'Your client was an adult; he could make his own decisions. He was nineteen years old.' My response to them was 'I understand that from your point of view, but tell me, how old were you when your father started having sex with you? How old were you when he said it was okay to have sex with your stepmother? How old were you when your father started eating your feces?'

"That is something I have no place in my life to put into context, and hopefully, no one else in this room does. We can imagine ourselves what T.J.'s level of responsibility on that day should have been and how he should have behaved, but we can't put into context the life he lived before that. We don't have a frame of reference for that because, hopefully, it was a life the rest of us have never known.

"To the hierarchy of responsibility for that offense, however horrible it may sound, it is the fantasy of Mr. Soria senior's that he [T.J.] lived, and not one of T.J.'s. The evidence that we have been able to review—that the state has provided us—is not necessarily inconsis-

tent with T.J.'s version of events that he gave in the pre-
sentence report. He did participate in getting Krystal
to that apartment, in secreting her from her mother,
and providing her to his father and ultimately disposing of her body.

"Your Honor, did he know that she would be killed?
Now I can hear even the audience behind me saying,
'Yes, he knew.' There's not evidence of that, Your
Honor. In fact, what there is—there is a history of Mr.
Soria taking over the women in T.J.'s life. There is a history of Mr. Soria senior seeking to have T.J. introduce
him to girls, to girls from high school, to girls that he
refers to as younger girls, and in each of these instances, Your Honor, the girl is not harmed physically
beyond the relationship she has had with Mr. Soria. It
becomes a sexual relationship and the girl is released,
set free. . . .

"In those letters, Tasha talks about T.J.'s affinity for
his father and how close the two of them are. She
would like to be able to keep secrets with T.J. or be
able to talk with him without T.J. passing everything
on to his father. She says in one of the letters, 'I'm
close to my dad and love my dad, too, but I don't tell
him absolutely everything.' I think that's further evidence of the dependence of the relationships. In T.J.'s
dependence on his father. He is completely domi-
nated in this relationship. There is someone who
overbornes [*sic*] him.

"Your Honor, T.J. says at five or six years old, his father began sexually assaulting him. But here is a boy
who adores his father, who clearly doesn't have a decent relationship with his mother at all. This person
(his father) who would sexually assault him, who would
force him and teach him that this is what a father and
son did. This is the normalcy of their life. This is real.

This is several times a week. 'This is what we do,' he tells him.

"Mr. Soria senior is an evil man, in my estimation, and I guess I get to give my opinion here. And that's it. But he's not the only influence in T.J.'s life. His mother, Francine . . . T.J. constantly hears her call him 'the little son of a bitch.' 'The little bastard.' 'I didn't want him. He's your son.' How does he align himself? Deeply with his father. He does that because his father, while sexually abusing him, has told him that that's love. 'I will always be there for you.'

"Family is so strong. Family is so important. 'You're the one who does favors for me, T.J., and I'll always be there for you.' And in the tape, T.J. says his father told him, 'Your mother just doesn't love you.' I don't know how devastating that is because, again, that is not part of my experience, but I can only imagine.

"In that interview, T.J. is asked, 'Did your mom know about what your dad was doing to you?'

"He says, 'Yeah. She must have. We'd always go back to the room and lock the door.'

"So there's your mom, and you know she doesn't love you, and she makes a point of saying that she never wanted you. And your mom knows that you're being raped and doesn't do anything about it.

"I would ask you, Your Honor, to consider giving T.J. the opportunity for parole. You're not paroling him. You're not granting him parole. That is for people at least twenty years down the road, and if you make sentences consecutively, twenty-five years down the road. People who aren't even on the parole board now, people at that time will consider whether T.J. has gotten some maturity normally. Whether, in fact, he has been punished enough. Your Honor, he didn't stab this little girl. He didn't rape her. He did provide her to his dad. He did dispose of her body. He must be punished. But he spent a life of punishment and has known nothing else . . . I ask you give him a chance for parole. Thank you."

Now it was the prosecutor's turn, Deputy District Attorney Thomas Perkins. He opened by saying, "The law protects children in a special way. That's because they are our future. I think the circumstances of his [T.J.'s] life have to be put in context of what happened. What was taken away from her and from us. Not only was it taken away from Krystal's mom and sister, her grandpa and cousins, aunts and uncles and father, but the children in this community. Is there a child in Lake Tahoe or Carson City whose life is going to be exactly the same? It's not just a shock to the family; it's a shock to the community.

"That's why I say this defendant owns this crime. He owns every single detail of it. Because he is the one, Your Honor. . . . This recidivism only goes so far and I've used it myself. My heart breaks for this man [T.J.] for the way he was raised. But he is the one who put this child in the hands of a killer. He owns every detail of her kidnapping. He owns every detail of her rape. And he owns every detail of her murder.

"Nothing we've heard this afternoon can tell us that twenty or twenty-five or thirty years from now he is going to be able to overcome the deficiencies that were given to him. Here is a man that worked for the Boys and Girls Club as a baby-sitter and knew the children. Knew the parents in their little apartment complex. What did he do? In that presentencing report, he says that his dad said, 'Get me a girl.' He goes upstairs and he says, 'I think I have one.' Then his dad says, 'Well, go get her.'

"He goes down and he waits until she is by herself

and gives her some candy and takes her back to the house. Now, you want to get a glimpse of his character? He is portraying himself as a victim here, and I think he is. But he is also responsible for his conduct and he knows it's wrong, because the first thing he did after he picked up this child and take her to that room to have sex with his dad—he left while his dad took her there.

"What does he tell us then? 'I didn't know that she was in there when I came back.' Your Honor, there's a word for that kind of statement. It's a 'lie.' He knows that it was wrong and he knows when her mother came there looking for her and she asked, 'Where is my child?' What did he say? 'She's not here. I saw her going down the street.'

"Why did he tell her that? Because he knew it was wrong and he knew that she was being ravaged inside that room.

"Your Honor, there has never been a single reason in this case from the very start to take his word for what happened. When he tells you he does not know what was going on in that room, then how can he possibly explain his sperm cells on her panties? He says, 'Wait, no, the sperm cells are on her panties, not on her body. I masturbated in my own room while this was going on.'

"We don't have to believe that, Your Honor. He was doing the same thing when he was interviewed that night about Krystal's disappearance. Asked, 'Where is she?'

"'I don't know,' he says.

"'Did you harm her?'

"'No.'

"'Did you dispose of her body?'

"'No, I want to help children.'

"That's what he told the officers while he had her

blood on his shirt and on his boots and on his car, while he tossed her over the side of the road like a piece of garbage.

"That's why I say his life has to be put into context of the crime because, I think, he owns it. There's a reason that deceit in kidnapping is the same as force. There's a reason for the felony murder rule. It's because the life of a child is likely to be lost when they're kidnapped for purposes of rape.

"Your Honor, as much as our hearts go out to this man for the way he was raised, the law does not excuse him because of the way he was raised. There's a reason he is not going to trial or death row, and that reason is because of the way he was raised. We can understand that. And our law understands why when somebody acts under the domination of another person, or when they are under extreme mental or emotional disturbance, we still allow for that. Look what he has won by his plea. He was relieved of the chance of life without the possibility of parole on two counts of sexual assault. He was relieved of the same penalty under the kidnapping charge. He was relieved of spending the rest of his life on death row and being executed for this crime. What else has he won? He won his life.

"As much as our hearts go out to him, there's nothing that we have learned about him today that makes us ever want to see him in this community again. Because really, it's not just about punishment, and it's not just about rehabilitation. It's also the protection of the community. How can somebody with a character as flawed as his be rehabilitated in the prison? How could he be rehabilitated anywhere? How can we expect somebody with his character, with his heart as flawed as it is, to overcome the disappointments of middle age, to overcome the bitterness of confinement, to overcome the losses that he has suffered or the vacancies in his life that we have been told about today? Our community demands to be protected from somebody who would so casually take a child away from her family and away from the community and hand her over to be tortured and killed. Our community demands that it be protected.

"Your Honor, I've never been comfortable with people hollering for a man's life or for a particular sentence. Justice requires that T.J. Soria be confined for the rest of his life with no chance of release. He has to carry the whole weight of what he did. And what he did requires that he be confined for the rest of his life with no chance of ever being released. As I say that, I apologize to him. I feel like we failed him in some way. There must have been something we could have done to stop it, but after all, Your Honor, none of that can diminish the weight of his crime and he has to carry it on his back. If he finds redemption in his own way, if he finds that the life we saved for him can be valued, so much the better. But justice requires that he be confined. Thank you."

It was now T.J. Soria's turn to say something from the stand. He turned and spoke directly to Krystal Steadman's family and friends. "I'd like to apologize to the entire family of the Steadmans and their relatives. Every day I will hold this burden on my shoulders. It will be on my conscience the rest of my life. It was a very big mistake, to say the least. I realize I will never be forgiven for what I've done."

Finally the man who would decide if T.J. Soria would ever see the light of day beyond prison walls spoke. Judge David R. Gamble said, "There is an inevitable anticlimactic sense to this. There are two potential sentences for the first count. The difference between these two sentences on Count One determine one thing and one thing only, and that is whether Mr. Soria will ever be released from prison. That is a momentous issue to you, Mr. Soria. It does nothing, however, to calm the hearts of or take away the pain of the victim in this case, or to restore a delightful little girl. I can't do that. Our system is not able to do that and I only wish I could.

"The issue of Mr. Soria's upbringing is an important one in this case. As Mr. Young eloquently pointed out, I don't really have parameters to use to examine that kind of upbringing. There were horrible crimes committed. It's too bad that they weren't found out about sooner. It's too bad that there wasn't prosecution of them or delivery of Mr. Soria junior from that circumstance. The fact that I am confronted with is that there was not.

"So we have a young man arriving at the age of nineteen years with certainly a screwed-up set of values, but what came across most importantly to me in the totality of the material that I have here is in spite of the screwing of those values, Mr. Soria knew full well the rightness and wrongness of his actions in this circumstance and in even prior circumstances that he was not prosecuted for, the other procurements, the other offenses that have been described.

"That knowledge, that certainty of the wrongness of the acts, leads us through a factual trail concerning this kidnapping, which then certainly encompasses, as Mr. Perkins said, all facets of this horrible murder. What I intend to sentence Mr. Soria to or for is his involvement in these crimes, for his ownership of these crimes, to use Mr. Perkins's words. I believe that I can only come to one conclusion about that.

"If you will stand please, sir—you will be sentenced as follows: On Count One, you will be sentenced to a term of the rest of your natural life in the Nevada State Department of Prisons without the possibility of parole."

A chorus of "Yes!" erupted from the Steadman clan and their friends seated in the second row.

There were also reactions that echoed from the community that Deputy DA Thomas Perkins had spoken of. A resident of Lake Park Apartments who knew T.J. Soria, and asked to remain anonymous, told a *Tahoe Tribune* reporter, "Everyone was surprised when the news first came out [about T.J.'s ties to the abduction and murder of Krystal Steadman]. When it came out that it was actually his father, it made more sense. There's no way T.J. thought this up himself and could do something like this. He seemed like a nice young, polite kid. As far as the atmosphere around here goes, everyone knows T.J. is going to spend the rest of his life in prison, and hopefully, his dad will get the death penalty."

Eleven-year-old Deborah Middlebrook said, "Most of the kids knew Krystal and it was really sad. [T.J. Soria] should get life in prison because he'll live his life in horror and maybe he'll feel real guilty. People will still be sad, but they might feel a little better because they know a killer isn't running around on the streets."

Both of these comments pretty much matched the opinions of others in the area. There were still a few who wished T.J. had received the death penalty, but for the most part, they felt justice had been done and that the death penalty should be served on one person only, Thomas Soria Sr.

SIXTEEN

Two Versions
of Death

Minden, Nevada, is the embodiment of a small western town. Lying in the lush Carson Valley and surrounded by sagebrush hills on one side and ten-thousand-foot Job's Peak and the Carson Range on the other, the residents take pride in their beautiful location. Fabled Virginia City, with all its silver riches, lies not far away, and Lake Tahoe is just over the Kinsgbury Grade.

But Minden has always been tied more to agriculture and ranching than mining and tourists. The Minden Flour Milling Company Building still dominates the skyline along Highway 395, and the Overland Hotel serves huge Basque dinners in the old style. Minden had been spared the detritus and mining dumps of so many Nevada towns. And it had been spared the violence so inherent in those towns that became part of the Western myth. In fact, Minden had never seen anything like the forthcoming Thomas Soria Senior trial.

As purely Nevadan in his own way was the main prosecutor in the case, Thomas E. Perkins. He had grown up in the Nevada mining town of Tonopah, once known for its fantastic silver boom, and had gone on to the University of Nevada, Reno. He earned a B.A. in political science there in 1973. Perkins took a short hiatus from Nevada at the University of Denver, College of Law, where he earned a law degree. But he was back in Sparks, Nevada, by 1978 as the city's law clerk. His legal career took a deviation from 1979 to 1995 as he practiced on the defense side of the law, first as a public defender at the regional office in Winnemuca, Nevada, and then in private practice.

All this changed in 1995 when he took on the job of deputy district attorney in Douglas County. Since then, he had tried several homicide cases. But none of them came close to the Thomas Soria Sr. trial.

On January 25, 2001, for the first time in months, T.J. was brought into the courtroom in front of his father. Soria senior sat between his two lawyers wearing a blue pin-striped suit, large gold-framed glasses and black dress shoes. In contrast, T.J. entered the court wearing a prison-issued orange shirt and blue pants. Their eyes met only once.

For the next forty-five minutes, T.J. went through the litany of sexual abuse he had suffered at the hands of his father. Several times, he broke down crying. When he was through, John Springgate asked, "Why did you wait until after your arrest to tell authorities about your father's abuse?" And then Springgate told Judge Gamble, "So what! It's inflammatory and doesn't prove anything. It may prove why Mr. Soria junior is a monster, but that's a question for another day. Who cares whether my client wanted a hooker or said he had sex with guys?"

Judge Gamble mused on all of this and said he would review the evidence and decide if the jury would ever hear any of this. Then he said he would review a seventeen-page file of computer text retrieved from Soria senior's computer. Thomas Perkins argued that the text was strikingly similar to how Steadman's murder was carried out. And Perkins's assistant, Kris Brown, said, "Mr. Soria's computer text is not just fantasy. He was living them on a daily basis."

Since she had done such a stellar job at the T.J. sentencing hearing, Thomas Perkins let his assistant, Kris Brown, begin the prosecution's opening statement to a jury on Friday, January 26, 2001, at 9:00 A.M., at Thomas Soria Sr.'s trial. Before her in the jury box sat four men and eight women.

Brown began by saying, "Good morning, ladies and gentlemen. First thing I want to talk to you about today is the defendant. What's in his mind? What he thinks. Not as he sits before you here today, but in the past, before Krystal was killed. At that time, he had thoughts of rape; he had thoughts of murder; he had thoughts of hurting children and women.

"He wrote those thoughts down in a computer. He wrote about hurting children. He wrote about brutal rape. He wrote about brutal sodomy. He wrote about his fantasies of cutting women to shreds with a knife. Cutting little girls up with a knife. Destroying what's feminine on a woman or a little girl's body with a knife.

"He wrote about taking what he couldn't have. He wrote about murder. One of the things he wrote was, 'Lupe is gone. It makes me have bad thoughts. I want to rape a blond in the forest. I want to plan how I'm going to rape a milky white, blond-haired, blue-eyed kind in the forest. I need to rape and possibly kill a woman. They all deserve to be raped and killed. I enjoy raping and hurting and killing women and little girls. It's what they deserve in life and what they're good for. If they can't fucking comply they will be killed. I will take revenge on the female species by seizing every opportunity to sexually exploit, sexually molest, savagely mouth fuck, brutally rape, brutally sodomize, whip, beat, torture, use as my personal toilet, and kill these beautiful stuck-up bitches.' This includes raping, sodomizing and killing a little blond-haired, blue-eyed woman or little girl.

"These were random thoughts, not directed at a specific person. Not directed at Krystal. The state will prove to you that on March nineteenth, he acted on those words. The state will prove to you that on March nineteenth Lupe, the defendant's wife, was gone.

"Krystal Steadman disappeared from the apartment complex where the defendant lived. Her body was found the next day. Bloodied. The defendant's sperm was on her body. Inside her body. The throat had been cut.

"Krystal was only nine years old. She was just a little over four feet tall. About half my weight. Blond-haired. Blue eyes. She was last seen wearing black pants and a white T-shirt with Tweety Bird on it.

"Her mother will tell you that Krystal was an athletic little girl. She enjoyed sports, like soccer and gymnastics. She was at the defendant's apartment complex just by chance. Just there visiting. And her mother last saw her about two o'clock in the afternoon of March nineteenth of last year.

"The state will prove to you on the early morning of March nineteenth that the defendant was at his computer, and he thought of rape, and he thought of murder. He thought of brutalizing children.

"The state will prove to you later that day, using his son, his teenage son, he lured Krystal away from safety. The son brought her to the apartment. The state will prove to you that was the day she was killed.

"Krystal can't tell you what happened. She's gone. But when her body was found and an autopsy done, there were numerous injuries documented. Those injuries will tell you what the defendant did to this little girl.

"You know, her wrists were bound. The evidence will show that there was tape residue on both her wrists and they were bruised. The evidence will be that the defendant beat her, battered her. There are bruises covering the side of her face and on the back of her head. The evidence will show you that she was bound and gagged. There's tape residue on her cheeks. There's marks of a gag across her face. The defendant stabbed her in the back of the head. The defendant punctured her arm. The defendant raped her. The defendant sodomized her.

"The evidence will show you that Krystal was raped vaginally. The evidence will be the defendant's sperm was found inside her body. There's injuries to her vagina, bleeding, hemorrhaging.

"The defendant raped her anally. The defendant's sperm was found inside her anus.

"The defendant murdered Krystal. The throat was slashed several times. Some of the cuts just barely went through the skin, leaving a crease where the knife went. Others were deeper. Above her clavicle. Under her chin. There's a group right at the base of the neck where there's two or three wounds that come together. Finally there's a slash on the right side of her neck that severed an artery, eventually causing her death.

"The evidence will show you that Krystal fought against this on both her hands. The evidence will show defensive wounds.

"And after the defendant raped and killed Krystal, he wrapped her up in a garbage bag and he called his son in and told him to go get rid of the body.

"The son, acting at his direction, did. He took the body from the apartment, drove down Highway Fifty as he was told, and threw Krystal's body over an embankment still wrapped in the garbage bags, and they ripped and tore as the body tumbled down the embankment.

"It was discovered there the next day, the trash bags intertwined in her legs; you can see the spots of blood coming down the embankment where her body had rolled. The injuries were injuries on her body that showed that she was dead when she was thrown over the embankment.

"An autopsy was done the next day by Dr. Ellen Clark and she'll talk to you about the injuries she documented, the injuries I've just told you about. And during the autopsy and also at the scene, there were some swabs taken from Krystal's body. What they do is they take Q-Tip–like things and moisten them with distilled water. At the scene, they took a swab from Krystal's buttocks. During the autopsy, swabs were taken from her vagina, from her anus, from the skin surrounding those areas and from her left cheek. Also collected during the autopsy and at the scene were little fibers that were on Krystal's body. And the swabs and the fibers were sent to the Washoe County Crime Lab.

"The Washoe County Crime Lab is the lab that's authorized to do DNA testing. Renee Romero is the one that conducts the DNA testing. She has a master's degree in biology, microbiology, and she's on a national committee that studies and does DNA testing.

"She'll tell you of the nine swabs that were taken from Krystal's body . . . eight of those swabs under the microscope . . . She could see that there was sperm. And a sample of the defendant's DNA was obtained. An analysis was done from that and a profile of his DNA was done. Then Renee Romero examined the results of each of those and compared those.

"And what she'll tell you is of the nine swabs that

were taken from Krystal's body, eight of which showed sperm, there were seven of them that she would say were a conclusive match of the defendant's DNA.

"Now, you've heard me mention a little bit about the defendant's son. A DNA sample was also collected from him, and he was completely excluded as a person who was the source of the DNA from the sperm that was found on Krystal's body. The only DNA that connected him with Krystal was found on a piece of clothing.

"And I told you there were fibers also found on Krystal's body, and those were also submitted to the Washoe County Crime Lab, where they were examined by Investigator Berger. And what they tell you is he examined those fibers microscopically—color, chemically—and that they were the same or similar to ones that were taken from the defendant's bedroom.

"The garbage bags that were found were examined chemically and under a microscope. You'll see the pictures of those garbage bags—one from the defendant's apartment, the other from where Krystal's body was found lying—side by side, and the manufacturing marks that are produced when these bags are extruded match across the two different bags.

"Now, why would the defendant do something like this to a little girl? Why would he seek out a little girl to rape and virtually destroy? The evidence in this case will be that the defendant was obsessed with sex. He wrote about sex. He wrote things like he didn't like to work because of sex. He had no shame when it came to sex.

"He had fantasies about raping and sodomizing little girls, little boys. He wrote that he was continually honing his brain to rape a woman or little girl. It was this obsession that gave birth to a deadly rage.

"I have read a little bit of what he wrote, and I want to read a little more so you can understand what this man was thinking. And I said sometimes he wrote specifically about one particular person, other times it was just directed to no person in particular.

"They describe the very type of thing that happened to Krystal. He wrote, 'I want to rape Debbie Sloan. I destroy all that is feminine on her body with my knife. I cut her into bloody shreds. She asks why. Because someone like you would never give a guy like me a chance to have sex with you and do nasty things to your body and allow me to worship you. Because I'm in love with you. So this is the way I will have you.'

"And in another part he wrote, 'I will find the kind of woman I've always wanted to fuck. I'll find a young white blond-haired blue-eyed girl. The kind of woman who would never be interested in me. So the only way that I can have sex with her body is to rape her. It's the only choice I have, and the only way I will ever have sex with a beautiful blond, so I must rape her.'

"We can't prove to you where this rage came from, but we can prove to you that it existed. We can prove to you that it was fatal. Krystal was a little blond-haired girl.

"The defendant wrote those words in a computer room that was off his bedroom. Off the master bedroom there was what used to be a walk-in closet. It was windowless. And in that room was a computer on the desk, and above that were shelves and there were dolls, toys, games and stuffed animals on that. But no little kids lived in the apartment. Only the defendant and his teenage son, T.J.

"After Krystal's murder, the computer from that room was seized and it was sent to the high-tech crime lab at the Sacramento County Sheriff's Office. It was looked at by Investigator Mannering, and he'll tell you all about the investigation he did on that.

"And I have read you small samples of it. It goes on

for pages and pages. Some of it is like what I've read. Some of it talks about things that are personal to the defendant and about his ex-wife, Fran. About Lupe, about Debbie Sloan, about Sara Stein and Julie Drayton, women he used to work with in Sacramento.

"There's a list of books at the beginning of the text. A *Color Atlas of Child Sexual Abuse, Pediatric and Adolescent Gynecology.* Books found in his apartment that he admitted to the Sheriff's office were his own.

"Most of the computer texts are like what I've read to you, expressing rage, expressing desires, expressing the desire to rape, murder and brutalize women and little girls.

"The state will prove to you, on March nineteenth, early in the morning, about one-forty, this file was opened. The state will prove to you that Lupe was gone that day. The defendant asked his teenage son, T.J., to bring a little girl up to the apartment. And T.J. did that.

"From the evidence you hear will be that the defendant sexually abused T.J. from his earliest memories. He can remember back when he was six or seven and would be called into the defendant's bedroom. He would be subjected to numerous sexual acts that he would have to perform on the defendant. Some that the defendant would perform on him. The defendant would ask T.J. to lick his body all over. His armpits, his testicles, his penis, his anus. And T.J. would do this because, in his mind, he grew to equate this sexual expression with his father as love.

"T.J. was always told, of course, he would have to keep this secret. The defendant told him there's other people like us in the country, but we can't talk about it. You can't talk to your friends about it. Don't talk to schoolteachers, school counselors. Because if you tell, then our family will be destroyed. They'll take you away from me.

"T.J. also felt isolated from his mother. He recalls hearing his mother and the defendant during arguments and hearing her say, 'I never wanted the little bastard. He's your son. I never wanted him anyway.'

"The defendant reinforced that with T.J. Telling him, 'Yeah, your mother doesn't love you. But I'll always be there for you. I love you.'

"There was very little contact with extended family when T.J. was young. He heard from or met with grandparents, aunts and uncles. But that dwindled until there was very little contact even with extended family. T.J. grew up pretty much tied to his father, thinking his father was the one that loved him and his father was the one that would always be there for him.

"And as he grew older, the sex between him and his father diminished some, and T.J. took on a new role as procurer. He tried to find girls to introduce to his father. They even came up with a plan that T.J. would call the defendant 'Uncle,' because that would make it easier for the girls to get acquainted with him.

"T.J came back and lived with Lupe and the defendant at Lake Park Apartments. And that's why that morning when the defendant told T.J. to go out and get him a little girl, T.J. suspected it was for something sexual, but he did it anyway. So he went out and played with the kids and that's where he met Krystal. She was just there visiting. And he befriended her. And then later when she was alone, he invited her up to the apartment to get some candy.

"When you come into the apartment, there's the entryway, then there's a kitchen, living room area open to each other, and then a hallway. T.J.'s room's right when you come in the door, and then the hallway on the right-hand side, there's the bathroom and then the defendant's room is the one back at the very end of the hallway.

"So, at two-thirty P.M. Krystal has not come back and checked in with her mother. Her mother and Dan Simmons go out in the complex and start looking for Krystal. Sandi Taylor takes Krystal's mother up there [to the Soria apartment]. She knocks on the door and it's T.J. that answers the door. He says he doesn't know anything about Krystal.

"So Betty [Elizabeth Steadman's nickname] leaves. And she and Dan Simmons look around more for Krystal, and again T.J.'s name comes up. So Betty Steadman and Dan Simmons go back to the defendant's apartment, knock on the door, and T.J. answers the door again.

"[Betty] is allowed to check the living room, kitchen area, [T.J.'s] room. Betty checks the bathroom. And then she's at the end of the hall where the defendant's bedroom is and then T.J. steps in between her and the door and says, 'No, you can't go in there. My uncle is in there asleep.'

"And she says, 'Well, let Dan go in. Let my boyfriend go in.'

"'He's indecent.'

"'Well, Dan's a man. Let him go in there.'

"But T.J. turns her away and she leaves.

"Betty Steadman will testify here today, and you're going to see a broken woman. A woman who is overcome with grief for the loss of her child. And also a woman who wonders if she had been more insistent, had [she] been ruder, could [she] have gotten into that bedroom? Could [she] have saved [her] little girl, or was it already too late?

"The fact of the matter was, that apartment wounded Betty Steadman so much, that even after the Sheriff's office had been called, she went back to the apartment and knocked on the door later that evening. But she received no answer. All she heard was the sound of the search helicopter overhead.

"By that time, there was a massive search going on for Krystal. There were citizens involved in it. Various law enforcement agencies involved in it. And as the sun set and the night temperatures grew colder, the people were concerned about finding Krystal. But by that time, Krystal was no longer feeling the cold. And the darkness no longer held any fear for her. She was dead.

"Now, the Blazer was taken that night and it was towed to the Washoe County Crime Lab. And there was an examination of it. Blood samples were taken from various locations in the Blazer. There was a swipe on the passenger seat, and that was tested, and it was determined that it was Krystal's blood and that was done by DNA testing.

"An investigator from the lab also did some testing. What [he] tells you is that the bloodstains are consistent with the type of movements that T.J. described. Seepage. They are not consistent with what blood spatter experts talk about as bloodletting events. The cutting, the stabbing and the blood would spray out in a more diffuse pattern.

"The blood had been determined in the Blazer to be human blood and so T.J. was arrested at that point. He was arrested around noon and later officers went to the apartment with a search warrant. And these officers had been out most of the night looking for Krystal. They had been at the location where Krystal's body was found. And they were tired. They did make mistakes.

"Some of the mistakes just came from lack of information. At that time, they still didn't know about Maria Gonzales seeing T.J. at the apartment complex with the

Blazer. But maybe the biggest mistake was that they treated the defendant with courtesy. They treated him as an ill, grieving father, whose son had just been arrested for murder. So, they allowed the defendant and his wife, Lupe, to remain in the apartment while they conducted the search and they searched for the things authorized in the search warrant.

"The next day, they saw new information and another search warrant was obtained. The officers came back to the apartment to do a more thorough search. They knew about the fibers found on Krystal's body. So the search warrant they came back with authorized them to look for and collect fibers. To collect trace evidence.

"When they came to that apartment that time, when they opened the door, they noticed a very strong odor of bleach. And it was at that time that they thought possibly they had made a mistake. That evidence had been destroyed. Bleach is one of the things that can destroy DNA evidence.

"Officers continued to investigate the case even after T.J.'s arrest. Witnesses were contacted; information was taken. T.J. was completely eliminated as the source of sperm on Krystal's body. But what Renee Romero will tell you is that half of your DNA comes from your mother and half comes from your father. She was able to determine as the source of the DNA of the sperm on Krystal's body [that it] came from a close relative of T.J. and was later confirmed to have come from the defendant.

"For his part in Krystal's death, T.J. pled guilty to first-degree murder and first-degree kidnapping. He was not charged with, nor did he plead to, actually killing Krystal. What he pled to was that he aided and abetted. He's now doing life in prison. As part of the agreement in his case, he agreed to give officers a statement about what he saw that day.

"This is the defendant's case. In this case, the state will prove to you that on March nineteenth of last year Lupe was gone. We'll prove to you that the defendant had bad thoughts. Thoughts of hurting children. Thoughts of brutal rape. Thoughts of brutal sodomy. Thoughts of cutting women with knives. Thoughts of beating women unconscious. Thoughts of taking what wasn't his. Thoughts of murder.

"The state will prove to you the defendant kidnapped Krystal through the use of his son and took her away from safety. He sexually assaulted her, he raped her, he sodomized her and finally he murdered her. You're going to have to see the shattered lives. And I know many of you during the jury-selection process struggled with this. Struggled with your emotions on this. I want to thank you at this time on behalf of Mr. Perkins and myself for taking the burden you've taken on. At the end of the evidence in this case, Mr. Perkins will have a chance to talk to you, and at that time, he will ask you to find the defendant guilty of the crimes charged. Thank you."

It was now Michael Roeser's turn to defend his client. And he had a totally different take on what had happened on March 19, 2000, in apartment 22. He began by saying, "Ladies and gentlemen of the jury . . . ugly thoughts, repugnant thoughts, have never killed anybody. Ugly language, repugnant language, language that makes us feel horrible inside . . . language which we can't understand, has never killed anybody. If I raise a child and that child turns into a monster and that monster kills somebody, that doesn't mean I killed somebody.

"Who killed Krystal Steadman? Who kidnapped her that morning of March nineteenth? Who asked the other little girls about her? Asked about her name? Where she was from? Who she was? Who lied to her?

Who stole her off the street? Who put her body into the Blazer and drove it and threw it down an embankment? Who owned a knife with a serrated-edged blade? The answer to those questions is Thomas Soria Jr.

"On March nineteenth, we submit, the evidence will show you that Krystal was with her mom visiting her boyfriend at the Lake Park Apartments. They had gone there the previous evening on Saturday night. About 10:30 A.M. [on Sunday], Krystal went outside to play with her friends. Now Tom Soria Jr. went out that morning. He ran into a young girl named Sandi Taylor. He asked Sandi—one, two, three times—who is that young girl? Who is the young blond-haired girl? Now, some of the testimony you will hear [from the young girls] is somewhat confusing. Of course, as you might expect, their recollections are not as keen as those of us who are older. . . . Naturally, when Krystal did not check in, her mom and her friend, Mr. Simmons, started to look for her. They talked to Sandi and the other girls and other children out in the apartment complex and asked where she was. Have you seen her? And they were told about the bicycle. They were told the last time [they] saw Krystal was two o'clock. You'll also hear that during one of his many interviews, Soria junior said quite early that the last time he saw Krystal was at two o'clock. But that would be yet another lie that you will hear coming from Mr. Soria junior.

"Mrs. Steadman was frantic, as you would expect. It would be hard to really put yourself in the position of her then and think what she was thinking as she searched for her daughter. She went to the apartment that was described to her as where T.J. lived. She opened the door and she met the monster. Because this man, Thomas Soria Jr., looked her in the eye after having taken her daughter and said, 'If you need any-

thing, let me know. I'll be glad to help.' He even offered to put his shoes on to help look for the girl that
he kidnapped.

"Mrs. Steadman was only in the apartment for probably two minutes, according to Mr. Simmons. Maybe
four minutes by her own recollection. Those time
frames are probably even faster when you think about
the adrenaline and how she was feeling. Her heart had
to be pounding. Her mind had to be pushing the fear
and panic she had to be feeling. She looked at that
young man and he lied to her. He offered to help find
Krystal—the person that stole Krystal.

"Tom Soria Jr. was next seen somewhere around three
forty-five P.M. by Maria Gonzales. She'll testify that she saw
junior standing at the open driver's side door of the
Blazer. He had the [door] open and holding a box. A
box that a moderate-sized television would fit in. He
wasn't holding the box like a person would hold a heavy
object. He was holding the box with his hands on the
side of the box and his one leg supporting it. But this leg
was not resting on anything. He was holding it in the air.

"Krystal died a horrible death. You are going to see
and hear evidence that will make you sick. The knife, according to the testimony you are going to hear, was
probably serrated. Her body was placed in a garbage bag
and Soria junior had taken that bag and thrown it down
an embankment. You will hear evidence that there was
vegetable matter and dirt and debris inside of her."

Roeser took the jury through T.J.'s first interview at
the Tahoe substation with Detectives Duzan and Minister. Then he spoke of Deputies Cable and Lowe's first
encounter with Thomas Soria Sr. and their search of
the apartment while T.J. was still at the Sheriff's substation. "You are going to hear that junior will say that
he still loves his father and that he cares for him. If, in

fact, his father had just killed a young girl in that apartment . . . he still gave these officers the key to go up into the apartment where his father was. The crime scene—if, in fact, she had been killed there. So they went up. Deputy Lowe and Deputy Cable from Douglas County went up to the apartment and they did knock on the door. It was not answered, so they opened the door with the key that they had obtained from junior and they went inside. They searched the apartment for Krystal. Deputy Lowe primarily went into the second bedroom, which belonged to junior. He went into the bathroom. He looked in the kitchen and he didn't see any evidence of her, nor did he see any evidence that a crime had been committed in that apartment. He didn't see any blood. He didn't see any clothing. He didn't see anything out of the ordinary which would cause him to believe that a crime of murder had occurred in that apartment, or any crime for that matter.

"So he went into the back bedroom and he opened the door. Our client, Mr. Soria senior, was asleep. He woke him and said, 'We're police officers and we're investigating the missing girl.' Mr. Soria got out of bed at their request. He didn't argue with them. He didn't say, 'I've got nothing to do with this.' He didn't say, 'You're bugging the wrong person. What are you doing in my apartment?' He obeyed their directions and requests. They asked him to get out of bed and put some clothes on and he did. And they didn't see any blood in that apartment or on him. In that back bedroom, they didn't see any blood in the bed or around the bed. They didn't see any blood on the floor. They didn't see any evidence of a crime whatsoever. Mr. Soria did as they asked. He answered their questions.

"Deputy Lowe searched the apartment. He looked in the apartment for Krystal and, of course, he looked for anything that would cause a law enforcement officer to believe that a crime had been committed there. That would only make sense for him to look for evidence of her person or anything that might cause them to believe that she had ever been in that apartment and/or something had happened to her in that apartment. He saw nothing.

"Meanwhile, T.J. had been released to go back to the apartment. He spent the night there. And the next morning, after Krystal's body was found, they arrested him. He had some lawyers that immediately came down to see him and talk to him. And those lawyers represented him in his case. Those lawyers got him a plea-bargain agreement in a minute.

"Now, back in the apartment. You are going to hear that Lupe Soria came back up on Monday, the twentieth of March. When she got to the apartment, things seemed just like they were when she left. She is going to come in and testify that things were just normal there. The apartment was basically as clean as it ever was. When you see the pictures, you'll conclude not very clean.

"Now, the investigation, of course, continued. The Sheriff's office went ahead and got three subpoenas the next couple of days to look for evidence in the apartment of a murder, the murder of Krystal Steadman. It's important for you to understand a couple of things about these searches. As I said, Krystal died a horrible death. Her throat was cut. It was cut as if a jabbing motion occurred. She had other wounds on her which caused her to bleed out. So her entire body, by the time they found it, was pretty much empty of blood. You are going to hear evidence when something like this, as horrible as this is, happens to a human being, it's not a clean thing. It's not something where you put down a piece of plastic on the floor and catch all of this blood. It's not the

kind of thing where there's any control over the blood
that gets in your fingernails, the blood that gets on the
wall, gets into the sheets of the bedding, into the carpet.
You are going to hear evidence about how horrible this
was. When you hear this evidence, you have to realize,
and we hope you stay with us on this, look at this evidence and think about what impact [it has]. Because the
Sheriff's office wanted to find evidence to figure out
what happened to Krystal Steadman. Who killed Krystal
Steadman. Because if she was killed there at the apartment, there had to be some evidence of it. So they went
in with these search warrants and this went on for quite
a while.

"They inspected the apartment as recently as a couple of months ago. They took the diverter from the
bathtub. It diverts the water from the shower to the
bath. They took out the drain. They took out the drain-
cover plate. They took out the linoleum. They took out
the toilet seat. They took out the floorboard. They went
in later on and took out the carpet, sections of the hallway and out of the bedroom. They took out the
plywood subfloor. They checked all of those items and
they found no blood. Nothing. Not one strand of DNA
or one cell of blood that belonged to Krystal Steadman
did they find in all of the analysis.

"They took some Luminol. Luminol is a substance
which will detect whether or not there is blood, or has
ever been blood in a particular place. I believe you will
hear testimony that even if somebody was to try to wipe
blood away, clean blood up, that Luminol will detect
the smears. So, while you visibly cannot see any trace of
blood, you'll see a smear through the use of Luminol
where the person wiped it.

"And they went in with alternative light source into
this apartment and they basically tore it apart. And they

didn't find one cell of Krystal Steadman's blood. They found the blood in the Blazer that T.J. was driving. They found Krystal Steadman's blood on his foot, on his shoes, but not a speck of blood or DNA in that apartment to tie the murder of Krystal Steadman to the interior of that apartment.

"That's important in the context of this case because you are going to hear evidence that our client, Mr. Soria senior, was in that apartment that day. What they are going to want you to believe is that he killed her. You just heard that junior is going to come in and say, 'I went into the bedroom and there was her dead body on the bed in a plastic bag.' That's their theory. This is not about a computer text that you will read. You will say the person that wrote this is disgusting. But this is about evidence. This is about who killed Krystal Steadman and where was she killed. How did she have debris and dirt and vegetable matter inside of her if she was killed in that apartment?

"Meanwhile, junior is arrested. He has got lawyers. They work out a plea agreement. He doesn't get death. Krystal got death. Krystal got thrown down an embankment by him. Her blood was around him and on his clothes, but he worked out a deal with his lawyers that got him no death. What did he agree to do in return? Give a statement. Who do you think the statement is about? His father. Because who else could he implicate in this crime? They wanted to hear bad stuff about his dad.

"Back on May 19, 2000, T.J. had an interview with an FBI agent named Rinek. At that time, he was looking at a number of possibilities as far as sentencing. And he knew that in exchange for his plea, he was expected to give a statement. And he knew that they were

looking for evidence against his dad. And so he told
Rinek his story.

"It was in that story that he told them about his supposed sexual abuse as a child. This is the first time you
will hear any testimony that he ever told anybody about
it. He had gone for fourteen years in his life and never
said anything about it until they wanted to know about
his dad. So he told a story about going in and finding
a girl's body on the bed. He said, 'I didn't see any
blood. There was an odor. I don't know what it was. I
don't know how she was killed.' He told a story that de-
fies the laws of physics.

"It's the first time that he came up with these stories
and denied his involvement, other than a few things
that he would admit to. The kidnapping. Throwing of
the body. Other than that, he didn't do anything. Even
though he had come in and pled guilty to first-degree
murder."

In essence, attorney Michael Roeser stated that T.J.
Soria alone was responsible for the murder of Krystal
Steadman and he may have not even killed her in
apartment 22. The lack of blood there would certainly
point in that direction. According to Roeser, T.J. had
killed her and blamed everything on his father to save
his own life.

And then the parade of witnesses began. Elizabeth
Steadman was called first. Through a stream of tears,
she recounted the entire terrible day of March 19,
2000, at the Lake Park Apartments. Of her time in the
Sorias' apartment, she said, "I had a feeling. I had a
sense. I felt something was wrong. Though everything
seemed to be quiet and calm and nothing seemed to
be disturbed, I went down the hallway and T.J. said—"

At this point, Roeser objected that this was hearsay.

This brought an immediate rebuttal from Thomas

Perkins. "Your Honor, it's not hearsay. It's part of the res gestae of the crime."

Judge Gamble overruled the objection and Elizabeth Steadman continued. "He said, 'Oh, I remember. She just went down to the trailer park."

Roeser, during his turn, said, "[T.J.], at that point, tricked you, did he not, by lying to you?"

Elizabeth answered, "Yes."

"I have no further questions."

And then it was time for Sandi Taylor.

Kris Brown asked Sandi, "Can you give me an idea of what you think is true and false?"

"Well, like, if you break a vase and say the dog did it."

"If you break a vase and say the dog did it, is that the truth or a lie?"

"That's a lie."

"Which of these is the better?"

"The truth."

Kris Brown took Sandi through the entire afternoon of playing in the field and the rides with the other girls on T.J.'s Chevy Blazer. Then she asked, "You said you went up to T.J.'s apartment a second time. When was that?"

Sandi answered, "When Krystal was missing."

"Who did you go with?"

"Krystal's mom."

"What happened?"

"He [T.J.] looked scared and didn't know where she was."

"When you got to that apartment, who knocked on the door?"

"I did."

"Did T.J. answer it?"

"Yes."

"When was the last time you saw him that day?"

"When he said he wasn't feeling good."

Michael Roeser also took Sandi through the sequence of events of March 19, 2000, and asked, "You said that T.J. acted differently than when you normally saw him?"

"Yes."

"Tell us what you saw again."

"When I went up with Krystal's mom, he seemed really weird. Like he was in trouble."

"Did his eyes look different to you?"

"Yes."

"What did they look like?"

"Wide. Like they never looked before."

"Did you notice that he was breathing like a normal person?"

"No. Like he was breathing really hard."

"How did you feel?"

"I thought he was in trouble or something."

The trial took a break over the weekend and Thomas Soria Sr. had plenty of time to think about what was still in store for him. The most painful thoughts of all must have concerned the allegations by his son, T.J. He had always controlled the boy, but all of that was now gone forever. With such a bleak future on the horizon, Thomas Soria Sr. cooked up a plan reminiscent of Douglas Mozingo, his violent uncle. He, likewise, had a trick up his sleeve, and it would catch everyone by surprise.

SEVENTEEN

"A Sign from God"

Thomas Soria Sr. turned forty years old on January 27th, 2001, but he certainly didn't have much to celebrate. Incarcerated at the Douglas County Jail between court dates, he had plenty of time to ruminate about what T.J. had said about him in court.

Soria senior was being held in a medical cell at the jail next to the control center. As Sheriff Ron Pierini said, "It was for his protection and everyone else's." Soria senior had been receiving medication for a heart condition as well as antidepressants. Soria had valvular defect and got his meds twice a day. Guards checked him at least every two hours to see that he was doing all right and medical personnel also came by on a routine basis to monitor his symptoms.

There was one thing, however, that no one knew except for Thomas Soria Sr. himself. He wasn't swallowing his medication. Instead, he would pretend to swallow it and when no one was looking, he would remove it from his mouth and store it away. On Sunday, January 28, 2001, his cell was checked at 1:00 A.M. and at 3:00 A.M. by a guard, and Soria seemed to be sleeping okay. But at some point in the early-morning hours of

January 28, Thomas Soria Sr. swallowed all of the anti-depressants he had been hoarding.

At 5:00 A.M. the jailers realized that something was wrong in Soria's cell. As Sheriff Ron Pierini said later, "[Soria] was normally up and about at 5:00 A.M. Sometime around then it was noticed there was a problem. There weren't any signs of life."

Soria Senior had not been on a suicide watch, despite his use of antidepressants. Sheriff Pierini added, "There was no sign of trauma. He was lying in bed and it looked like he was asleep. But we're not ruling out anything until the investigation's done. Nothing is foolproof, but the officers are to make sure to the best of their ability that medications are swallowed."

The Douglas County jail authorities summoned medical personnel a little after 5:00 A.M., but by then it was too late. Thomas Soria Senior, just like his uncle Douglas Mozingo, had robbed the executioner by committing suicide in jail.

His lawyer John Springgate told reporters, "If we had thought anything was out of the ordinary, we would have alerted the jail staff. But [he] had never expressed suicidal thoughts as the trial began."

Douglas County had budgeted $350,000 for what was expected to be at least a six-week trial. Instead it had only run a few days and $100,000 was spent. Investigators who were lined up to give testimony were reassigned to other cases. District Attorney Scott Doyle said, "I think they're relieved. We feel very comfortable we had the right suspect. It's not an issue of whether we had a conviction. We felt confidant we would get that."

Deputy DA Thomas Perkins was even more adamant about Thomas Soria's guilt. He told reporter Christy Chalmers of the *Record Courier*, "The evidence against Soria senior was overwhelming. The murder of Krystal

Steadman put a gaping hole in humanity. We're relieved we don't have to go through this trial."

If Thomas Perkins was relieved, the same was even more true for the friends and family of Krystal Steadman. Her sister, Sonya Klempner, told reporters, "It's unbelievable. Miracles do happen. Inevitably, that's what we were going for. The death penalty. He was going to pay anyway. We didn't know it was going to come that quickly. But it will never fulfill that space that Krystal gave each of us. That wonderful warmth and love. It will never fulfill that emptiness. [Now] I'm definitely changing my plans. I'm just going somewhere a little more warm where I can smile and laugh a little more."

Leslie and Irene Bucknell, Krystal's grandparents from Florida, were in the area as well, ready to spend whatever time the trial necessitated. At 9:30 A.M., on Sunday, January 28, they received a phone call from Thomas Perkins as they were about to leave for church. He asked if they were all there and then said, "I'm going to come over and see you with what you might consider to be good news." About an hour later, he and Kris Brown arrived at their door and told them of the suicide of Thomas Soria Sr.

Leslie Bucknell later told a *Tahoe Daily Tribune* reporter, "We were very, very relieved. Betty had a very good day. It was a hell of a relief to her. She was dreading the whole proceeding."

Leslie and Irene Bucknell were so relieved and grateful, in fact, that they composed an open letter to the public, which was then printed in the January 30, 2001, issue of the *Tahoe Daily Tribune*.

Speaking for the family, we are all elated with the news of Soria's death. I personally believe it was a sign from God. After Soria listened to Krystal's mother on the witness stand what little kernel of conscience left in him kicked in, and he found he could no longer live with himself. Or perhaps he had a heart attack which would also be a sign from God. I have also heard from some people that the karma police took over, which is also God's sign.

This latest event will bring closure for all of us much more quickly than going through the agony of a protracted trial and the interminable delays which would be encountered in the state and federal courts. It's over and we can start rebuilding our lives.

Another of God's signs was the coming forth of the lady who witnessed Soria Jr. throwing Krystal's body down the embankment on Highway 50. This was the key lead which the Douglas County Sheriff's Office used to reconstruct the evidence pointing to Soria Sr. and Soria Jr.

The family will be forever grateful to the Tahoe and Minden police in so diligently pursuing the crime. The speed in which this was accomplished is outstanding in crime annals. Special thanks and recognition are due the Sacramento Police in finding Soria Sr.'s personal computer which contained damning evidence linking him directly to the crime.

All things considered, justice has been done!

The family is also impressed with the overwhelming response of grief and compassion felt and shown by the whole Tahoe community. It has meant so much to us all. God bless you.

We would be remiss if we did not mention the Minden District Attorney's Office headed by Tom Perkins and their constant diligence in bringing these proceedings to a speedy trial. In addition their compassion for the family victims was over and beyond their normal duties. The immediate members of the family who came into contact with the D.A.'s office express their heartfelt gratitude to them.

Not only the family of Krystal Steadman, but the entire community weighed in on Thomas Soria Sr.'s suicide. South Lake Tahoe resident Krystal Sanchez told *Tahoe Daily Tribune* reporter Emily Aughinbaugh, "I'm mad because he didn't even go to trial. He got the easy way out and I don't think it's fair. You should torture him. Do you know how much pain that little girl went through?"

Reno resident Katie Kendell told Aughinbaugh, "Too bad [Soria's death] couldn't have been a long, ongoing process. I would have rather paid the money to see him tortured."

And Kendell's coworker Sue Secord agreed. "I have a child and if [Soria] would have done that to my kid, I would have killed him myself. You don't touch children. I don't think too many people are going to be sad about his death."

Perhaps one of the few people who was saddened by Thomas Soria Sr.'s death was T.J. He was in jail when he was given the news. The jailers immediately put him on suicide watch.

In the weeks after Thomas Soria Sr.'s death, a team of Washoe and Douglas County investigators delved into his demise to make sure it was suicide and not from normal causes. From the evidence gathered, it was ascertained that his blood contained fatal levels of amitriptyline, a prescription antidepressant that had been prescribed by a clinical psychiatrist. Sheriff Pierini surmised that Soria senior either hadn't swallowed or else had coughed up the pills that he was administered at ten o'clock each night. He had hoarded the antidepressants and then taken them all at once in the early-morning hours of January 28, 2001. In a long, strange and twisting road, he had gone down the path of two men he despised—Ronny Mozingo and Douglas Mozingo. Just like Ronny, he had ended up torturing and murdering a female; just like Douglas, he had committed suicide within the confines of jail. The spark of destruction that had been ignited on September 25, 1979, when Thomas Soria's mother was violently murdered, ended on January 28, 2001.

By the one-year anniversary of Krystal Steadman's murder, most people in the region no longer thought of Soria senior or junior. Their thoughts turned instead to the bubbly little girl who had so tragically been snatched from their midst. In faraway Tennessee, Krystal's father, John Steadman, told *Record Courier* reporter F.T. Norton, "I cry most every night. She was a little girl. How could someone do that to a little girl? I still have a hard time believing she is dead. But what can you do? She's gone and only now do I definitely know where she is."

Closer to home, a candlelight vigil was conducted on El Dorado Beach at Lake Tahoe on March 19, 2001. Organizer Cathy Buffa, whose children had known Krystal, told *Record Courier* reporter Jill Darby, "My daughter was a friend of Krystal's. It still affects us. I want this to be a reminder that we all need to keep an eye out on each other's kids."

South Tahoe Middle School student Tayah Del Vecchio said, "There are so many wonderful memories of her."

And Dot Magnall, a member of Compassionate Friends, who had lost her own ten-year-old daughter,

Lori Beth, said, "We're going to have events like this for the healing, but also to remind us that this can happen, even up here. The more we recognize grief, then the more we are willing to accept death and work through the grieving process."

Eleven-year-old Kaylee Davis said that she cherished Krystal's friendship and their time together. "I forgive myself and I forgive her for fighting with me. I want to say, 'Krystal, we miss you and we love you.'"

There was no doubt that the entire community did miss and love Krystal. They erected a memorial on Highway 50 where her body had been discovered on the chilly morning of March 20, 2000. Any traveler driving down the road toward Carson City, Nevada, can see the small white cross and the scores of stuffed animals left there in remembrance of Kyrstal Dawn Steadman. As Tom Perkins had said, "It helps to mend the hole in the heart of humanity."